Proactive

SCHOOL SECURITY

and

EMERGENCY PREPAREDNESS PLANNING

D1261843

This book is dedicated to my loving and supportive family, whose patience, understanding, encouragement, and reality-checks motivate me to continue my advocacy for safe schools and communities.

Many thanks also go out to my close friends and colleagues who have consistently continued to stand with me through the long haul.

Ken Trump

KENNETH S. TRUMP

Proactive
SCHOOL SECURITY
and
EMERGENCY PREPAREDNESS PLANNING

CORWIN
A SAGE Company

CORWIN
A SAGE Company

FOR INFORMATION:

Corwin
A SAGE Company
2455 Teller Road
Thousand Oaks, California 91320
(800) 233-9936
Fax: (800) 417-2466
www.corwin.com

SAGE Ltd.
1 Oliver's Yard
55 City Road
London EC1Y 1SP
United Kingdom

SAGE India Pvt. Ltd.
B 1/I 1 Mohan Cooperative Industrial Area
Mathura Road, New Delhi 110 044
India

SAGE Asia-Pacific Pte. Ltd.
33 Pekin Street #02-01
Far East Square
Singapore 048763

Acquisitions Editor: Arnis Burvikovs
Associate Editor: Desirée A. Bartlett
Editorial Assistant: Kimberly Greenberg
Production Editor: Veronica Stapleton
Copy Editor: Amy Rosenstein
Typesetter: C&M Digitals (P) Ltd.
Proofreader: Dennis W. Webb
Indexer: Sheila Bodell
Cover Designer: Michael Dubowe
Permissions Editor: Karen Ehrmann

Copyright © 2011 by Corwin

Printed in the United States of America

Library of Congress Cataloging-in-Publication Data

Trump, Kenneth S.

Proactive school security and emergency preparedness planning / Kenneth S. Trump.

p. cm.
Includes bibliographical references and index.

ISBN 978-1-4129-7431-8 (pbk.)

1. Schools—Security measures—United States—Handbooks, manuals, etc. 2. Schools—United States—Safety measures—Handbooks, manuals, etc. 3. School crisis management—United States—Handbooks, manuals, etc. I. Title.

LB2866.T79 2011 363.11'9371—dc22 2011000469

This book is printed on acid-free paper.

11 12 13 14 15 10 9 8 7 6 5 4 3 2 1

Contents

Ongoing updates and news items regarding school safety and security can be found on Ken's blog at www.schoolsecurityblog.com

Disclaimer and Legal Notices

Although the author has attempted to ensure the accuracy of information contained herein, we do not warrant that it is complete or accurate. The author and publisher do not assume, and hereby specifically disclaim, any liability to any person or entity with respect to any loss or damage alleged to have been caused by any error or omission as well as for the use or misuse of strategies described, herein.

All specific individual concerns should always be directed toward qualified professionals in those areas on an individual basis. Nothing in this book is provided as a substitute for legal, medical, mental health, public safety, or other professional advice or intervention.

Information contained in this book is not applicable in states or localities with laws, ordinances, regulations, and/or other legal restrictions that specifically prohibit any suggestions or recommendations made in this book.

Material from this publication may not be used in for-profit training without the express written permission of the publisher and the author.

Foreword

Only a few decades ago, school personnel were worried about students running in the halls and chewing gum, and parents were worried that their child might die of embarrassment from something that happened to them at school. The concerns for school personnel and parents in the United States have changed dramatically, and we are very fortunate to have Ken Trump who has dedicated his career to making our schools safer. It is my distinct pleasure to write a foreword for his third book.

I have been very fortunate to not only have read his books and countless articles, but to have heard Ken speak about school safety and to have partnered with him on several projects. Ken is an exceptional, tireless, and very knowledgeable spokesperson on school safety who knows the inside story of what really needs to be done, having worked firsthand in the school security field. He is very familiar with the politics of school safety, knows how to lobby for better funding for school safety, and knows how to get the most benefit from the shrinking funding for school safety that schools are currently experiencing. This book covers everything from conducting safety audits and crisis drills to how to help the school board shape better policies for safer schools.

Ken and I share that our highest professional priority has been prevention of school violence. We have both testified several times before the U.S. Congress on this topic, and in July 2009, we testified before the same committee on strengthening federal school safety policy. Ken's testimony, which stressed the need for better data about the incidence of school violence, was eloquent, thoughtful, and practical based on his unmatched knowledge of school safety and school crisis planning.

I have been working in the field of school safety and crisis prevention and intervention for more than two decades, as my first book on the subject was published in 1989. I have also served on a national emergency assistance team for the past decade and have personally responded to provide assistance in the aftermath of 11 school shootings and many other school crisis situations. My background is in psychology, and I have been concerned that some experts in school safety seem only to be interested in promoting hardware measures such as metal detectors, surveillance cameras, and more police presence.

Ken Trump believes in a comprehensive and balanced approach to school safety that includes all school personnel, parents, and students. He especially recognizes the important roles for support staff such as counselors and psychologists in both crisis prevention and intervention. Ken knows that one of the keys to school safety is creating a climate where close supportive relationships are developed between all school personnel and students.

Students also must be involved in safety planning, as much of school safety is an inside job. There is no substitute for knowing all students and knowing them well. Ken knows that the student who was just bullied and harassed and who is humiliated or fearful is not in a state of mind to learn at an optimal level.

Crisis planning is never a done deal, and our plans must be continually evolving. School faculty meetings and school board meetings must regularly include reviews of crisis plans and safety initiatives. Ken's book outlines what he has demonstrated throughout his career: how schools can work collaboratively with key community partners such law enforcement, emergency management, and mental health professionals for better crisis planning.

I believe many of the incidents of school crises could have been, and should have been, prevented. The information in this landmark book will reduce school violence and save lives. I recommend it with the highest possible praise.

Dr. Scott Poland

Associate Professor, Center for Psychological Studies
Coordinator of the Suicide and Violence Prevention
Office at Nova Southeastern University
Member, National Emergency Assistance Team
Past President of the National Association
of School Psychologists

Preface

Today's school administrators are under enormous pressures to boost academic performance, maintain safe and orderly schools, and address many societal issues crossing their schoolhouse doors each day.

School administrators are increasingly faced with tighter budgets. Time is the only thing scarcer than money in many school districts. Educators need practical, cost-effective school safety strategies from credible sources without a lot of theory and fluff.

Proactive School Security and Emergency Preparedness Planning is designed to meet the needs of today's school leaders. Within it, readers will find straightforward information on school security and emergency preparedness. The book first looks at threats to school security and the politics surrounding it, and then moves right into the nuts-and-bolts strategies for preventing violence and preparing for crises.

A number of best practices in school safety have remained constant since my first two books were published in 1998 and 2000. Yet this book is timely in refocusing on the fundamentals and in advancing conversations on current hot topics and future threats to safe and secure schools. School safety planning is an ongoing process, not a one-time event, and this book builds significantly upon the knowledge base covered in my first two books.

Proactive School Security and Emergency Preparedness Planning introduces new, dedicated full chapters on managing the current national hysteria around bullying, preparing schools for terrorism, managing school safety on tight budgets, parents and school safety, and managing media and parent communications in the postcrisis stage of school emergency planning. These five new chapters offer practical, commonsense frameworks and steps school leaders can take to proactively manage and respond to highly visible, emotional, and political aspects of school safety leadership in today's security-sensitive school community. The guidance in these chapters will help school leaders navigate complex school safety issues while operating under unprecedented budget constraints.

Educators and safety officials will also benefit from new subchapter sections on hot topics that have emerged over the years since my first books. Administration building and board meeting security, after-hours school security; athletic and large event security; cell phones; Election Day security; elementary school security; Federal Educational Rights and Privacy Act (FERPA) and school privacy exceptions; Tasers and school police; training staff on school security and emergency preparedness; transportation security; diversifying emergency drills; tabletop exercises; and financial and continuity of operations plans are among the new and expanded subchapters. Readers who found my earlier publications helpful in covering a wide range of school security issues will find more best practices and issues to consider with the addition of these new topics.

School safety continues to be an evolving field, and keeping up with new information on school safety is as important as following the latest research in academic achievement. Updates on topics in this book will be added to my website at www.schoolsecurity.org. For timely and breaking updates on current trends, hot topics, free resources, news, opinion, and interactive dialogue on the latest developments in the school safety field, visit my blog at www.schoolsecurityblog.com and sign up for daily e-mail alerts.

About the Author

 **Kenneth S. Trump**, M.P.A., is the President of National School Safety and Security Services, a Cleveland-based national firm specializing in school security and emergency preparedness training and consulting. He has more than 25 years of experience in the school safety profession and has advised school, public safety, and government officials from all 50 states and internationally.

Ken served as a school security officer, investigator, and youth gang unit supervisor for the Cleveland City Schools' safety division. He also served as a suburban Cleveland school district security director and assistant gang task force director on a federally funded antigang initiative.

As a graduate of Cleveland State University, Ken has a Master of Public Administration degree and a Bachelor of Arts degree in Social Service (Criminal Justice Concentration). He has extensive specialized training in school safety, gangs, and emergency/crisis preparedness.

Ken has authored three books and more than 75 articles on school security and crisis issues. He is one of the most widely quoted school safety experts, appearing on all national news networks and cable TV and in top market newspapers. Ken also blogs on school safety issues at www .schoolsecurityblog.com.

Ken is a four-time invited Congressional witness, testifying on school safety and emergency preparedness issues. He has briefed Israeli educators and safety officials on school safety issues at the request of the U.S. State Department and was an invited attendee at the White House Conference on School Safety in 2006.

For updated biographical information, visit Ken's website at www .schoolsecurity.org.

Part I

Understanding and Managing School Safety

School leaders face a tense struggle between maintaining welcoming and supportive schools with a positive climate for students while also keeping schools safe, secure, and prepared for managing crises that cannot be prevented.

Effectively managing school safety requires the combined skills of a juggler and tightrope walker. School administrators must juggle school safety and the many other aspects of leading schools: academics, facilities, finances, district politics, school-community relations. They must also walk a tightrope by beefing up security and preparedness for an emergency while maintaining a supportive environment where students feel they are a part of the school, teachers can focus on academics, parents feel welcome as visitors and volunteers, and the school is part of the broader community.

This is not an easy job. School leaders must understand the evolving threats to school security, know how to navigate the "politricks" of school safety, and develop a comprehensive and balanced approach to school safety planning. Chapters 1–3 provide guidance for addressing these complex, and sometimes competing, interests.

1 The Evolving Threats to School Security

A series of school shootings and violent acts rattled the American education community between 1997 and 1999. The 1999 attack at Columbine High School was a watershed event in the field of school security and emergency preparedness planning. But more than a decade later, schools still struggle in managing safety, security, and emergency preparedness issues. Schools have made many safety improvements in the post-Columbine era, but glaring gaps remain.

THE SCHOOL SECURITY THREAT CONTINUUM

In my first book, *Practical School Security: Basic Guidelines for Safe and Secure Schools* (Trump, 1998), I wrote about aggressive and violent behavior, drugs, weapons, gangs, and stranger danger. In *Classroom Killers? Hallway Hostages? How Schools Can Prevent and Manage School Crises* (Trump, 2000), I talked about homemade bombs and bomb threats, computer-related offenses, adult-originated violence, teen suicide and self-harm, bullying and aggressive behavior, and schools as terrorist targets.

More than a decade later, I realize that all of these issues plus new threats can, and do, challenge school leaders at various times and in various communities still today. We cannot frame school security threats in the form of a top-10 list of specific threats at any given time. Instead, school leaders must prepare for a continuum of threats that could potentially affect the safety of their school at any given point in time.

On one end of the continuum, on a day-to-day basis the worst threat to maintaining a safe school may be verbal disrespect, physically aggressive behavior, and bullying (all important issues not to be minimized). On the other end of the continuum, threats may include a school shooting or a terrorist attack upon our nation's schools. Somewhere in between these extremes rests a host of other threats, such as a student or staff suicide, weather or natural disaster, large-scale student fights or riots, or a gun discharged in a restroom.

Any of these situations could potentially occur at any school at any point in time in the school year. Gangs may be a priority threat in a given school this year, but 2 years later gangs may be a nonissue. Today's focus on bullying and teen suicide by the media and school-community could shift overnight if terrorists strike our schools.

School leaders must therefore view potential threats to school safety as being on a continuum. The threats evolve from school to school and from one point in time to another. Planning and preparedness must evolve accordingly.

INTERNAL AND EXTERNAL THREATS TO SCHOOL SAFETY

Today's school leader must prepare for both internal *and* external threats. Too often we see school administrators overemphasizing the source of potential threats to their school's safety. Some say they are less worried about violence by a student inside a school but are more worried about outsiders who may come into the school to cause harm. Others will overemphasize potential student violence while failing to recognize factors beyond the school property line that pose a risk to their schools.

For example, I'm often surprised at how many schools that sit adjacent to, or within a very short distance of, a railroad track have never addressed the risk of a hazardous material spill incident. Administrators and crisis teams at these schools have often given detailed thought to reducing access to their buildings, training staff on assessing student threats, and planning for a school shooter. But so often we find these schools have had little if any discussion and planning on one of the biggest threats facing them: a train derailment, hazardous material spill, or other emergency related to the railroad track in their vicinity.

As another example, one of the top reasons we see elementary schools go into lockdown to secure their buildings is the result of the police or other activity outside of their school in the broader community. It is not uncommon for schools to lockdown after being alerted of police in pursuit of a bank robber or fleeing suspect from a traffic stop nearby. Yet over the years I have frequently had elementary school administrators and teachers say they do not want to practice lockdown drills out of fear they will traumatize young children and that there is no need to do so since there is little likelihood of violence impacting a school with elementary children.

School officials must recognize that threats to their school's safety can originate from both within and outside of their school. It is unrealistic to believe that student-originated violence or a disruption from an irate parent could not potentially occur inside a school. Likewise, ignoring potential risks from our broader community, such as a felon fleeing police or a hazardous materials spill from the highway next to your school, is also a risky move.

ASSESSING THREATS AND PRIORITIZING RISK REDUCTION

Each school district, and every school and support facility within that district, should assess the potential threats and prioritize their risk reduction measures. This means the priorities at one school may differ from those of another school within the same district.

For example, in one county school system where I conducted a school security assessment, one school was located within a few feet of a railroad track. Priority for planning at that school should have been for a hazardous material or other railroad incident. But in the same district, on the other side of the county, another school was in the flightpath of a small regional airport, and an airplane accident was of significant concern.

It is this uniqueness of each school, district, and school-community that requires educators, public safety officials, and community partners to conduct ongoing assessments and reevaluations of their school's security and planning for a crisis. Too often, schools put a one-time emphasis on assessing security and creating a crisis plan, relying on checklists or templates used districtwide rather than requiring a site-by-site assessment and emergency plan. Reassessments and updating of emergency plans must be conducted at least annually. School safety planning must be an ongoing process, not a one-time event.

Higher Risk Threats

Some types of individuals, situations, times, and places encountered by school officials are, by their nature, higher risk than others in terms of safety threats. These include the following:

- Athletic events, especially when there are a large number of observers or when the games are between rivals.
- Dances and similar social events where there are a large number of individuals gathered together and engaging in increased social activities.
- Locations within and around the school where there is a high level of student movement but little responsible adult supervision, such as restrooms, isolated hallways, stairwells, cafeterias, and bus drop-off and pick-up points.
- School opening, class change times, and dismissal.
- Irate parents or guardians, especially when they have ongoing encounters with school officials that they perceive to be negative or adversarial.
- Disgruntled employees who cannot resolve their conflicts through formal and legitimate mechanisms.

It is logical to believe that, because we know what types of situations pose a higher risk, we should be able to take more risk reduction measures to counter them. Unfortunately, this is not always the case.

ROLLER-COASTER AWARENESS, POLICY, AND FUNDING: THE BIGGEST ONGOING THREAT TO SCHOOL SAFETY

Although specific threats such as gangs or bullying change over time, the most serious threats to school safety have remained constant since I wrote my first two books more than a decade ago. These threats are adult-generated threats, not threats from students or outsiders who come onto school property. These threats are not violent, per se, but instead involve how school and other public officials manage policy and funding for school safety.

These threats include the following:

1. Inconsistent or AWOL leadership on school safety. We have worked in school districts where school safety is a top priority, from the school board to frontline staff such as school secretaries and custodians. Likewise, we have been in school districts where school safety is a priority by the leadership in one school, yet in another school in the same district the attention to safety is almost nonexistent. Inconsistent or nonexistent leadership on school safety issues, from the school board and superintendent to each school building principal, is one of the biggest threats to school safety. Specific issues such as drugs or fighting will likely evolve over time, but if school safety is not held forward as a consistent priority of the board, superintendent, and principal, schools will be less prepared than they possibly could be.

2. Complacency by school staff, students, and parents. The first and best line of defense for school safety is a well-trained, highly alert school staff and student body. When students open doors for strangers or fail to report another student who has a gun in school, and when staff members prop open doors and fail to challenge or report strangers in the hallways, school safety is at risk. Parents who fail to follow building entry and visitor procedures put safety at risk. An "it can't happen here" mentality puts school safety at risk. All of the security technology in the world cannot overcome the threat of human complacency, which is truly the biggest enemy of school safety.

3. Inadequate funding for prevention, security, and preparedness. Our state and federal legislatures, as well as local school boards, legislate and fund by anecdote. When there is a high-profile school safety incident in the headlines, legislators look for legislation and funding for that particular issue. When parent and media pressure is on at the local level, school boards *find* money to fund prevention and security programs that otherwise have had funding cut to the bare bone. Long-term stability is needed in both policy and funding for school safety, and legislating and funding by anecdote creates knee-jerk reactions, not the consistency needed for long-term success in addressing school safety.

Roller-coaster public awareness, policy, and funding present a danger to long-term school safety as great as the danger of specific threats such as gangs and bullying. When programs are created and then cut 2 years later, when school resource officers or security staff are in place for years and then suddenly eliminated, and when school safety falls to the back burner because there is not a crisis in the local news, long-term, sustained school safety planning loses.

2 The "Politricks" of School Security

"**P**olitricks"—political tricks—is unquestionably the biggest obstacle to having professional school security in many districts. A focus on image, power, control, and money (ironically the same features that motivate many gangs) often takes precedence over reporting crime and implementing professional security measures to truly protect children, staff, and property. This creates varying degrees of denial, rhetoric, underreporting and nonreporting of school-based crime, and a general state of paralysis for those educators, students, parents, and community members who often falsely believe that the people creating this type of environment are actually sincere in their claims of commitment to safe schools.

DENIAL, IMAGE, AND UNDERREPORTING

Denial, image, and related political motivators play a significant role in how, or even whether, many school officials report school crime and respond to school security needs. Although the phrase "zero tolerance" has gained national use by a substantial number of political and school officials, the action or inaction of many of these individuals fails to place meaning behind the rhetoric.

Every board member, superintendent, and principal is not in denial. Many school leaders are committed and sincere in their concern, talk, and action in enhancing school security. Although there has been a shift in school administrative culture to improved reporting and partnerships with law enforcement since the 1999 Columbine attack, the political problems associated with school security are still far too prevalent across the nation.

Denial of security problems by elected and administrative school officials exacerbates security problems and increases the risk of further threats. For example, the scope and effect of denial have been cited as major obstacles to the effective management of gang problems, especially in schools. In his first study of Ohio gangs, Huff (1988) described the effect of denial on schools by noting that

> it is probable that the official denial of gang problems actually facilitates victimization by gangs, especially in public schools. School principals in several Ohio cities are reluctant to acknowledge "gang-related" assaults for fear that such "problems" may be interpreted as negative reflections of their management ability. This "paralysis" may actually encourage gang-related assaults and may send the wrong signals to gang members, implying that they can operate within the vacuum created by this "political paralysis." (p. 9)

Unfortunately, Huff's finding was one of the first of numerous reported concerns about the issues of nonreporting, underreporting, and the lack of data on school-based, gang-related crime across the nation (Kodluboy & Evenrud, 1993; Lal, Lal, & Achilles, 1993; Spergel, 1990; Taylor, 1988).

Similar problems of nonreporting, underreporting, and denial exist with nongang, school-based crimes. Concerns about poor reporting of school crimes and inadequate reporting practices have been cited repeatedly for more than three decades (Kodluboy & Evenrud, 1993; Quarles, 1993; Rubel & Ames, 1986; U.S. Department of Health, Education, and Welfare, 1978). Yet three decades since the first documentation of the problem, efforts to improve school crime reporting have been haphazard and inconsistent across the nation, while the issue of school crime and its associated level of violence has grown to be a major area of public concern.

Numerous examples of underreporting and nonreporting of school crimes to law enforcement have been exposed in recent years through news reports, academic studies, law enforcement, reports by school employees and students, after external audits and assessments of school districts, and sometimes, through internal audits and subsequent reports. Offenses not reported by school officials range from such property crimes as vandalism, theft, and arson (many involving thousands of taxpayers' dollars) to such crimes against persons and society as assault, drug possession and trafficking, extortion, rape and other sex crimes, and weapons possession and use. About the only offense missing from the examples (so far) is murder!

The exact extent of nonreporting and underreporting is difficult to specify in numbers because there is no central tracking authority for such problems. Nevertheless, increasing indicators of school-crime reporting problems strongly suggest that they are more prevalent than many people would like to believe or admit. It is becoming increasingly difficult for persons to deny this problem, as a national concern, by labeling documented cases of nonreporting as "isolated incidents," "atypical," or "only characteristic of large, urban districts."

Why do officials fail to report school-based crimes? According to the American Association of School Administrators (1981), the reasons educational administrators refrain from notifying law enforcement officials of school-based crimes include the following:

- They want to avoid bad publicity, litigation, or both.
- They fear being blamed for the problem or considered as ineffective in their jobs.
- They consider some offenses "too minor" to report.
- They prefer to handle the problems using disciplinary procedures.
- They believe the police and courts will not cooperate.

Almost 30 years after the American Association of School Administrator's report, the reasons for nonreporting remain largely the same.

Far too many cases of nonreporting are intentional and sanctioned by some principals, central office administrators, superintendents, or board members. Other instances of nonreporting are less intentional and more a by-product of bad past practices and distortions of outside influences. The reasons for intentional nonreporting are described as follows.

1. School officials fear that if crimes are reported to police, they will be perceived by the public as poor managers. Some principals and central office administrators, including superintendents, fear that they will be removed from their positions if it appears that there is "too much crime" in their schools. In some districts, the number of incidents reported has a direct negative effect on administrator performance evaluations and, in turn, on salary increases or continued employment in these positions.

2. Politricks exist not only between the school system and the community but also within the school system. Even when the data exist, countless examples exist of manipulation, largely owing to internal competition and the fear of negative consequences to careers (Hill & Hill, 1994). Such behavior exacerbates denial, nonreporting, and an organizational culture focused more on its image than on school security.

3. Some principals submit only selected statistics and information to the central office. Some central office administrators submit only selected statistics

and information to the upper administration. And some superintendents "spoon-feed" only selected statistics and information to the board. So even when board members are sincere in dealing with security issues, the information they receive from the administration may be grossly distorted.

4. A number of cases have been documented, largely through investigative news stories, where local school districts have reported school discipline and crime statistics inaccurately to state education agencies that require annual reports from schools. Reporters have often uncovered discrepancies among local school district data, police department data, and data provided by the school district to state education officials. Typically school officials feign ignorance, claim a misunderstanding of state reporting procedures, or blame clerical errors for the discrepancy. They get a warning from the state and black eye in the local media, both of which tend to go away quickly with few long-term consequences for intentional or grossly neglectful underreporting of school discipline and crime incidents. (For an ongoing list of school crime underreporting incidents, see my Web page on the issue at www.schoolsecurity.org/trends/school_crime_reporting.html.)

5. School board members fear that negative publicity of reported crimes will contribute to their not being re-elected to their positions. Political images and egos are easily bruised. Few bruises are worse than those stemming from the perception by the community that the individuals they elected to the school board have no control over the district. The tide is slowly turning, however, as public displeasure and distrust for schools not being candid with their communities is coming back to haunt elected officials, especially when the distrust involves the safety of children and schools.

6. School leaders fear that if crimes are reported, parents will perceive the schools as unsafe and remove their children from the school system. A related fear is that if crimes are reported, parents and other voters will not pass school tax proposals for those communities that require funding increases through elections.

7. Some administrators believe that no data mean no problems. If incidents are not reported and data are not collected, then there will be no concrete evidence of a problem. Should the media, parents, or others ask for data or documentation related to school security, administrators can honestly say that there are no reports of, or statistics on, such occurrences.

8. Some educators have control issues, especially relating to image. Educators are indoctrinated in an environmental culture based on control. Teachers must control their classrooms. Those who are successful in classroom control may be promoted to assistant principals when they are given

responsibility for control of discipline in the school. These assistants may be promoted to principals and now would be responsible for controlling the entire school operation. Principals may be promoted to central office positions and would be responsible for controlling an entire school service department. And some will be promoted to superintendent, when they must fully control the entire school district.

The real and perceived need to control, although certainly not the only evaluation factor in determining the promotion of school personnel, can have a detrimental effect on school security. Those who falsely interpret security-related incidents to be a personal loss of control inevitably will make decisions contrary to professional security practices. Nevertheless, those who interpret security-related incidents to be a problem requiring a proactive and preventative response will accurately perceive any inaction as a personal loss of control and, in doing so, will likely pursue proper practices.

In fairness to school administrators, the failure to report crimes can truly be unintentional. Reasons why administrators unintentionally fail to report crimes may include the following:

1. School administrators have a history of handling all student behavior administratively as disciplinary issues. Administrators traditionally have full authority to discipline students for violations of school rules with such consequences as detention, suspension, or expulsion. This is indeed within their realm of authority.

The problem arises, however, when the student misbehavior is also a crime. Principals still have the authority to administer disciplinary action within the realm of established policies and procedures. Nevertheless, they also have a responsibility to process the case criminally by reporting the offense to police.

Some administrators falsely believe that by handling the criminal incident administratively, they have fulfilled their obligation. Others inaccurately view handling an incident administratively and criminally as double jeopardy. Nevertheless, there is no double jeopardy.

Students are not punished twice for the same offense when they are disciplined within the school and reported to law enforcement officials for a violation of the law. Administrators are fully justified and should be mandated in reporting crimes to police besides administering disciplinary action. Failure to do so sends a strong message to students that their criminal behaviors are immune from consequences so long as they are committed under the supervision of school officials. This, in turn, increases the likelihood of further criminal behavior.

2. A large number of educators, including administrators, have received little or no training in distinguishing crimes from disciplinary

offenses. For example, a difference exists between fighting and assaults. Fighting implies that there are two willing, intentional participants who choose to engage in combat. Assault, however, suggests an intentional act by one individual against a victim who is not inclined to fight. A difference also exists between "bullying" and extortion, when the bullying involves a student shaking down another student for his or her lunch money in the school restroom.

Although law enforcement, prosecutors, and school security specialists are readily available to provide such training, it appears as though few school personnel see its need or importance until an unreported incident becomes high profile. School administrators should seek this training for themselves and their staff with updates at least once a year. They also should incorporate legal definitions of offenses into their school policies and student handbooks to ensure that school definitions of crimes are consistent with legal codes.

3. Some educators believe that certain crimes are too insignificant for law enforcement to be notified or that they can be better handled internally without law enforcement involvement. One of the best examples of this is the occurrence of thefts. School officials have been known to choose to not report thefts of school property, even in cases involving thousands of dollars, because, in their minds, it serves no purpose as their districts are self-insured. What they seem to forget is that, not only has a felony crime occurred but also that they are self-insured with public taxpayer dollars! Replacement or repair costs for thefts, vandalism, and similar offenses contribute to a significant loss of public dollars that, if prevented, would be better used toward classroom education.

Other administrators are hesitant to involve law enforcement because they fear parental complaints, lawsuits, or both, for their actions. It is not uncommon for central office administrators or board members to provide *less than anticipated* support for principals who take a strong stand when parents complain about discipline or related issues. A lack of central office support discourages principals from firm, fair, and consistent discipline, crime reporting, and security practices when principals know, or perceive, that the district's leaders will reverse their positions when the "squeaky wheel" calls central office to complain.

Law enforcement and criminal justice systems can, at times, contribute to the problem of nonreporting of school crime by school officials. Especially in larger, urban areas where law enforcement and court resources are stretched to maximum capacity, school officials may be unofficially encouraged to not report certain such offenses as possession of small amounts of marijuana or other misdemeanors. By doing so, the police and courts imply that school officials are creating an unnecessary burden by calling the police, leading school administrators to avoid reporting other offenses that they may interpret as minor. Problems then arise, because school administrators generally do not have the training, experience, or legal right to judge which crimes should and should not be reported.

AWKWARD CIRCUMSTANCES ENCOURAGE DOWNPLAYING OF SCHOOL SAFETY

School administrators have also been put in an awkward position on reporting school crimes and fully addressing school safety threats.

Persistently Dangerous Schools

As a component of the federal education No Child Left Behind law signed into law by President Bush in 2002, state education departments were required to create definitions of "persistently dangerous schools" in order to create a trigger for allowing parents to remove students from such a designated school to send them elsewhere. Although states typically created definitions in such a manner that most schools would never meet the criteria (nor did they want to), the mere existence of the definition cast a shadow over schools, which discouraged the accurate reporting of school crime and violence. Most school administrators privately acknowledged they would rather their schools be labeled "academically failing" than "persistently dangerous" if they had to pick between the two negative labels. Common agreement grew over time that this requirement was counterproductive and problematic.

School Climate Survey Scores

As this book heads to press, President Obama's Education Department is proposing policy and funding to have schools complete school climate surveys for which schools would subsequently receive school safety scores based on criteria yet to be disclosed. The proposed approach of providing school safety scores based on climate surveys pushed by federal and state governments risks being the current administration's version of the "persistently dangerous schools" component of the No Child Left Behind law. Although the pitch to receive federal funding for school climate may sound attractive on the surface, especially given other cuts to school safety funding, in the long haul this approach will likely lead to discouraged school crime and climate honesty rather than increased accuracy and openness.

Lack of Federal Mandatory School Crime Reporting

No federal mandatory school crime reporting and tracking exists in the United States. Federal data are limited to a hodgepodge collection of a handful of academic studies, many of them unrelated to one another, based primarily on surveys. Federal school safety policy and funding has been largely driven by this limited, questionable data.

Local school officials and education associations have not been quick to support mandatory federal (or state) school crime reporting. On the one hand, local schools enjoy state and federal school safety grants as a source outside their local operating budgets for providing prevention and safety programs. Yet on the other hand, local schools are hesitant to accurately report school-based crimes out of fear of adverse media and public attention.

Ironically, the failure of local schools to accurately report school crimes and the failure to have incident-based federal mandatory school crime reporting increases the risks of reduced federal funding for school safety. In fact, using their questionable and limited academic survey reports, the federal government has actually repeatedly claimed that school crime is down nationally since 1992. Although it is hard to understand how they come to that conclusion given there is no federal mandatory school crime reporting and data collection, the lame federal survey data have directly or indirectly contributed to reduced funding for school safety under the facade that school crime is declining.

Terrorism and School Security

The discussion of schools as potential targets for domestic and international terrorism has been muted due to fears of alarming parents. As I address later in this book, the 2004 terrorist attack upon a school in Beslan, Russia, is one of many concrete examples of schools and school buses being targeted internationally for terrorist attack. Although there has been some study of the issue, including a National Strategy Forum publication titled *School Safety in the 21st Century: Adapting to New Security Challenges Post-9/11: Report of the Conference "Schools: Prudent Preparation for a Catastrophic Terrorism Incident"* (2004), and a 2007 Congressional hearing by the House Homeland Security Committee, greater public discourse has been stifled due to the politics and public reaction concerns. Of course, if federal and other leaders more publicly acknowledged this threat, they would also be under pressure to better fund school security and preparedness—something that has not happened since that 2004 report and 2007 hearing.

Politicization of School Safety

In *Classroom Killers? Hallway Hostages? How Schools Can Prevent and Manage School Crises* (Trump, 2000), I lay out an extensive review of how school safety was politically prostituted before and after the Columbine High School attack in 1999. The political abuse and misuse of the issue of school safety range from Congressional and political party spin in Washington, D.C., to how local school boards and administrators capitalized on the frenzy about school safety to use it as leverage to pass local school financial issues on the ballot by including safety and security components to proposed bonds and levies. It makes for an interesting historical read, but for the purposes of this book I will point readers to the 2000 publication for details.

The politicization of school safety continues, though, up to the printing of this book. At the national level, bullying became the focus of opportunistic elected officials in the late 2000s and became a tool for political manipulation at the federal level in 2009, rising to a frenzy level by elected officials, special interest groups, and the media as of the writing of this book in late 2010. Bullying has especially become the centerpiece for gay rights advocates calling for anti-bullying bills to protect students who are or are perceived to be gay, to their Christian conservative opponents who claim that such advocacy is less about bullying and more about a deeper political agenda to get gay-friendly policies, training, and curriculum into public schools. (See Chapter 6 on bullying issues as well as www.schoolsecurityblog.com for a detailed look at this storyline of school safety politics.)

Parents and most frontline educators have no clue as to the extent to which school safety is a political issue. Parents don't know what they don't know, and nobody is rushing to tell them. Aspiring school administrators, as well as those currently holding the position, had best take a closer look both locally and nationally to better understand the politicization of school safety so they can learn to navigate the politics while making sure their policies and decisions meet the best interests of keeping kids and schools safe, not furthering a broader political agenda of special interests locally or on a state or national level.

REALITY, NOT RHETORIC

Administrators must establish a strong foundation that includes the consistent reporting of school crimes to law enforcement before new policies, procedures, and programs can be developed to enhance school security. Without this foundation, security threats cannot be identified, trends cannot be established, and prevention and countermeasures cannot be deployed.

Most people on the front lines do know what is going on in the schools, even in the absence of formal reporting mechanisms and data. It is false to think that members of the school community live in isolation and do not know that crimes occur in school. Similarly false is the perception that the community will perceive school leaders as poor managers if they report crimes.

The reality is that they will be perceived as poor managers for not reporting crimes and for not handling problems head-on. It is then that parents might not pass tax proposals or might move out of the system. Administrative inaction, not action, will eventually lead to their downfall on security issues.

The failure to report school-based crimes and to deal with security matters proactively has negative consequences on several levels. Most important: It is not good for kids and is wrong. Regardless of the perceived benefits of nonreporting, the reality is this:

- It teaches children that there are no repercussions for committing criminal acts.
- It sends a message to students that schools are islands of lawlessness where the criminal laws of the broader community do not apply, thereby subjecting the school to even more potential offenses.
- It states to the parents and community members that there is a lack of concern about the safety of their children.
- It states to school employees that there is a lack of concern about the safety of their workplace.
- It contributes to an atmosphere in which teachers cannot teach and children cannot learn at their maximum capabilities.
- It creates an inadequate knowledge base regarding the true extent and nature of crimes committed in school and on school grounds across the United States, thereby reducing our ability to develop effective intervention and prevention strategies.

Veteran school security specialists and law enforcement officers are not the only professionals finally talking publicly about the seriousness of this basic tenet of professional security. In its report titled *Risks to Students in School*, the Office of Technology Assessment (OTA) for the U.S. Congress (1995) cited the lack of data on school-related injuries, noting that information had not improved much since 1985. The report concluded:

Definition inconsistencies, the lack of accurate baselines, underreporting, and the absence of a national—and, in most cases, state-level—surveillance system complicates the characterization of trends in injuries at school and undermines public health intervention efforts to stem the impact and severity of risk factors related to school injuries. (p. 108)

The OTA's finding reinforces the position that many U.S. schools have bypassed the first step of acknowledging, reporting, and identifying security problems. One can only ask how these officials attempt to create policies, procedures, and programs to address a problem that they allege does not exist.

It is sad to hear the phrase "zero tolerance" as a political buzzword in many communities. Given the politics of school security, the repeated abuse of such sayings as "zero tolerance programs for violence, drugs, weapons, and gangs" should be followed with a simple question from students, staff, parents, and the community: What percentage of tolerance did the school system previously have for violence, drugs, weapons, and gangs? Seventy percent tolerance? Fifty percent tolerance? The honest reporting of discipline and crimes should be in place at all times, not as a new program or political rhetoric.

Congress should also pursue federal school crime reporting and tracking laws for K–12 schools that focus on law enforcement and incident-based data. Although this is a politically charged issue, federal policy and funding cannot continue to be based upon a hodgepodge collection of a half dozen or so academic surveys limited in scope and depth. Our lawmakers must have improved data on actual criminal incidents reported on campuses, not just surveys based on perceptions and self-reports alone.

By consistently and accurately reporting school-based crimes, educators, and school security and police officials can reverse the tragic trend of political priorities taking precedence over school security. This step, taken via a national legislative mandate, would send a stronger message to the students, staff, and community that they can expect schools to be the safe and secure havens that they were in the past. Done properly, it can also be a positive public relations tool and provide justification for increased school safety funding for local school districts.

3

Comprehensive School Safety Planning and Leadership

Overall, educators, law enforcement officers, parents, students, and other community members want to do the right thing in providing safe learning environments. The political issues described in Chapter 2 present some major obstacles. No quick-fix solution or simple checklist exists for putting and keeping everything in its proper place. Rarely will it be easy. But it can be done. And it can be done in a win-win manner for all.

Although no one can guarantee that a school will never experience a tragedy, school officials should be able to identify specific, balanced, and comprehensive steps that they have taken to reduce the risks of such an incident occurring and to prepare to manage a serious incident effectively, should one occur.

The trend of pitting security and crisis preparedness strategies against prevention strategies as an *either/or* option highlights the tendency Americans have of going from one extreme to the other in their perspectives on how to solve complex problems. Likewise, the inaccurate framing of security and crisis preparedness, equating them with scores of police and tons of equipment in our school hallways, also contributes to a skewed picture of what needs to be done to improve school safety. To stand a chance of making a significant impact on the issue of school safety, those who are working on safe schools issues must acknowledge, accept, and use a balanced and comprehensive framework.

SCHOOL SAFETY AS A LEADERSHIP ISSUE

School safety is not just a funding issue. It is largely a leadership issue. Parents will forgive school officials if test scores go down, but they will be much less forgiving if something happens to their children that could have been prevented or better managed.

School leaders have the power to reduce risks, improve preparedness, and protect their reputations in the process if they choose to do so. The positive impact of being a school board and administration that is proactive with school safety includes the following:

- Safer schools.
- Improved attendance and reduced dropouts.
- Primary focus on academic achievement, not discipline and safety.
- Increased parental confidence, which leads to greater faith in school leaders, stable schools and communities, and greater likelihood of support for school funding requests.

School officials can no longer view school safety as a grant-funded luxury. Long-term costs must be budgeted in school operating budgets for items such as the following:

- Security and police staffing.
- Physical security measures (security equipment, communications systems, etc.).
- Professional development training for all staff, including support personnel such as bus drivers and schools office support staff.
- Consultant services (security assessments, emergency planning evaluations, etc.).

School administrators must also exercise leadership in making school safety a part of their school's culture. Professional development time must be allocated for school safety training and planning time dedicated for updating school crisis plans. Incorporating discussions of school safety into faculty meetings and communicating safety in parent communications must be a normal part of school activities.

Too often, we see limited budgets used as an excuse for not addressing school safety issues. Many tasks for improving and maintaining school safety require more time than money. Leadership is often a bigger missing component of school safety than money.

GETTING ON THE SAME PAGE

The first step to safely managing the problem is to get everyone on the same page. This is probably the most difficult step. The following is a

5-point continuum on which individuals, organizations, and communities often fall in addressing school safety issues:

1. *Lack of Awareness.* This is defined as "simply not recognizing a problem or not knowing how to address a problem that is recognized."

2. *Denial.* This "occurs when officials are aware of a problem, and possibly even know an appropriate response to the problem, but refuse to admit that the problem exists."

3. *Qualified Admittance.* This is a position by which "the problem is partially recognized and confronted, but only in a limited manner and not to the actual degree to which it needs to be addressed."

4. *Balanced and Rational Approach.* This "incorporates all components of prevention, intervention, security, and preparedness.

5. *Overreaction.* This is characterized as a "point where many people perceive most schools as being filled with gun-toting, drug-dealing gang members who spend their entire school day committing crimes on campus. . . . The resulting tension and hysteria can lead to increased violence by students and to progressively harsher reactions by adults, who respond more to the perception of fear than to the reality of the threats that may actually exist" (Trump, 1997, pp. 266–268).

The key to successfully getting on the same page is to assess where each key individual and organization falls along this continuum and then to get everyone to adopt a balanced and rational approach. The process of assessing where individuals, organizations, and communities are on the continuum frequently involves the formation of task forces or committees, often with duplicate and nonproductive meetings, descriptive assessments or reports, and many times in the end, few concrete steps or products resulting in true security improvements. School administrators need to be aware that this process can consume a great deal of energy, waste time, and what is most important, have minimal effect.

Progress can be made. Understanding different professional and personal perspectives is critical and should be included in the problem identification and assessment process. But a deadline needs to be placed on doing this and then moving on to action. Everyone cannot agree on everything, but they can agree to disagree and move ahead with concrete steps. Paralysis by analysis is one of the leading contributors to poor school security, and talking about a problem for the sake of feeling good about talking about it is, in reality, still doing nothing.

OVERCOMING DENIAL

The first and most important step toward reducing security and crisis risks is to acknowledge that the potential for an incident exists in any school district and community in the nation, regardless of location, size, demographics, or other social and economic factors. Although it is logical to believe that this would be a basic premise in the minds of all, denial on individual, school, and community levels is still alive and well. Reasons for denial include the following:

- A perceived need to protect the image and reputation of individuals, schools, and/or communities.
- Belief that acknowledgment of the possibility of a security or crisis incident occurring in a school or community equates with a loss of management power, control, and professional or personal security.
- Fear that parents and members of the school community will not support levies or other funding drives, and that they may relocate from the community out of fear that schools are unsafe.
- Disbelief and distrust of the motives of individuals who publicly persist in putting safe schools on the agenda (i.e., the belief that these individuals are grandstanding, have personal or professional aspirations behind their efforts, or that they are alarmists).
- The sincere belief that "It can't happen here" or that "It won't happen in *my* school or *my* community."

The hazards of continued denial include the following:

- Denial in the short-term only leads to higher losses in the long-term.
- Increased, not decreased, safety risks.
- Promotion of the wrong message to offenders, leading them to believe that their behavior is acceptable and tolerated.
- Reductions in the productivity of individuals on the front lines who perceive—many times appropriately so—a lack of support from those who are higher up and in denial.
- Denial communicates that school officials are not concerned about safety and that they are not responsive to the needs and desires of members of the school community.
- A reduction of the knowledge base on a problem, because, as a result of denial, the problems are not fully identified, researched, or funded to find solutions.
- An adverse impact on an organization's or community's economic base because the failure to acknowledge and act upon a problem or

concern is interpreted as neglect or a cover-up. This perception generates a lack of trust in and support for the organization and its leaders, which can lead to a lack of support for funding drives or relocation from the community.

In the end, the costs of denial are far greater than the benefits. Once everyone acknowledges a problem or the potential for a problem, they can then move on in their efforts to prevent and manage the problem.

FINANCIAL OBSTACLES

I have listened to school board members, superintendents, and other educational administrators dismiss security and emergency preparedness suggestions by claiming, "Whatever it is, it costs too much. It is either security or textbooks and, since we're a school district, education is our top priority and the money must go directly to learning." Several inherent problems exist with this line of thinking.

Foremost, the first priority must be school safety. Common sense (something often lacking in policymaking and legislative decisions) dictates that children and teachers who are preoccupied with their safety will not have their maximum attention focused on the educational process. For true education to occur, school officials must first create a safe and secure environment in which to deliver the educational programs.

A second problem with this line of thinking is that security and crisis preparedness are automatically framed as such high-ticket items as manpower or equipment. Ironically, in our assessments of school security for districts nationwide, we typically find that these items are often last on the list, if they even make it at all, in terms of safety needs. A lack of training and awareness, combined with inadequately enforced security policies and procedures, top the list of safety needs in most schools.

Realistically, some areas for improvement simply require dollars, especially those associated with physical security improvements. Schools cannot duck and dodge the need to pay for some risk reduction measures, although incorporating such needs into capital improvement budgets and long-term strategic plans may be one appropriate step toward reducing risks and still managing the financial end of school operations. Creating schools without some costs is unrealistic and impractical.

Perhaps the best way to look at the financial aspect of implementing safe school measures is to look not at the cost of doing *something*, but instead at the cost of doing *nothing*. By taking no steps to reduce school safety risks, educators face the following potential costs:

- Increased risks for successful legal action against a school district and/or its individual employees because of inadequate security, and increased legal costs associated with defending unsuccessful lawsuits or paying off settlements for cases that do not go to trial.
- Increased insurance claims against the school district from injuries and losses associated with violence, property damage, and other criminal activity.
- Potentially massive unplanned costs associated with a recovery from a crisis or disaster, such as increased manpower and overtime costs, major repairs to the physical facility, and increased legal and public relations support services.
- An inability to recruit and retain quality staff because of real or perceived unsafe workplace conditions.
- An inability to improve test scores and other areas of student achievement because of a decreased focus on academics stemming from an increased focus on safety.

In the end, the costs of doing nothing certainly outweigh the costs of taking practical, cost-effective measures to reduce school safety risks.

SCHOOL SAFETY AS A PUBLIC RELATIONS TOOL

School safety has experienced a complete turnaround in terms of public relations. Previously, many educators felt that by publicly addressing school safety and crisis preparedness, they were setting themselves up for a public relations nightmare by talking about the subject. Today, the credibility, reputations, and potentially the careers of school leaders rest on their ability to meet parental expectations for providing safe and secure schools.

The use of the issue to gain some positive public relations by a school district is not a bad thing as long as the district is doing what it says that it is doing. Public relations has, unfortunately, become a negative phrase, when in reality it should simply mean communicating the good behavior of school district officials in an effective manner. As long as the school officials are sincere and are doing something in addition to talking about doing it, there is nothing wrong with school safety being a positive public relations tool.

COMMUNITY OWNERSHIP

Collective ownership of the problems of school violence and the solutions, including security enhancements, is often the best way to manage this issue. Schools alone do not create violent children; nor do police departments, social service agencies, community centers, or political bodies. But all of these entities and many others must deal with the outcome.

Any of these agencies or their members will have little success with taking public ownership of the problems or efforts to control the problems by themselves. They will quickly realize minimal success of their policies, procedures, and programs, and increase their political liability as the problems continue to grow and the community looks to those who took sole ownership for answers. It is programmatic and political suicide to try to take them on alone.

The key stakeholders must collectively and publicly acknowledge the problems as a community problem. These stakeholders include representatives from schools, law enforcement and other first responders, emergency management agencies, social and other youth service providers, political entities, businesses, community-based organizations, faith-based organizations, neighborhood groups, media, parents, and most important, students. None of these groups alone created the problems, but they all must deal with them.

Progressive leaders have realized that shared ownership can lead to shared success. Funding sources for youth and other programs are mandating collaboration before they will fund many projects.

Collaboration is great when it is sincere and results in action. Problems arise, however, when stakeholders get together for a press conference and do damage control after high-profile incidents and create the false perception that they are doing something for the right reasons when, in reality, it is all a smoke screen. If collaboration exists for developing such a final, concrete product as improving school security, then great. If collaboration exists for political reasons or because it is the popular thing to do, and all that results is rhetoric, then administrators should focus their energies elsewhere on more productive tasks.

TOOLS FOR BALANCE

How do you get everyone on the same page and how do you stay focused?

Five simple tools, along with strong leadership, can help maintain focus and prevent stakeholders from falling into the counterproductive positions of lack of awareness, denial, qualified admittance, or overreaction. These include the use of the following resources.

1. Concrete Data and Facts

Facts, figures, and case studies must be assembled, and in some cases, be indisputable to reduce the risk of stakeholders resting on preconceived notions or posturing on political platforms. Even with data and facts, it can be difficult to persuade people to move forward with a security program. Without data and facts, it will be even more difficult.

What are the sources of data related to school security? Some include:

- *Police calls for service to schools.*
- *Police offense or incident reports for schools.* Note that this may be different from police calls for service to schools; police may be called to schools, but a report may never be made as a result of the call.
- *Security incident reports.* School security personnel, administrators, and staff should complete standard incident reports for security-related incidents and offenses. Incident reports should be categorized and periodic summaries compiled to analyze data trends. Many schools, even those without security departments, have such forms in place. Those that do not should establish one immediately.
- *Discipline data.* Most schools regularly compile data on student discipline. Larger school districts have student services offices or similar departments that coordinate discipline-related services throughout the system. Suspensions, expulsions, and other figures should be available with a breakdown by offense categories.
- *Federal and state data.* Many states require local districts to report discipline and other demographic data on at least an annual basis. Federal data are also required, including those for grant-funded programs. Grant programs in the school system should be reviewed for data collected and reported in grant applications, evaluations, and reports. The absence of such data usually makes obtaining a grant much more difficult.
- *Surveys.* Many school districts conduct student, staff, or both types of surveys periodically to assess particular issues. Student surveys on drug use have been common over the past decade, and a number of them are now being conducted on violence and safety concerns. Larger employee unions and professional associations also survey their members as a potential source of additional information.
- *Audits, assessments, and consultant reports.* Review prior audits, assessments, and consultant reports related to prevention, security, preparedness, or other aspects of school safety.
- *Community reports.* A variety of criminal justice, social services, and other youth service agencies, as well as chambers of commerce, private businesses, colleges and universities, philanthropic foundations, and others conduct studies, assessments, or write reports related to juvenile crime and violence. Although the information may not always be school specific, it will provide insight into community youth safety concerns. As school officials know, the schools reflect the community.

- *Unions and professional organizations.* In addition to conducting member surveys, a growing number of unions and organizations for school employees are establishing data collection mechanisms to gauge measures related to school security. Some larger district teacher unions are requiring teachers to fill out special incident reports so the union can check on school administrators to ensure no statistical manipulation or such accidental misplacement of reports and data as underreporting and nonreporting.
- *Physical evidence, videos, photos, and other visuals.* Nothing beats physical evidence to illustrate a point. Take a look at items confiscated by the school district and police for evidence for student expulsions and/or criminal prosecution. This may put a realistic face on an abstract problem being discussed.
- *Student, parent, and community input.* Involving the stakeholders in the school community helps keep a balanced picture of the problems and required strategies. Ownership of safe and secure school plans on the front end reduces the risk of ineffective plans, lack of support, and negative publicity after the fact.

Several problems may be encountered when trying to locate data. First is the absence of data, suggesting that questions then need to be asked about why data are not collected (no data, no problem?). Second, reluctance may exist on the part of some school officials to provide the data. Although these data are usually public information and must be provided on reasonable request according to the law, the benefits of having data outweigh the risks of having to release them because of public inquiry. Partial information or sanitized versions of the full reports should not be created in response to these requests simply to paint a better picture of the school, district, or both, than the actual data suggest. Trust and honesty are critical elements of effective collaboration, which could be damaged if school officials attempt to distort reality.

2. College and University Support

Academic studies are not a substitute for internal school data or professional school security assessments. Nevertheless, research and analysis of data and other information related to school security can help focus more on facts and less on perceptions. Many colleges or universities have education, social service, or public administration departments that may be able to design surveys and analyze data. Some of these departments may be able to provide this support at reduced costs as a part of student projects or internships, saving the school system money.

3. Education Programs for School Personnel, Students, Parents, Community Members, and the Media

People often base opinions on false perceptions or their fears of the unknown. Beyond media stories, many individuals have little knowledge about gangs, drugs, weapons, youth violence, school security, and school crisis issues. Schools should provide education programs for all stakeholders to present a balanced understanding of the problems, and the rationale behind security measures and emergency preparedness plans taken by schools. No school official would disagree that education is the key, so why should this stop with security and emergency preparedness issues?

4. Youth Involvement

The importance of student involvement in identifying security concerns and in making recommendations for corrective and preventive action cannot be overstated. Too often we forget to involve those directly affected by the problems: the students. Not only is their input important but their solutions for dealing with problems are often more creative and practical, and less complex and costly, than those proposed by adults. Student involvement adds a touch of reality and balance to the process.

5. Professional Security Assessments

Officials frequently attempt to *attack* security problems either haphazardly or with extreme measures. Although it is wise to avoid paralysis by analysis, it is equally wise to have a plan for enhancing school security methodically and logically. Professional school security assessments by school security specialists can provide a strategic plan for taking short-term and long-term measures in a rational, balanced, and prioritized manner.

RISK REDUCTION FRAMEWORK

General Approaches

From a practical, frontline perspective, I have found that the following approaches contribute significantly to safe schools:

- Order, structure, and firm, fair, and consistent discipline.
- A genuine balance between prevention, intervention, security, and emergency preparedness strategies.

- Individual assessment and intervention with children experiencing academic and behavioral problems.
- Sincere relationships between students and staff, and staff and the broader school community (e.g., with parents, social services, law enforcement, support personnel, etc.).
- Information sharing, within legal boundaries and not in violation of legitimate confidentiality parameters, between schools and law enforcement, criminal justice officials, social service representatives, parents, and relevant other youth service providers.
- Youth service providers, parents, and others who are consistently alert, informed, and proactive in addressing youth and violence prevention issues.
- Simple, apolitical, and youth-focused action.

Most of these items require more time than they do money. But, we cannot continue to ask ourselves why our efforts at preventing school and youth violence are not working when we are not willing to invest fully both our time and money into doing so.

The Security and Emergency Preparedness Components

Steps should be taken in at least four basic risk-reduction categories associated with school security and emergency preparedness. These include the following:

1. Firm, fair, and consistent enforcement of safety-related policies and procedures, along with adequate and effective levels of adult supervision.

2. Training, as appropriate, on security and crisis threat trends and strategies for *all* school personnel, including support staff, such as secretaries/office support staff, custodians and maintenance staff, food service staff, and transportation staff, as well as other key members of the school community.

3. Professional school security assessments conducted by qualified professionals, such as in-house school security specialists, school resource officers, or qualified outside school security consultants, and the implementation of appropriate recommendations stemming from such an assessment.

4. Creation, testing, updating, and revising emergency preparedness guidelines for natural disasters and crises stemming from man-made acts of crime and violence.

These four broad categories, and the many specific measures that are a part of the respective processes or process outcomes, can contribute to reducing security and crisis-related risks.

A Comprehensive Safe Schools Framework

Security and crisis preparedness represent only two pieces of a comprehensive safe schools framework. A balanced and comprehensive safe schools framework includes these parts as the first line of defense and prevention, but also will include them as a part of an overall plan that includes but is not limited to the following:

- Proactive security measures.
- Emergency preparedness planning.
- Firm, fair, and consistent discipline.
- Effective prevention and intervention programs.
- Mental health support services.
- A school climate stressing respect, acceptance of diversity, belonging, trust, pride, ownership, involvement, peaceful resolution of conflicts, and related characteristics.
- Strong and challenging academic programs.
- Diverse extracurricular activities.
- Parental and community involvement, support, and networking.

These components should receive equal attention in developing a safe schools plan. To focus too strongly on only one or a handful will reduce the likelihood of having an effective, comprehensive strategy for reducing safety risks.

Part II

Proactive School Security: Focusing on Fundamentals

My analysis of school safety progress in the decade following the 1999 Columbine attack found that although many schools made progress in addressing security and emergency preparedness issues, many glaring gaps remained. The progress made in the immediate months and years after Columbine has stalled, and in some cases slid backward, because of school safety budget cuts and competition for time as pressures mount on school districts to improve test scores.

We have also seen the need to return to a focus on fundamentals in school security and emergency preparedness planning. Many people forgot the lessons from some of the earliest school shootings in Pearl, Mississippi; Paducah, Kentucky; and Jonesboro, Arkansas. As time passed after Columbine and subsequent school shootings, conversations often jumped to extreme and ridiculous ideas such as arming teachers, bulletproof backpacks, and other so-called "solutions" for preventing school shootings.

Meanwhile, the students who were in school at the time of Columbine moved on. So did many school staff. Many of today's school board members, superintendents, and principals were not in these leadership positions at the time of the Columbine tragedy. And many of today's frontline teachers and support personnel were also not in their current positions a decade ago.

Our most recent call has therefore been to returning to the basics—to focusing on the fundamentals of school security and emergency planning. Our school safety assessments, training, and other consultations consistently find security and emergency preparedness gaps in some of the more basic practices in these areas. Mastering fundamentals is the first step in addressing more complicated safety issues that may arise as the challenges to school safety evolve.

4 School Security Assessments

ASSESSMENT DEFINITION AND USE

The purpose of a professional school security assessment is to provide educational leaders with an evaluation of existing security conditions within their school or school district and to make recommendations for improving these conditions at the building and district levels. An assessment, which educators call *safety assessment* and *security assessment* interchangeably, identifies vulnerabilities and risks related to school safety threats. It also makes specific recommendations, short-term and long-term, for corrective action to reduce these risks or to continue effective practices.

A professional assessment should provide educators with an independent evaluation by school security professionals of existing positive safety measures in place and recommendations for building upon existing measures with school safety improvements at the building and district levels. School leaders should use security assessments as

- a risk management tool for reducing crime and violence threats, risks, and potential liability;
- a school-community relations tool to demonstrate a district's commitment to school security prior to a crisis;
- evidence of having conducted a professional needs assessment that can be used in meeting federal and state grant proposal requirements to receive grant funding for safe safety and emergency planning.

Progressive school administrators assess school safety prior to a crisis and can use a quality security assessment as a strategic plan for making safety and emergency preparedness improvements over a multiyear period during tough budget times.

The assessment must be unique to the school, district, or both being assessed, and not be a canned package of generic recommendations. It must also reflect more than a mere walk-through look at doors, locks, and other physical security features. Anyone who claims to provide a thorough security assessment of a school with just a 15-minute walk-through and no other evaluation methods will most likely not give school officials the best possible evaluation of their strengths and needs.

Individuals who conduct professional security assessments should clearly indicate the assessment scope and limitations. Information contained in the final assessment report should be consistent with the most current recommendations and practices in the school security field at that time. Even then, school officials should consult with their legal counsel when implementing specific policies, procedures, and programs developed as a result of the assessment.

Although there will be some common areas of agreement, every school security assessment likely will be different. Some districts want in-depth assessments at each school or at selected sites. This type of assessment will be specific to individual building issues.

Other districts desire a district-level assessment of the big picture of school safety. This type often looks at such broader issues as policy and procedure consistency across schools, security staffing needs and operations, political and administrative contextual issues, and school-police-community coordination. School leaders may request a district and a building-specific assessment covering both district and building-level issues.

Because no two assessments are exactly the same, it is important to clearly define assessment expectations and responsibilities at the onset of the process, especially if an outside consultant or resource is used to conduct the assessment. Regardless of who does the assessment, an ongoing dialogue between assessors and school personnel will be critical.

The assessment should be viewed as a process, not a product-driven inspection. Generally, it should not focus on specific brands of equipment or services from a particular company. The final recommendations may include suggestions for types of corrective measures, but the assessment itself should not be a marketing mechanism for selling products.

ASSESSMENT EXPECTATIONS, BEST PRACTICES, AND LEVELS

Assessments help to keep balance without overreaction or denial, while serving as a strategic plan to reduce risks and to improve school safety. School security assessments should not, however, be presented as the following:

- A guarantee that a crisis will never occur.
- An attack on individuals or their management ability.
- Single-strategy focused, such as curriculum-only or equipment-only.
- Product-driven instead of process-driven.
- Generic, canned, or rhetorical one-size-fits-all reports.
- A panacea or final cure for all school safety concerns.

Best practices in conducting school security assessments include the following:

- Distinguishing safety, which is freedom from accidental injuries, from the concept of security, which is freedom from intentional harm.
- Avoiding relying solely on checklists for assessing school security.
- Remembering not to compare excessively the security issues of one school or district with another.
- Accounting for unique issues and needs of individual schools and districts.
- Avoiding the use of security equipment vendors, nonsecurity professionals, and security specialists with no K–12 school security experience to conduct school security assessments.

School officials also need to recognize that multiple levels of assessment exist with accompanying pros and cons:

- *No assessment* requires no immediate costs but increases risks for security problems and higher liability in the long term.
- *Self-assessment* typically has low costs except for time investments, but may lack specialized knowledge in security and crisis areas and also has a higher risk of a flawed process, especially considering the potential for political and personal influences in self-assessments.

- *Assessment by other governmental agencies* may have no cost or low costs and may offer more area-specific knowledge, but may also afford no control over the quality or experience of the assessors and could involve other bureaucratic issues.
- *Assessment by outside specialists* offers an independent and specialized expertise working for the school district, but one which typically costs more than the other options.

WHO SHOULD ASSESS

School security assessments should be performed by individuals with experience in professional school security. They might include school security directors, school resource officers, specially trained police officers, or similarly experienced consultants or outside resources. It is important that those conducting assessments be trained, knowledgeable, and experienced with professional school security best practices and in school climate, culture, and school-community relations dynamics.

It is equally important to remember that, whereas the security assessment can be attempted by educators and others, using checklists and fragmented pieces of information from various seminars or reference documents, the outcome will be limited. A lot of good information is shared at many school safety conferences and workshops. But we get a little nervous when we see well-intended educators attend a 1-day workshop and leave believing they are now an expert in school safety.

Likewise, outside consultants and overnight experts should be scrutinized to avoid getting packaged assessments that fail to focus on the uniqueness of individual schools and school districts. The number of self-proclaimed school security experts continues to grow after each school shooting. Former educators, administrators, police officers, and others with peripheral affiliations with schools are now eager to sell your district their security "expertise," regardless of whether they have professional education, training, or experience in this area.

Can administrators, educators, and other school staff conduct a self-assessment? The answer is yes. Improvements can be made by conducting self-assessments, and every school should be doing internal reviews on an ongoing basis.

Nevertheless, the outcome will be much more limited than if the assessment were to be conducted by a school security professional or other experienced, trained professional. Oftentimes outside professionals view the situation through a different lens and unique professional perspective, and they can often be more candid and less fearful of political retaliation for being blunt, when necessary. Self-assessments serve a purpose, but if school leaders want to take their school safety to the next level, a professional assessment is a bump up in the process.

AVOIDING A TEMPLATE APPROACH TO SCHOOL SECURITY ASSESSMENTS

Would you let your plumber do your heart bypass surgery just because he had a template on how to do so? Of course not.

For a template to be effective and useful, the person completing it must be qualified to do so. Having directions on a checklist, using a template after attending a 1-day or 1-hour course, or taking a similar approach to assessing school security is a risky thing to do. It raises safety risks and also increases the risks for potential liability.

Yet, so many school districts today are trying to do school safety cheaply that they believe a template approach to school security is acceptable. They are dangerously wrong.

Too often school officials, who are increasingly busy and competing with other hot button issues in schools, look for a quick fix by seeking school security assessment checklists or templates to "fill in the blanks" or "check off the boxes" so they can say they have conducted an assessment. Although using templates may solve a short-term need for school administrators, they can also create longer term safety deficiencies and potentially greater liability.

Oftentimes school security assessment checklists are primarily focused on physical security issues. This means the assessment is not taking a comprehensive look at school safety, but more on the hardware and equipment side of the equation. The result focuses heavily, if not exclusively, on physical security recommendations, while likely missing potential gaps and liabilities in areas such as awareness, training, policies and procedures, security or police staffing, and special event security. And a narrowly focused assessment on physical security also increases the likelihood of resulting recommendations skewed toward the purchase of new equipment and other costly physical facility changes.

FOCUS ASSESSMENTS ON MORE THAN HARDWARE AND MANPOWER

Educators wish to take a balanced, rational approach to improving security without adopting a knee-jerk, siegelike mentality. Security assessments, done properly, will approach the process with the idea that security needs and strategies often vary by community, district, and school.

Although factors identified in assessments may result in recommendations for security equipment or staffing, these tools are a supplement to, but not a substitute for, an overall comprehensive security program. A predisposition toward equipment or any other single approach is unfair, and potentially costly, to schools.

A camera, for example, could create unnecessary expenses—or it could save a school thousands of dollars. An assessment of the unique security needs at a given school could determine if a camera is needed in a certain area, what potential problems it is trying to address, how and where to best use it, and what to expect from its use. Or, a different approach without equipment might be in order. A quality assessment helps schools manage their limited resources effectively by making case-by-case decisions versus taking a hardware-driven lens to evaluating each school.

EVALUATION METHODS AND IDENTIFYING POLICY-PRACTICE DISCONNECTS

Professional security assessments often include the following:

- Analysis of policies, procedures, emergency and crisis guidelines, and other safety-related documents.
- Interviews of staff, students, or members of the school community, including key community partners (first responders, emergency management).
- Crime and discipline data review.
- Examination of physical facilities and grounds.
- Analysis of related news, crime, and other public information sources.
- School-specific analytical methods based on unique issues, concerns, facilities, and operations of the particular school or district.

One of the key focuses of using the previously described methods for an assessment should be to identify disconnects between what is on paper and what is in practice. Too often, we find schools have extensive policies, procedures, manuals, and other written documents proclaiming they do many things related to school safety, security, and emergency planning. But an experienced school security assessment team can, in a short period of time, identify gaps between what a district says on paper it is doing and what is really occurring, or oftentimes not occurring, in practice in each school building.

Why is this important? First, it poses a potential safety risk to students and staff if district leaders say and believe their people are taking steps to reduce risks and improve school safety, and in reality they are not. Second, it poses a higher risk for legal liability if the district is not doing what it says it is doing. Third, it poses a greater risk for loss of credibility and confidence when parents and the community believe a district is taking steps to protect their children when in reality it is not.

AREAS THAT MAY BE EVALUATED IN A SCHOOL SECURITY ASSESSMENT

Areas reviewed in a professional school security assessment can include the following:

- School emergency and crisis preparedness planning.
- Security crime and violence prevention policies and procedures.
- Physical security measures, including access control, communications capabilities, intrusion detection systems, perimeter security, after-hours security, physical design, and related areas.
- Professional development training needs related to school safety and emergency planning.
- Examination of support service roles in school safety, security, and emergency planning, including facilities operations, food services, transportation services, pupil services, physical and mental health services, technology services, and associated school departments.
- School security and school police staffing, operational practices, and related services.
- Linking of security with prevention and intervention services.
- Personnel and internal security.
- School-community collaboration, school and public safety agency partnerships, and school-community relations issues on school safety.

This is not an exhaustive list, nor does it mean that each assessment will include every area depending upon the scope of an assessment desired and agreed upon by a school district. But the list does point out that assessing school security goes far beyond a checklist of physical security measures. School security is more than hardware only or curriculum only. An assessment must take a look, from a policy and administrative level, at a more comprehensive package of what makes up a balanced approach to school security.

BENEFITS OF ASSESSING

The benefits of conducting professional security assessments include the following:

- Identification of such practical strategies as procedural changes, which require minimal to no costs for better safeguarding staff, students, and property.
- Creation of a final report that serves not only as a strategic plan for strengthening school safety over multiple years but also as a risk management and public relations tool.
- Demonstration of a commitment to the security of students, staff, and facilities through a professional and methodical review without paralysis by analysis, overreaction, or panic response to a crisis situation or to legal action.

The professional security assessment is a proactive tool for meeting the security needs of the school and the political concerns facing average school leaders. Assessments provide a fresh perspective for administrators from one generally not available elsewhere on staff: that of a school security professional. The final assessment report provides administrators with a tool for balanced, rational, short-term and long-term school security planning.

5 School Security Strategies and Issues

W hat about metal detectors? What about drug-sniffing dogs? What about uniforms? Questions arise on a host of school security strategies and issues in most every school safety conference, parent meeting, and other discussion on the subject. Unfortunately, research is limited, and professional opinions on many of these subjects are often anecdotal. Some common themes and considerations on these various hot topics and evergreen school safety issues follow.

ADMINISTRATION BUILDING, BOARD MEETING, AND SUPPORT SITE SECURITY

School board members, superintendents, and other district-level administrators often shy away from implementing security measures, creating crisis teams, and developing crisis plans for administration buildings and support service sites in their districts. Well-intended school leaders want to put their primary focus and limited resources on school facilities housing students. Although this is understandable, today's public safety climate requires reasonable security and preparedness measures at all school facilities, including those primarily in which adults occupy the space.

Workplace violence has been a growing concern for large and small corporation offices nationwide for some years now. School administration offices and support sites should be viewed no differently. Consider, for example, the following:

- School district administration offices typically house the offices of the board members, superintendent, human resources department, payroll staff, the treasurer, special education staff, and student services hearing officers and staff. Disgruntled current and former employees, suspended and expelled students, irate parents, job applicants, and other high-risk individuals are very likely to attend hearings, meetings, or visits for other purposes at such offices.

- School board meetings in many districts are often held in administration buildings. The ever-increasing political nature of school board meetings, and, for that matter school politics in general, can draw large groups of community members to these locations depending upon the issues being addressed. It is not unforeseeable that highly charged meetings and emotional issues could result in escalated undesirable and threatening behavior at board meetings.

Stand-alone facilities separate from district central offices often house transportation, food services, maintenance, warehouses, and other support departments. These facilities can experience a great deal of traffic in and out each day by district employees, salespersons, outside vendors, delivery personnel, and other individuals conducting legitimate business with the district. These departments often have limited (if any) administrative support staff to greet and monitor visitors, the facilities are often physically challenging to monitor for security purposes, and the nature of their operations involve a lot of open doorways, delivery docks, and other entranceways.

School leaders can, and should, require reasonable security and emergency preparedness measures at district administration and support site facilities just as they require such measures of their schools. A number of measures can be taken to reduce safety risks and to be better prepared for crisis situations that may occur. These include the following:

1. Develop a threat assessment protocol that applies to threats made to school administrators, administration building and support site staff, and board members. A number of cases have been documented where threats have been made to harm district-level coordinators, supervisors, directors, superintendents, and board members.

2. Assess board meeting security measures, including the meeting sites, physical security measures such as panic buttons and member egress, security or police staffing, training of board members in emergency plans, and related measures.

3. Include administration offices and support sites in school security assessments conducted for the district.

4. Develop emergency guidelines for school administration and support sites as would be done for actual school buildings, including having site-specific crisis plans, site-specific crisis teams, and practicing of the same drills that would be expected of school sites (fire, evacuation, and lockdown drills).

5. Train central office administrators and support staff (including secretaries and receptionists) on appropriate security policies and procedures, threat assessment and management, office safety measures, and district and site-specific emergency guidelines.

6. Incorporate crime prevention into central office and support site design, including in reception areas, secretarial offices, and inside administrative offices and meeting rooms.

7. Evaluate methods for reducing and controlling access to district administration offices and support facilities.

8. Establish basic procedures for conducting potentially high-risk meetings and hearings.

9. Assess physical security measures, including the use of security technology, for reducing administration office safety risks and for preparing to manage incidents of crime and violence in administration and support site settings.

10. Evaluate communication methods that would be used in administration offices and support sites in a threatening situation, including public address systems, telephone systems, two-way radios, and so on.

Many risk-reduction measures can be taken to improve school administration and support site safety. The failure to take appropriate steps for reducing security risks at these locations could place school employees at greater risk and may also lead to greater liability should an incident of crime or violence occur that could have been prevented by reasonable safety measures.

ADULT-ORIGINATED VIOLENCE

School officials often focus only on security threats that originate from youths. Many times this youth threat is perceived as being only from the inside (i.e., from students) or the outside (i.e., from nonstudent trespassers). Not only should the youth threats be anticipated from both inside and outside of the school, but educators should also recognize adult-originated security threats.

Angry and Irate Parents

Educators historically have faced angry parents on a rather frequent basis. Nobody likes to see his or her child fail classes, be disciplined, or in some cases, be arrested and prosecuted. School crime and disciplinary incidents have increased the chances of educators facing angry confrontations.

Some basic steps that can be taken to reduce risks associated with dealing with angry parents include the following:

1. Schedule conferences in advance, whenever possible.

2. Establish procedures to ensure that parents do not disrupt classes or ambush teachers or other staff during regularly scheduled business that should not be interrupted.

3. Recognize the need for parents to vent. Their frustration may stem from months or years of problems with their children. (So may yours!) Also recognize, however, the point at which you must draw the line when parents' venting turns to abuse. Make sure there is an agreement between staff and administrators, in general and in advance, of where that line is acceptable to both staff and principals. Nothing is worse than having a staff member draw the line, only to have an administrator reverse the decision and place the staff member in an even more confrontational position.

4. If a problem is anticipated, ask another staff member to join in a parent conference or notify someone else about when you enter and will complete the conference and that you may call on him or her for assistance if a problem occurs.

5. Do not meet in isolated areas or where there is no way available to communicate with other staff members.

6. Leave your conference room door slightly ajar in case you need assistance. Also, consider establishing code words or statements with other nearby employees that indicate a problem exists and you need help. For example, one principal believed that the mother in his office had a gun in her purse. As she became loud, the principal's secretary entered the office to give him some papers. Then he said to her, "Mrs. Smith, please schedule that meeting we discussed for this afternoon." Although it seemed normal to the parent, the secretary's real name was Mrs. Jones. The phrase was a code to send for assistance.

7. Focus parent conferences on how their concerns can be resolved in the best interests of the child. In other words, talk about what action needs to be taken from that point, not just what happened yesterday.

These are a few simple considerations. It is not an exhaustive list. Common sense and good planning will help reduce risks and may identify many other helpful steps that can be taken to prevent problems.

Alcohol, drug, and mental health problems experienced by some parents further enhance the risks some administrators must face. Parents facing economic stress, along with these personal stressors, understandably could be at higher risk for aggressive or unstable behavior.

School officials need to be cognizant of potential irate parent situations and, when possible, to take such preventative measures as organizing a parent conference when they perceive a risk. Educators also need to remember the importance of greeting and questioning parents whom they know by sight or who may even be in the building on a daily basis, because the moods, influences, and motivations of these individuals could change because of circumstances. Educators might think that they know these parent regulars, but they may not necessarily know if that person is under the influence of mind-altering substances that day, if they are angry at a particular staff member, or if there are family conflicts being brought into the school unless those educators communicate with the parents and ascertain their purpose during each visit.

Noncustodial parents also present safety concerns for school officials. Rarely do we find an elementary school where there are not, or have not been, concerns about parents wanting to remove or potentially to harm children who are not in their legal custody. More on noncustodial parents can be found in the section on elementary school security (p. 64).

Domestic Spillover

The spillover of domestic conflicts from staff and parent homes should also be considered in developing crisis guidelines. Serious conflicts between spouses, where at least one spouse is a school employee, or by parents of students can easily be continued on school grounds or in school buildings. Administrators need to be aware of potential related crime and violence ranging from vandalism to vehicles all the way to murder.

Such conflicts present administrators with a difficult situation, because these matters are perceived both by the participants and by school employees as being personal. The none-of-your-business attitude might be appropriate as long as the conflict does not affect the school setting, but when it comes to the school, or has a potential to come to the school, then the antagonism does, to some extent, become the school officials' business. Administrators need to be attuned to such problems, and they need to ensure that their staff and parents feel comfortable in giving them a heads-up warning of potential problems.

Workplace Violence

Working for a school district can be a wonderful experience. Working with children can be quite rewarding. However, it can also be quite stressful. Added to this normal amount of stress is the fact that school districts are, in essence, government and political entities. Not only is the school bureaucracy a world of its own in many districts, but so, too, is the world of school politics. Some of the most unique personalities and political games that I have ever come across have been within school districts across the nation.

We often talk about personal safety with principals, counselors, office staff, human resources supervisors, and others who frequently meet with potentially disgruntled parents, visitors, and employees. In particular, we raise the issue of how these school employees arrange their office furniture. Very often, they set up their offices in a manner where they are trapped into a corner of the room where they sit, while potentially hostile or armed individuals with whom they meet are seated closest to the exit of the room. We suggest they rearrange their furniture so they, not the potentially hostile visitors to their office, have an easy exit if needed.

One need not look too far into this picture to see the perfect formula for workplace violence: workload stress from the youths, plus bureaucracy stress and political stress. It is somewhat surprising that there have not been more incidents of workplace violence by disgruntled school employees considering the amount of adult-driven stress and the political games played with individuals and their careers. As school districts continue to become increasingly politicized and stressed from the boardrooms to the classrooms and custodial offices, we can anticipate a growing potential for workplace violence.

AFTER-HOURS SCHOOL SECURITY: ACTIVITIES AND COMMUNITY USE OF SCHOOLS

School leaders want school and community use of their buildings after-hours. In many communities, the single city high school in town is often the center for community activities. This not only helps the community but encourages the community to feel pride and ownership of the school, which in turn provides an incentive to keep the school safe.

The challenge for administrators is how to encourage community use of the school while taking steps to reduce safety risks after hours when most school employees have gone home for the day. Adult supervision is decreased while the various afterschool activities are often spread throughout the building. The end result is a school building left fairly wide open and unsupervised in many parts of the school.

No quick fix exists for this gap in school security. Educators often look to those of us who are school safety consultants for some type of miracle cure for this situation, but there isn't one.

The first and most logical option is to increase adult presence. In an ideal world, this would mean having an evening administrator on duty, hiring security, or police personnel for afterschool and evening times. Another option would be to staff an after-hours activities coordinator who serves to coordinate evening events. The world is not ideal, however, and because of tight budgets such hiring is typically not done.

Another option is to section off areas of the building to concentrate after-hours activities in a limited area or areas. Gating off unused areas, when consistent with local fire department expectations, has been done in some schools in conjunction with concentrating activities in limited areas. Sometimes, though, the nature or extent of the use of the building does not allow for this type of access reduction.

One approach used in new school design is to build new schools with the most commonly used areas in one section of the building. For example, the auditorium, cafeteria, media center, office, computer lab, and gym would be built in one section so the rest of the academic areas of the school could be gated off from public access. This requires either new construction or major remodeling, something not being done in most school communities because of financial constraints.

A few other options include the following:

- Training custodial, cleaning, and related after-hours staff on security and emergency preparedness procedures, as well as verbal de-escalation and nonviolent crisis intervention, cardiopulmonary resuscitation (CPR)/first aid, and other safety-related topics.
- Equip evening shift custodians, cleaners, and other with two-way radios to enhance communications capabilities.
- Require in contracts for community groups that contract with the school for space to provide security staff or off-duty police once they reach a certain level of use, number of participants, or higher risk rival group activities.
- Supervision, supervision, supervision. One of the most common issues in discussions with attorneys considering lawsuits against schools is supervision. Kids get in trouble, and in some cases educators

get in bigger trouble, when adults are not supervising kids. Coaches, activity sponsors, parent groups, and others must supervise children and the activity for which they are in charge.

Afterschool and evening hours are some of the most vulnerable times in school safety. Most school leaders are simply playing the odds that something won't happen. Risk-reduction steps need to be taken during these times just as we expect to be done during the regular school hours.

ARMING TEACHERS AND SCHOOL STAFF

The vast majority of teachers want to be armed with textbooks and computers, not guns. Yet from time to time, typically after high-profile school shooting incidents, some elected officials and gun-rights advocates propose arming teachers and school staff as a strategy for preventing and responding to school shootings. Although on the surface this may sound worthy of debate, the devil rests in the details of implementation, and there are far too many questions and risks compared with alternative approaches, such as having school-based certified police officers as the only armed persons on campus.

School districts considering arming teachers and school staff with guns would take on significant responsibility and potential liabilities beyond the expertise, knowledge base, experience, and professional capabilities of most school boards and administrators. Fortunately, most school district leaders around the nation do not even consider arming teachers as a viable alternative or worthy serious discussion item. Although I support the right of citizens to carry concealed guns consistent with the requirements and laws of those states allowing concealed carry of firearms, I believe giving school staff this responsibility raises the bar above that of general citizens allowed to carry a concealed gun by sanctioning them to perform in a public safety capacity that is outside the scope of their professional training, responsibility, and expertise.

Arming teachers and school staff raises a number of questions and issues:

- Would a school board have appropriate and adequate policies and procedures governing the carrying and use of firearms by teachers and school staff?
- What type of *use of force continuum* would the school district create for staff who may use firearms? How does that stand up in comparison with such standards held for police officers and others who are armed and deployed in a public safety capacity?
- What types of firearms (types of guns, caliber of weapons) would staff be allowed to carry and not allowed to carry? Would staff carry

their own personal firearms or school district-issued firearms? If the school allows staff to carry their personal weapons for the purpose of protecting staff and students, what responsibilities do school boards and administrators thereby assume for making sure the firearms carried are functional? Would the school district have regular inspections of staff firearms to make sure they are functional and appropriate to policy, and if so, who on school staff would be responsible for that function and what is their level of expertise and training to make such decisions?

- What type of firearms training would the school district provide on a regular, ongoing basis to those staff it authorizes to be armed with guns? Would the school district build and operate its own firearms range? Who on school staff would be qualified to provide such training, operate a firearms range, and so on? Would firearms certification and recertification be added to the school district's professional development training program each year?
- What type of weapons retention training would be provided to staff who are armed, and what steps would be taken to reduce risks of a teacher or staff member being intentionally disarmed by a student or other person, or for having a firearm dislodged from a staff member's control when the teacher breaks up a fight in a cafeteria or hallway?
- How would the district be prepared to prevent and manage situations where teachers or staff members lose, misplace, or have stolen their firearms while on campus?
- How would the school district manage an accidental shooting that could occur?
- What would be the impact of this type of board policy and practice on the school district's insurance and potential legal liability posture? If self-insured, would the district be able to handle potential lawsuit judgments against it for cases resulting from this practice? If insured by a private carrier, what would be the insurance provider's position and concerns, or would it even insure the district for such a practice?
- Most importantly, what other options have we considered as school leaders? For example, if the school district is concerned about first-responder response time from the community to the school, has the school district considered employing a School Resource Officer (SRO) or its own trained, commissioned and certified school police officer who is a school district employee, such as what is allowed in Texas, Florida, and other states?

I continue to be a strong advocate for SROs/school-based policing programs. Law enforcement officers working on a school campus who are trained, certified, and commissioned to carry a firearm should be allowed to do so. School employees who lawfully carry a concealed weapon outside of the school setting as private citizens certainly may do so, but their roles and responsibilities in school settings should be focused on their expertise in education. Law enforcement and public safety responsibilities should be left to those who are trained, certified, and experienced in such functions.

ATHLETIC AND LARGE EVENT SECURITY

A significant number of violent incidents occur at school athletic events around the nation. These incidents have included assaults, riots/fighting, stabbing incidents, shootings, and even murder. A review of incidents, along with communications from school and safety officials nationwide, suggests that increased attention is needed to school athletic event security.

Although this section is written to address athletic events, a number of the concepts can also be applied to other types of large events such as large dances, proms, and so on.

The success of school athletic event security can often be tied to strategies associated with the following three major categories:

1. Adequate staffing and supervision.

2. Advance planning of security strategies.

3. Thoughtful emergency preparedness planning.

Many school athletic events pose relatively low safety risks. Many middle school games, as well as certain high school games, attract smaller crowds of spectators, involve less emotional rivalries, and overall do not present major security concerns.

School athletic events such as high school football and basketball games, however, can draw large crowds, be highly competitive, and require significant attention to security issues. Reasons for such games presenting more serious security concerns can include the following:

- Large crowds of spectators, potentially by the thousands, depending upon the nature and type of event. Spectators at high school basketball and football games, for example, may include students from both participating schools, students from other schools, former students, parents, and community members.
- Crowd psychology tells us that some individuals who may otherwise not act aggressively in normal, one-on-one environments may act out aggressively in a crowd. This is often attributed to the real

and perceived anonymity provided by a large crowd as well as the crowd emotions created within the large gathering.

- Lower levels of adult supervision, visibility, and mobility. Too often schools under-staff athletic events, especially in terms of police officers and security personnel staffing, to save limited funds out of athletic department or school-based budgets.
- Increased emotions among spectator crowds, especially when there are intense rivalries between playing teams.
- Increased access to, and exposure of, the larger physical plant areas. These areas may include stadiums, athletic fields, parking lots, school gyms, locker rooms, and potentially the entire school itself if exit doors are not secured and inside gates are not used to section off and seal down unused areas of the building.
- Higher risk for drug and alcohol consumption before, during, and after games by spectators.
- Higher risk for gang member presence and potential activity in those school communities experiencing gang activity.

Advanced planning for security strategies for athletic events is very important. It is important to remember that advanced planning means more than saying on Thursday that "We need to get a couple of cops to work tomorrow night at the game."

Some security strategies will require funding. Hiring off-duty police officers, paying overtime to school security personnel, funding stipends for additional school staff, installing surveillance cameras, and other measures come with a cost attached.

But many operational strategies, policies, procedures, communications, and planning techniques require more time than money. In today's busy schools, getting people to find the time for security planning is often more difficult than finding the money.

Some practical strategies schools can employ to reduce security risks, especially at larger events, may include the following:

- First, provide adequate adult supervision and staffing. Factors to consider in determining what is adequate may include the anticipated size of the crowd, the size of the facilities and grounds (including parking lots) used for the event, past history of incidents at similar events, intelligence information received about current conflicts at the school and in the community that could spill over into the event, and other related considerations.

- Events with larger crowds should employ sworn law enforcement officers. School districts with their own school police or school resource officers (SROs) should give priority to using these officers at school athletic events since these officers typically know the youth who may be attending the event. If additional officers are needed, consider first using gang unit officers, juvenile detectives, and community policing officers who may know the youth and their families. The same concept applies with hiring in-house school security personnel, assigning school administrators, and using school staff members since they also know the students. These individuals typically know those students and nonstudents who have past behavioral problems in schools and at school-sponsored events. School officials should also employ adequate levels of teaching staff and other support staff. Parent volunteers may also help augment regular staff.

• Deploy police, security personnel, and school staff in a manner that provides adequate coverage to the facilities being used for the event. This includes at ticket gates, perimeter entrance/exit points, parking lots, common areas (restrooms, concession stands), on the playing grounds/inner field perimeter, in the stands, and at other key locations. Have police in uniform and security staff in clearly identifiable clothing. The use of plain-clothes, undercover police officers may be necessary in certain large-crowd events or situations where problems are anticipated.

• Train police, security personnel, and staff on techniques for monitoring crowds (and not the athletic event on the field), verbal de-escalation skills, procedures for handling fights and riots, handling emergency medical situations, evacuation procedures, tasks related to specific operations (ticket-taking procedures, concession stand operations), and emergency guidelines.

• Equip all staff with two-way radios. Issue school cell phones to select staff assigned to the event.

• Create policies related to admission, limitations of items that can be carried in (purses, book bags, backpacks), right to search spectators at admission point (metal detector scans, bag searches), no passes out and back in once admitted, spectator conduct, and other security protocols. Post rules outside and inside of admission gates, and elsewhere in the facility. Enforce the rules in a firm, fair, and consistent manner.

• Establish procedures for advance ticket sales and on-site ticket sales. Have staff ticket-selling and ticket-taking procedures with adequate police, security, and ticket-taking staff at admission gates. Stop ticket sales after a designated time, such as by the beginning of the third quarter. Have police or security staff escorts of ticket-takers and money from the admissions areas to a designated location for counting money and preparing it for bank deposits, which should occur with police escorts the same evening.

• Maintain separate locker rooms for home and visitor teams. Have team buses pick up and drop off at opposite sides of the playing facility to avoid interaction before and after the game.

• Separate spectator seating into clearly designated areas, that is, home team in bleachers on one side and visiting team on other side. If at all possible, have separate concession stands operating in each of these areas.

• Administrators and safety officials from the schools playing a given event should communicate with each other well in advance of the event to discuss procedures, safety concerns, security practices, emergency guidelines, investigation into rumors and any recent incidents that could result in conflicts, and associated logistics.

• Secure perimeter doors of schools and gate off sections of the building not used for the actual athletic event in a manner that is in accordance with fire safety regulations.

• Create a detailed plan for parking procedures, traffic flow, parking lot staffing during entire game, and related issues. Consider not allowing any cars into the parking lots after a designated time, such as after the beginning of the third quarter of the game. Advise students in advance to coordinate pickups by parents outside of the parking lots on the perimeter of the grounds.

• Conduct advance assessments of physical security needs and strategies. Consider use of surveillance cameras in admission areas, game field areas, common areas (concession stands, walkways and areas around restrooms), parking lots, and other areas as appropriate. Evaluate lighting in stadiums, athletic facilities, parking lots, and perimeter around the school and event grounds.

• Consider having dedicated staff for videotaping the game and, if necessary, areas of spectator misconduct that may occur.

• Establish code of sportsmanlike conduct and educate players, coaches, cheerleaders, the band, students, parents, and others on the code in advance of the game.

• Have public address (PA) announcers make announcements at the beginning of the game and at other times, as necessary, regarding sportsmanlike conduct behavioral expectations. Train PA announcers on overall guidelines for communicating with the crowd during the event, under emergency situations, and so on.

• Have clear procedures, roles, and responsibilities for clearing and locking down facilities upon completion of the game.

Thoughtful emergency preparedness planning is also important since incidents can occur, even with the best of prior advance security planning:

• Establish written emergency guidelines. Test and exercise the written guidelines to make sure they would work in an emergency. Train all staff involved in supervising events on the guidelines.

- Administrators and safety personnel from both schools involved in the event should coordinate information in advance and review security procedures and written emergency guidelines.

- School administrators and safety personnel should coordinate with emergency medical personnel in advance of the event. In the case of many larger games, a number of schools will have an ambulance on stand-by on-site before, during, and after the game. School administrators and safety officials should also notify their appropriate law enforcement district station or area commanders in advance of major games or high-risk events so on-duty safety personnel will be aware of the event even if off-duty police are being hired to work the game.

- Evacuation plans should be clear, and announcements regarding emergency evacuation expectations should be made to the spectators at the start of events.

- Staff assignments with roles and responsibilities in the event of an emergency should be clearly delineated.

- Create emergency communications procedures and protocols to be engaged in the event of an emergency incident at the event. Communications plans should include communicating with media, parents, school staff, students, and so on.

- Have plans for managing the postcrisis aftermath in the hours and days following an incident at an event (Trump, 2010d).

These are a sample of general suggestions for consideration and discussion. Plans and strategies must be tailored for each school and school district. No cookie-cutter plan will fit all schools, but adequate staffing and supervision, advance security planning, and thoughtful emergency guidelines can help keep school athletic events safe, secure, and well managed in comparison to the alternative of little-to-no planning for such events.

BOMB THREATS AND SUSPICIOUS DEVICES

Bomb threats to schools usually have been motivated by hopes of early school dismissal, instructional interruptions, and in some cases, anger or revenge directed toward school staff. School officials face a new challenge, however, with easy access on the Internet to formulas for making home-made explosive devices and the items to do so at most local hardware stores, terrorism threats, and heightened public attention to bomb scares. In too many cases, traditional bomb threats have been replaced with actual devices in school buildings and on school grounds.

Administrators should take these basic steps to properly manage bomb threats and suspicious devices.

1. Inform staff that all bomb threats and suspicious devices must be treated as if they are real. The shifting trend from hoax incidents to the real thing must be quickly recognized and treated seriously.

2. Coordinate with law enforcement bomb specialists in developing specific procedures for handling threats and devices before an incident occurs. Although some common issues in most response plans exist, local concerns and protocol must be adapted to individual school and district guidelines.

3. Assess physical security issues when developing bomb guidelines.

4. Incorporate these basic components into your guidelines:

   a. Bomb threat telephone call checklists and procedures.
   b. Procedures and roles of notifiers for informing law enforcement and other staff of a threat, suspicious device, or both.
   c. Guidelines for conducting visual search inspections of common areas and individual rooms.
   d. Procedures for securing an area where a suspicious device is located.
   e. Evacuation plans for the building and grounds.
   f. Contingency plans for an actual explosion incident.

5. Train all staff, including secretaries, custodians, and support staff, on bomb threat management procedures. Although secretaries often receive the threat calls and custodians may be the first to find suspicious packages, they are often not included in staff development training sessions. Practical exercises and search drills should be included in the training.

6. Discussions often arise over whether schools should be evacuated upon receipt of a bomb threat. In general, the best and common practice is not to automatically evacuate a school on a bomb threat call alone. School administrators and law enforcement officials should develop plans to evaluate cases on a case-by-case basis. This of course does not mean common sense and the presence of an obvious threat, such as suspected device, would not warrant evacuation. It simply means that in general, automatic evacuation on every bomb threat is not the normal practice.

7. A related question on conducting searches for suspected devices always generates discussion and debate. Teachers are particularly hesitant when they are told they, not the police or fire officials, are expected to search their areas when a bomb threat is made. The underlying idea is that those

individuals who work in the school are most familiar with what does and does not belong, so they are in the best position to recognize truly suspicious items. We typically point out the teachers and staff are usually asked to conduct a visual inspection of their areas and report anything usual and are usually not asked to pick up and move suspicious items.

Law enforcement bomb specialists are the best resource for school administrators to develop specific guidelines. Most police departments either have specialists on staff or access to specialists in other departments. Because they will be the individuals responding to an actual bomb-related incident at your school, including them in front-end planning is essential.

CELL PHONES, CAMERA PHONES, AND TEXT MESSAGING

Cell phone disruptions in schools can come in a number of forms. Ringing cell phones can disrupt classes and distract students who should be paying attention to their lessons. Text messaging has been used for cheating. And new cell phones with cameras could be used to take photos of exams, take pictures of students changing clothes in gym locker areas, and so on.

From a school safety perspective, cell phones can detract from school safety and emergency preparedness in a number of ways:

- Cell phones have been used for calling in bomb threats to schools and, in many communities, cell calls cannot be traced by public safety officials.
- Student use of cell phones could potentially detonate a real bomb if one is on campus.
- Cell phone use by students can hamper rumor control and, in doing so, disrupt and delay effective public safety personnel response.
- Cell phone use, including text messaging, by students can impede public safety response by accelerating parental response to the scene of an emergency during times when officials may be attempting to evacuate students to another site.
- Cell phone systems typically overload during a real major crisis (as they did during the Columbine tragedy, 9/11 attacks, and so on), and use by a large number of students at once could add to the overload and knock out cell phone systems quicker than may normally occur. Since cell phones may be a backup communications tool for school administrators and crisis teams, widespread student use in a crisis could thus eliminate crisis team emergency communications tools in a very short period of critical time.

School officials should maintain an adequate number of cell phones on campus for administrators, crisis team members, and other appropriate adults. School and safety officials should seek to provide such equipment as a part of their crisis planning. In addition, although I am not necessarily advocating that schools provide cell phones to teachers, school policies should allow teachers and support staff to carry their cell phones if they choose to do so.

I have long advocated for school administrators to completely ban cell phones from schools. Too many school boards and administrators have unsuccessfully tried playing both sides of the fence: Telling students they can have cell phones but not to use them during school hours is an unrealistic expectation, especially during a school crisis. Riding the fence or political waffling on the cell phone issue has not helped school leaders.

The issue is further complicated with the use of smart phones as an instructional tool in the classroom. It is impossible to allow cell phones for instructional purposes while expecting students not to use them for other purposes. Some school administrators have even suggested having adults encourage students with cell phones to send out agreed-upon messages to parents in a crisis; however, this seems to create a high risk for misinformation and rumors to be spread even by well-intended students.

Once the genie is out of the bottle, it is hard to get it back inside. In many districts, the horse is out of the barn, however, and politically and administratively it may be impossible to completely keep cell phones out of schools. School administrators should create their school security and emergency plans, and well-crafted crisis communications plans, under the assumption that a massive number of students, and even some adult staff, will use cell phones during heightened security and crisis incidents.

COMPUTER SECURITY MEASURES

How will your school handle bomb and death threats sent by electronic mail? How can you protect your school computer records, schedules, and employee payroll data from being changed by hackers? Can your students produce counterfeit money using school computers, scanners, and printers?

Schools continue to add new computers and technology to classrooms daily across the United States. One of the biggest challenges is not for the children and youths but for the adults. How can adults adapt to the new technology and keep one step ahead of the students or other hackers to ensure that it is not abused?

It is interesting, and somewhat scary, to see how far behind adults are in technology compared with our youth. It is even scarier to see that many of these adults are the teachers, administrators, and safety officials responsible for supervising, monitoring, and keeping safe these youth. The adults will typically be behind the students in technology awareness and use. The challenge, though, is to close—not widen—the gap between the two.

School officials need to address not only physical security issues related to preventing the theft of computers and other equipment but also the potential for abuse of services. Policies and procedures regarding abuse or misuse of school equipment, computer systems and networks, and the Internet should be implemented and modified as technology advances are brought into the schools. Staff should be fully trained in the use of all new technology used by students. Districts should provide training and resources for keeping their personnel up with the times. Administrators and staff can and should request such training.

Adults cannot endlessly police the Internet. The filters will not be those put on a school district or home computer system, but instead working to penetrate the filters of the brains of the computer users: our children. Education and supervision of the end user, our children, will be the key to keeping them safe in their online and offline activities.

CRIME PREVENTION THROUGH ENVIRONMENTAL DESIGN

The design of a school and its surrounding campus can play a significant role in preventing crime and facilitating school safety measures. An entire field of study known as Crime Prevention Through Environmental Design (CPTED) is dedicated to the study and application of concepts related to how design can impact safety. The writings of Tim Crowe serve as landmark resources on the topic.

School officials involved in designing new school facilities or remodeling existing school sites should consider doing the following:

- Insist on involvement in the design process, and work with architects and construction personnel in the early stages to provide input on how the school design can help improve supervision and safety.
- Consider carefully the placement of common areas, sites used extensively for after-hours events (e.g., gyms, auditoriums, cafeterias, and libraries), and other key locations to help control access and limit use requiring movement or open access to all areas of the school in the evening.

- Review parking lot placement, size, traffic patterns, separation of bus and parent vehicle areas, and related factors to best facilitate safe movement and supervision.
- Consider the importance of line of sight in hallways and areas requiring supervision.
- Take into consideration opportunities for natural surveillance and supervision by placing areas of greater activity or higher risk in areas where there will be higher levels of adult supervision.
- Involve school security officials, SROs, or outside school safety specialists in the planning and design of new or remodeled facilities. Their perspectives may provide very different, but valuable, insights.

It is much easier to put crime prevention measures into the initial designs of a school and its surrounding campus than it is to attempt to retrofit security measures after a structure is already in place.

DRUG-SNIFFING DOGS

Many years ago, one principal was overheard saying, "I bring drug dogs into my school all the time." When asked how often they check the lockers, the principal replied, "Oh, I don't let them check the lockers. I just bring them into an assembly to scare the kids!" The other principal responded, "You're so progressive. I only bring them in at night when nobody else is around."

Sad to say, this was not a joke. A great deal of the fear of using drug dogs can be attributed to the political and image issues discussed in Chapter 2. Other misconceptions may center on a fear that the dogs will somehow hurt the students. Many simply fear what the dogs may find.

Recommendations and considerations about the use of drug-sniffing dogs include the following:

- Recognize in advance that serious drug dealers will likely have their products concealed on their person, where the dogs cannot check anyway. Some traces of drugs stored in lockers at some point may be detected, even if the contraband is not there at the time of the search. Still, the chances are that the use of drug-sniffing dogs will not culminate in massive arrests with bulk drug confiscations.

- If you are going to do it, do it right. Drug dogs largely serve as a deterrent. To bring them in at night when nobody is in the building is not a deterrent. Not only is no one present to be deterred, but the chances are also good that students will not leave drugs in lockers overnight.

- Likewise, bringing dogs in for an assembly is a good idea if principals plan to follow through with actual inspections during the school year.

Dog demonstrations will show students what they can expect and the overall effectiveness of the dog in detecting drugs. This strategy is a deterrent. To hope that this alone will scare the students into not bringing drugs, without following up with some real enforcement of the inspection procedure, is at best an administrator's fantasy.

- Do not issue advance warnings about a specific inspection. This includes not only keeping it a secret from students but also from staff. Everyone knows the effectiveness of the lounge grapevine. If one staff member knows, the chances are that all staff members and a good number of students will know.

This does not mean that notice of a potential dog inspection should not be given at the beginning of the year. District policies and handbooks should include notice that the school is subject to such an inspection, without prior warning, at any time during the school year. Parents also should be notified of this potential. Nobody, however, should be notified of a specific inspection by a PA announcement that "Tomorrow we will have a drug dog search at 9:00 a.m."

In fact, one suburban school district leader reportedly decided that she was going to have zero tolerance with drugs in her high schools. After 2 years of ignoring pressure from local law enforcement officials to bring drug-sniffing dogs into her secondary schools, the superintendent coordinated a simultaneous sweep of all three public high schools shortly before the end of the school year. It was later learned by the police that 2 weeks prior to the sweep, with only several weeks left in the entire school year, school administrators had students carry home letters to parents announcing that drug sweeps would be taking place before the end of the school year. It was not surprising that the sweeps were not productive.

- Do not believe that drugs are not present nor available simply because a search comes up empty. As previously noted, the majority of successful drug dealers will have their product on their person or close at hand. It is ludicrous to believe that no hits on all of the lockers equals a drug-free school.

- Do not be embarrassed or apologetic if drugs are found. The purposes of the inspection are to find drugs and to send a deterrent message. If drugs are found and the perpetrators face consequences, the inspection has served its purposes.

Most parents, students, and community members will support such initiatives if they are properly educated on the subject and the process is done professionally. Problems tend to arise when the reasons for such actions are not made clear in advance and when such programs are implemented haphazardly. By setting realistic expectations and acknowledging that this is only one tool that is a part of a comprehensive approach to school safety, this particular strategy can be a helpful tool.

ELECTION DAY SECURITY

Although many school and community officials continue to make their schools available for Election Day voting, there is also a reasonable expectation for maintaining the safety and security of students and school staff as well as the community members using the schools on election day. Although practices of years past often allowed schools to be more open and relaxed on Election Day, safety threats in a post-Columbine and post-9/11 world have increasingly raised concerns with many school administrators, school staff, and parents about the vulnerability of their schools when schools are thrust open to use by any legitimate voter from the broader designated school community. Although the level of safety concerns may vary by school, community, and perhaps even election, school and community officials must take reasonable safety and security measures into account.

I have strongly supported efforts to remove polling places from schools. Unfortunately, many elected and administrative officials are hesitant, often for political reasons, to propose and strongly support removing polling places for schools. Although doing so will obviously require additional administrative work of finding new election sites and providing notice to voters, the additional work is unquestionably worth the added benefits toward creating safer schools.

Wide open doors and facilities, limited (if any) supervision, and leaving the school on autopilot during Election Day simply are not options in today's society. Our educators work hard throughout the school year to reduce access to school grounds and buildings, and they cannot summarily dismiss school security on any one given school day deemed as Election Day in a school community. Although we cannot prevent every potential crime and act of violence, our school, election, and community officials should explore ways to reduce safety risks and to provide a secure school site on Election Day.

A number of schools have designated Election Day as a *professional development* day for staff training only, with no students in attendance in their districts, and this option continues to be considered in other schools. However, although this has been done more since the late 1990 spate of school shootings, the majority of schools continue to provide regular educational services on Election Day. Until political and administrative leaders take the most appropriate course of action, that is, to remove polling places from schools, educators must take all possible risk-reduction measures to enhance security on Election Day.

Some specific steps schools can consider to address Election Day security risks include, but are not necessarily limited to, the following:

• School district administrators and safety personnel should meet prior to Election Day with their elections board administrators to discuss safety and security issues and guidelines for poll workers and poll operations. School officials should consider providing district guidelines for use of their facilities and site-specific information on assigned voting locations in advance of the actual elections. Elections officials should provide this information to on-site elections supervisors/polling place leaders so they have it prior to the day they report on-site at the school for Election Day.

• Building administrators and facility/custodial managers should meet with on-site elections supervisors upon their arrival to review school-specific polling locations, parking procedures, designated ingress and egress locations, emergency communications systems and protocols, and related information.

• Schools should restrict election voting to one location or area of the school for the election day. Ideally this location will have its own entrances and exits for ingress and egress to and from the outside, thereby requiring voters to enter and leave the designated voting area without going through the rest of the school building. Many schools use their gymnasium, for example, which has doors where voters can enter and exit to and from the outside without going into the rest of the school. Student classes normally held in the gym are relocated elsewhere in the building for that day.

• If at all possible, voter parking should be off-campus to reduce the number of vehicles parking on the school grounds and near the building. Schools should encourage parking on the streets around the school if this is logistically possible based upon the school's location and design. If parking on campus is the only option for voters, establish designated parking areas specifically for voters, preferably parking closest to the entrance to the designated voting area. Designated parking areas for voters should be clearly marked with signage.

• High schools where students drive to school each day may wish to consider encouraging student parking off campus on election days to reduce the number of cars on campus and to enhance visibility and supervision of overall parking lots. Although this may present a 1-day inconvenience to students, this option could be an extra risk-reduction strategy depending upon each specific school's parking situation, physical layout, and school-community dynamics. At a minimum, voter parking should be separate from student and staff parking, if at all possible.

• Provide clear signage for voter entrances and exits. Provide signage on secured doors not authorized for voter access to direct voters to the appropriate entrances for their use.

• Examine transportation drop-off and pick-up points used by school buses and parents to assess traffic patterns and potential conflicts with voter traffic. Reassign these locations to less congested areas of the school for the one Election Day, if necessary and logistically possible, should the voter traffic conflict with regular school transportation logistics. Strong consideration should be given to providing or increasing the amount of supervision in parking lots and transportation areas by school security personnel, SROs, or school administrators and staff throughout the school day and during student arrival and dismissal times. Bus drivers should be given protocols and training related to managing their transportation operations on election days, and they should be reminded and encouraged to maintain a heightened awareness at bus drop-off and pick-up areas, on streets around schools, and elsewhere during their travels.

• Provide two-way communications capabilities (telephones, two-way radio, or cell phones) in the voting area so polling workers or school staff have immediate communications capabilities to call for assistance if needed.

• If necessary, designate a restroom in the immediate voting room area for emergency use by voters. Avoid situations where voters have to walk throughout the building if they need to use restroom facilities if at all possible.

• Review school emergency plans for lockdowns, evacuations, and related guidelines prior to Election Day. Assess how the presence of polling operations would be impacted by the implementation of these procedures in a real emergency and what additional steps would need to be taken during the activation of such plans to secure polling areas.

• Provide an increased presence of school security staff, SROs, or police patrols in and around schools, including the time from the opening to the closing of the polls before and after regular school hours.

• Educate staff, students, and parents about Election Day security procedures and the need for heightened awareness ahead of time. Brief school staff the day before the election on specific heightened security procedures and the need for staff to be extra vigilant and highly visible on Election Day.

- Use existing surveillance cameras and associated security technology to monitor parking lots, entrances and exits, and related areas of concern. Although using cameras in the voting room itself may be inappropriate, existing cameras covering the parking areas, entrances and exits, and hallways leading to the voting area should be functional and employed as a support to overall security strategies.

- Conduct regular patrols/checks of building perimeter and grounds before the opening of school and throughout the day for suspicious items or persons and other unusual or disruptive activity. (Trump, 2010b).

ELEMENTARY SCHOOL SECURITY AND AGGRESSION BY YOUNGER STUDENTS

When people think of school security, their minds often envision high schools and middle schools. Elementary schools are frequently viewed as safe havens with few safety threats or concerns.

Elementary schools do, however, face a number of security concerns and deserve the attention and resources as their districts conduct school safety planning and security enhancements. One of the top concerns at the elementary school level is noncustodial parent concerns. Custody battles so often circle around elementary-aged children and can easily spill over into the schoolhouse.

School administrators can take a variety of steps to better protect elementary students:

- Enhance supervision. Nothing beats adult supervision of students. The absence of adequate supervision is where students get in trouble and educators get into increased liability risks.
- Aggressively monitor custody issues: Noncustodial parent concerns are big issues at elementary schools. Office support staff, administrators, and staff need to work closely to aggressively monitor custody issues.
- Train students not to open doors for strangers or for anyone they know, including students, staff, and parents.
- Create buddy systems for students who must travel to restrooms or for other out-of-classroom movement without the full class.
- Reduce school access, create visitor sign-in and management procedures, and train staff to greet, challenge, and report strangers on campus.

- Establish procedures for responding to student walk-away incidents where students leave the school without permission during the course of the school day.
- Train staff on verbal de-escalation and nonviolent crisis intervention, including office support staff who often deal with frustrated or angry parents.
- Create notification procedures for notifying parents when children are absent from school and the school has not been notified by the parent.

Schools and school communities also need to come to grips with the increasing aggression and violent behavior of younger and younger children. This violence obviously is not taught in our schools. Too many educators are seeing seriously aggressive behavior during the first years of a child's school experience.

John Weicker, a Fort Wayne, Indiana, well-respected, veteran school security director, educator, and school safety expert, speaks passionately about the need to recognize, acknowledge, and deal with the increasing number of cases of aggressive and violent behavior by younger children in schools. He argues that schools, and of course parents, must teach children early that there are consequences for their behaviors. Like some of us in the school safety profession, he recognizes that failing to do so in the early years leaves us with middle and high school students who pose substantial behavior and security problems, and whose trajectory into more serious disciplinary and criminal behavior is often irreversible if their behaviors have not been addressed up until that age and grade level.

Elementary sites, like secondary schools, have a number of school safety concerns. From noncustodial parents to growing aggression in younger children, physical security issues, aggressive younger children, and emergency planning needs, our elementary schools must be an integral part of a district's school safety planning process.

FAMILY EDUCATIONAL RIGHTS AND PRIVACY ACT AND SCHOOL SAFETY

The Family Educational Rights and Privacy Act (FERPA) is grossly misunderstood or misinterpreted by many school administrators. Far too often, we see school administrators hiding behind FERPA as a justification for not sharing information. Although there certainly are privacy limitations stemming from FERPA, school administrators need to have an understanding of the law so they are able to appropriately respond to school safety related issues.

The U.S. Department of Education (2007a) provides the following guidance on FERPA:

Health or Safety Emergency

In an emergency, FERPA permits school officials to disclose without consent education records, including personally identifiable information from those records, to protect the health or safety of students or other individuals. At such times, records and information may be released to appropriate parties such as law enforcement officials, public health officials, and trained medical personnel. See 34 CFR § 99.31(a)(10) and § 99.36. This exception is limited to the period of the emergency and generally does not allow for a blanket release of personally identifiable information from a student's education records.

Law Enforcement Unit Records

Many school districts employ security staff to monitor safety and security in and around schools. Some schools employ off-duty police officers as school security officers, while others designate a particular school official to be responsible for referring potential or alleged violations of law to local police authorities. Under FERPA, investigative reports and other records created and maintained by these "law enforcement units" are not considered "education records" subject to FERPA. Accordingly, schools may disclose information from law enforcement unit records to anyone, including outside law enforcement authorities, without parental consent. See 34 CFR § 99.8.

While a school has flexibility in deciding how to carry out safety functions, it must also indicate to parents in its school policy or information provided to parents which office or school official serves as the school's "law enforcement unit." [The school's notification to parents of their rights under FERPA can include this designation. As an example, the U.S. Department of Education (2007b) has posted a model notification on the Web at: http://www.ed.gov/policy/gen/guid/fpco/ferpa/lea-officials.html.]

Law enforcement unit officials who are employed by the school should be designated in its FERPA notification as "school officials" with a "legitimate educational interest." As such, they may be given access to personally identifiable information from students' education records. The school's law enforcement unit officials must protect the privacy of education records it receives and may disclose them only in compliance with FERPA. For that reason, it is advisable that law enforcement unit records be maintained separately from education records.

Security Videos

Schools are increasingly using security cameras as a tool to monitor and improve student safety. Images of students captured on security videotapes that are maintained by the school's law enforcement unit are not considered education records under FERPA. Accordingly, these videotapes may be shared with parents of students whose images are on the video and with outside law enforcement authorities, as appropriate. Schools that do not have a designated law enforcement unit might consider designating an employee to serve as the "law enforcement unit" in order to maintain the security camera and determine the appropriate circumstances in which the school would disclose recorded images.

Personal Knowledge or Observation

FERPA does not prohibit a school official from disclosing information about a student if the information is obtained through the school official's personal knowledge or observation, and not from the student's education records. For example, if a teacher overhears a student making threatening remarks to other students, FERPA does not protect that information, and the teacher may disclose what he or she overheard to appropriate authorities.

School leaders should always consult their district's legal counsel for development and implementation of policies and procedures related to FERPA. School officials should, however, discuss with their school attorney the various health and safety guidelines above. Not all school attorneys are equally versed in FERPA law.

Dr. Bernard James of Pepperdine University is an excellent resource on school law for school board members, school administrators, and school attorneys who want to learn about school law related to school safety issues. Unlike some school attorneys who focus in on what schools can get away without doing, Dr. James focuses on clarifying myths and misinformation to identify how schools *can* legally and proactively address school safety.

GANGS

Factors motivating kids to join gangs vary by the individual. A multitude of social and economic reasons can be involved. Power, status, security, friendship, family substitute, economic profit, substance abuse influences, and numerous other factors can influence kids to join gangs. Gang members also cross all socioeconomic backgrounds and boundaries regardless of age, sex, race, economic status, and academic achievement.

Each case must be evaluated on an individual basis, thus the importance of knowing what to look for and how to intervene early before the problem becomes entrenched!

Gang violence is different from nongang violence in several ways:

- Gang violence typically involves a larger number of individuals.
- Gang-related violence tends to be more retaliatory and escalates much more quickly than nongang violence.
- Gang activity is usually more violent in nature and often involves a greater use of weapons.

School and public safety officials must look at gang activity differently and not as one-on-one, isolated incidents. Otherwise, the problem can escalate so quickly that a school lunchroom fight between rival gang members will escalate into a potential drive-by shooting just hours later at school dismissal.

School officials must still discipline individual students involved in gang offenses on a case-by-case basis based upon their individual actions in violating school rules, but educators must see the forest with the trees and recognize that these offenses are interrelated and part of a broader pattern of gang-related misconduct and violence.

Historically, people looked for graffiti or bandannas as the main indicators of a gang presence. However, gang indicators can be quite subtle, particularly as awareness increases among school officials, law enforcement, parents, and other adults.

Depending upon the specific gang activity in a specific given school or community, gang identifiers *may* include the following:

- Graffiti: Unusual signs, symbols, or writing on walls, notebooks, and so on.
- Colors: Obvious or subtle colors of clothing, a particular clothing brand, jewelry, or haircuts (but not necessarily the traditional perception of colors as only bandannas).
- Tattoos: Symbols on arms, chest, or elsewhere on the body.
- Lit (gang literature): Gang signs, symbols, poems, prayers, procedures, and so on in notebooks or other documents.

- Initiations: Suspicious bruises, wounds, or injuries resulting from a jumping-in type initiation.
- Hand signs: Unusual hand signals or handshakes.
- Behavior: Sudden changes in behavior or secret meetings.

One or several of these identifiers may indicate gang affiliation. It is important to remember, however, that identifiers help recognize gang affiliation, but a focus on behavior is especially important.

Educators, law enforcement, parents, and other youth-service providers need regular training and updates to monitor the changing nature of gang identifiers and, most importantly, gang behavior in their schools and communities. Because of the ever-evolving nature of gang identifiers, and the increasingly common trend of gang members going lower profile with fewer visible signs of gang membership to avoid detection by authorities, the best training on gang identifiers is often provided by local law enforcement and other gang specialists who are familiar with the latest local trends.

Gangs thrive on anonymity, denial, and lack of awareness by school personnel. The gang member whose notebook graffiti goes unaddressed today may be involved in initiations, assaults, and drug sales in school in the near future.

The condition that makes the school environment most ripe for gang activity is denial. The most common initial response to gangs in almost all communities and schools is denial because public officials are more focused on image concerns for their organizations while they should be focusing on dealing with the problem. The longer they deny, the more entrenched the problem becomes and in the end, the worse their image will be.

School and community responses require a balanced approach of prevention, intervention, and enforcement strategies. Schools must work very closely with law enforcement to share information on gang activity since what happens in the community spills over into the schools and vice versa.

Practical steps schools can take include the following:

- Communicate to staff, students, and parents that schools are neutral grounds and that gang, drug, and weapon activities will receive priority response.
- Apply discipline in a timely, firm, fair, and consistent manner.
- Institute student antigang education and prevention programs.
- Establish a mechanism for student conflict mediation.
- Train school personnel and parents in gang identification, intervention, and prevention techniques.
- Obtain input from youth on violence-related concerns and prevention strategies.

- Establish cooperative relationships and communication networks with parents, law enforcement and other criminal justice agencies, social services, and other community members. Set up mechanisms and structures to promote informationsharing and coordination among agencies addressing youth, gangs, and related public safety efforts (Trump, 2010a).

Gangs are a community problem, but schools are a part of that community and cannot operate in isolation while hoping that the gang members will drop their gang alliances and activities once they cross the schoolhouse door.

HOTLINES AND OTHER ANONYMOUS REPORTING

A number of schools find success with school safety hotlines either at the building, district, or community levels. Some hotlines simply involve a dedicated line with an answering machine. Others are a bit more advanced, such as having a tie-in with local crime stoppers programs or by using e-mail or text message to transmit anonymous tips.

A hotline or other anonymous reporting mechanism is only as effective as the follow-up on tips and the publicity of its existence. Notices of hotlines should be included in PA announcements, student handbooks, posters throughout the schools, parent and community newsletters, and advertisements through the media. Many administrators find that student callers are less interested in rewards than they are in effective follow-through to resolve their safety concerns.

LOCKERS AND BOOKBAGS

Some schools have eliminated lockers. On the surface this sounds great, but there are many implications. It usually means that districts provide one set of books for the classroom and another set for students to take home. In many districts, this is not financially possible.

See-through bookbags serve as an extra tool for security. Of course, this is not a panacea. Students who want to carry weapons or other contraband can simply conceal them on their person or within something else in the bookbag.

Proper procedures related to student searches provide an alternative for those school officials unable to implement locker and bookbag elimination. Students should be given prior notice that they are subject to search if administrators have a reasonable suspicion that they violated school rules or the laws. They also should be advised, in advance, that lockers are the property of the school, and as such, they are subject to search at any given time during the school year.

Perhaps the most practical and likely step administrators could take is to require students to keep their bookbags in their lockers during the course of the school day. Today's bookbags and backpacks look larger than some luggage I see in airports around the country. In addition to creating increased risks for accidents from tripping over them, students' carrying bookbags and backpacks up and down stairwells, through tight hallways, and in smaller classrooms increase the risk of students being accidentally (or intentionally) hit with them, which in turn increases the risks of verbal and physical altercations.

PERSONAL SAFETY

During the past decade, educators have voiced a growing fear for their personal safety. Threats include potential injuries from dealing with angry parents (see the "Adult-Originated Violence" section, p. 43) or intervening in fights and conflicts. Educators are also concerned about their own use of force and how they can reduce their potential for victimization.

Intervening Safely in Fights and Conflicts

Many staff injuries are not received in student versus staff confrontations, but instead, occur when staff members break up fights or conflicts between two or more students. Many staff members subsequently may hesitate to break up student fights and conflicts, but their total inaction contributes to a likely increase in security risks. Unfortunately, students fight at school because they know that someone will usually break up the fight quickly.

Nobody can force staff members to physically intervene in a situation if they choose not to do so. Each staff member must assess in advance what his or her threshold is for physical intervention. Regardless of whether they physically intervene, all staff members can play a role in assisting to restore order. This can include dispersing crowds, documenting observed behavior, and providing similar supportive actions.

School officials who do decide to physically intervene should remember some basic points:

- Monitor for early warning signs of such conflicts as stare-downs, verbal exchanges, posturing, audience formation, and other clues that an altercation is about to ensue. Do not wait for the smoke, if you can put out the fire early on.

- Remain calm and do not draw additional student attention to the incident.
- Get assistance en route to the scene or as soon as possible.
- Briefly assess the situation, including the participants, the audience, and your surroundings, before jumping into the middle of a crowd.
- Watch hands as well as eyes. Remember that while someone may be looking in one direction, his or her hands could be going for a weapon.
- Identify an escape route and do not be afraid to take it, if necessary. Heroes are for television, not school hallways. Let your common sense prevail in all situations.

Administrative, teaching, and support staff members should be trained on verbal de-escalation and nonviolent crisis intervention techniques. It is not advisable to try to teach your staff a full form of martial arts in one 20-minute staff meeting. It is unrealistic to attempt to instruct staff members on how to disarm students in such a short time, and it often creates a false sense of security.

Reducing Staff Victimization

School officials often lay the groundwork for reducing staff victimization far ahead of an actual confrontation. Officials are often helped to deal more effectively with students in a state of alarm by building positive relationships with them prior to a crisis. Officials who have good relationships with many students will have a good reputation among the student body as a whole. This also can be potentially helpful in dealing with others who may not have had contact with the staff member before an incident.

Educators, as well as security or police personnel, must strike the delicate balance of being firm, fair, and consistent in how they administer discipline and exert authority with children. Individuals who are perceived to be too weak or too hard are likely candidates for increased victimization. Effective staff will be firm, fair, consistent, organized, confident, supportive, and friendly but alert and cautious to a reasonable degree. The fourth R in education today truly is *Relationships*.

Use of Force

School districts should establish policies and procedures regarding employee use of force against students. This issue also should be addressed in staff meetings and training programs. Some general suggestions include the following:

- Use of force by staff should be reasonable, necessary, and timely in the eyes of a prudent person.

- Use of force should escalate only in response to the level of resistance and without malice by the staff member using the force.
- Use of force should cease once compliance is achieved.
- Use of force by staff in any incident should be documented, and witness statements should be obtained immediately following the incident.

The potential always exists for liability. This potential will increase if severe injury occurs to students, when a staff member acts in anger, or when an action is disproportionate to the need. These issues and others, of course, are situational. The listed suggestions, and more important, advice from your district's legal counsel on sound school policies, will help staff prepare to face such incidents.

PERSONNEL AND INTERNAL SECURITY

In addition to not reporting student crimes, school systems are equally, if not more, notorious for handling employee misconduct internally. Many examples exist in which school systems have refused to prosecute employees who commit such crimes as improper relationships with students, thefts, embezzlement, and more. In lieu of prosecution, employee misconduct is frequently handled with administrative disciplinary action (similar to some student criminal offenses), and in more serious offenses, acceptance of a forced resignation from the employee.

Forced resignations may include an agreement that the district will not include any record of the offense in the employee's personnel file. It might also include an agreement that the district will not provide negative information when a prospective employer inquires about the employee for a position elsewhere. The result is that the problem employee moves to a different school system—a process known within the education community as *passing the trash.*

School systems also have a history of conducting limited background checks on potential employees. Although laws have been enacted in many states that require criminal history checks of new employees for school districts, many problems still exist regarding school hiring practices as they relate to background checks. These include the following:

1. As noted, the absence of a criminal history does not necessarily indicate the absence of past criminal conduct, even when such misconduct had been detected and confirmed. Criminal history checks are limited in that they show only those instances of arrests, prosecutions, or convictions. Considering the traditional practices of school systems in handling

internal matters, it is relatively safe to say that a significant number of employee criminal offenses have gone unrecorded.

2. State laws, district policies, or both regarding criminal history checks may be limited to such classifications of employees as teachers, counselors, or administrative personnel. Volunteers, uncertified support employees, or such contract personnel as school photographers, building tradespeople, or outsourced school service providers, may never even receive this basic check.

3. Criminal history checks historically were limited to a particular local, county, or state jurisdiction. Depending on the scope of the criminal history check, an applicant could potentially have a record in a neighboring county that will never show up on the records check. Access to national criminal history data has improved this issue, but costs for the checks are always an issue of concern to cash-strapped schools.

4. Even if the criminal records are checked for all new applicants, a bigger problem exists regarding employees hired prior to the start of this type of record check. In a number of instances, employees have been convicted of criminal offenses outside the workplace and the school system was never notified. The result: The employee continues working with children while he or she has a criminal record.

All school systems should have a policy mandating employees to notify the employer when they are arrested or convicted of any crime, misdemeanor, or felony. This is still not enough because, unfortunately, many people will not notify the employer in the hope that the incident will never be discovered. For that reason, school systems should be required to perform periodic criminal history update checks on individuals during their periods of employment.

Although this may sound harsh, those questioning such a practice should ask themselves if they want a convicted criminal to supervise and serve as a role model for their children. Individuals who accept positions of working with children should expect such actions to be a reality of the times. If they do nothing wrong, they should not have to worry about being checked.

5. Few districts conduct what security professionals would call a true background check. Some may go as far as to send letters to former employers and references listed on the applications. Few have enough staff to go out in the field to talk with people and dig deep for character references and concrete verification of application information. Unfortunately, some readily accept what is on the application or resume, and never check anything except the required criminal history.

6. School districts should have a standard procedure for investigating and documenting alleged employee misconduct. Statements should be taken from all victims, witnesses, and suspects. Criminal offenses should be immediately reported to the police once they are detected. As with students, criminal offenders should be prosecuted and handled administratively, not simply one or the other.

Another aspect of internal security includes the security of information. Student files, personnel records, computerized information, and other district files and records are frequently left open and accessible to anyone who wants to gain access. Although certain records are public information, school systems need to take a close look at the security procedures for maintaining the integrity of information.

Computer hackers, reporters, and others with an interest in obtaining certain information find schools easy targets. Schools have always been user-friendly, and school employees find it extremely difficult to challenge strangers or question individuals even when, at heart, they feel uncomfortable. Open doors, unchallenged strangers, unlocked file cabinets, and computer systems with no security measures provide unauthorized information seekers with perfect targets. In fact, a reporter once noted that if she wanted to know anything or to see what was new, she simply walked through and looked on the desks of central office administrators when they were away. She would always find something.

When assessing this area of school security, a close look should be taken at district hiring practices and background check procedures. Questions should include the following:

- Are background checks really conducted?
- Does the district require criminal history checks?
- What are the limitations of such checks?
- Are all employees checked or just certain classifications of employees?
- Does the district have a policy requiring employees to report arrests or convictions during their term of employment?
- Is there a standard process in place for investigating and documenting employee misconduct?
- Are employee criminal offenses prosecuted or simply transferred to another employer through forced resignations?
- Does the school system use appropriate information security measures?

School leaders also need to have clear protocols for conducting staff investigations and for providing checks and balances to avoid criminal activity in areas of higher risk and common inappropriate activity. For example, over recent years we have seen more thefts from student activity funds by principals, program coordinators, secretaries, coaches, and athletic staff. Districts should have reasonable checks and balances for handling and accounting for such funds, periodically unannounced audits of such programs, and investigation procedures for handling irregularities.

Security assessments should not be an adversarial process in which the assessors are treated as though they are enemy spies. When assessing personnel and internal security, however, security professionals often find that this is the case. School officials need to view this component of school security with as much seriousness as the others. It could save a great deal of embarrassment and legal liability down the road.

PHYSICAL SECURITY

The majority of elementary and secondary schools in the United States were not designed with security in mind. In fact, many of them are unintentionally designed for disaster, in terms of professional security standards. Poor visibility, inadequate communications, excessive access points, varying levels of lighting, limited intrusion detection systems, nonexistent key control, inconsistent or inaccurate inventory control, and inoperable or nonexistent locks characterize the state of security in many of these schools.

Clearly, this section alone could easily be developed into a book. It is for this reason that many of the individuals selling security assessments to school districts often focus largely, if not solely, on the physical security component.

The following sections identify some key physical security areas.

Access Control and Visitor Management

Most schools have far too many access points. Not only do they have many doors, but in many districts, most of these doors are left unlocked and accessible from the outside. This problem could be corrected rather easily by using panic bars that secure the door from the outside but will facilitate egress from inside the building in the event of such an emergency as a fire.

School officials often mistake this type of reduction in access points as a fire hazard. Chaining doors from the inside creates a fire hazard. Proper use of panic bars on doors creates no fire hazard if occupants can leave the building in an emergency.

The reality is that access control is more an issue of convenience than anything else. Whereas some say that parents or other visitors will complain about having all doors secured from the outside except one designated entrance, it is often more an inconvenience for staff. If school officials educate parents, staff, students, and visitors of the necessity for access control, resistance should eventually decrease.

Some schools have secured all doors from the outside and established one designated entrance point. This designated entrance door is also secured from the outside and access is controlled by electronic buzzer, frequently integrated with video surveillance, speaker systems, or both. This works particularly well at the elementary level but can be less effective at larger schools with a significant amount of pedestrian traffic.

One elementary school principal felt that she had the most secure building in the district. All doors were secured from the outside and the designated entrance had a buzzer system. What the principal failed to consider was that more than half of the main entrance was made of glass, creating an easy target for those choosing to simply knock out the glass and open the door from the inside, particularly at night. Fortunately, a security assessment at that school resulted in a change in the type of door.

Open windows accessible from ground level and unsecured roof hatches also present access control problems. Many schools have adjacent playgrounds where children and youths spend many evenings and late nights. It is not uncommon for them to climb onto the roof of the building or crawl inside through an open window. It is also not uncommon for vandalism and other damage to follow.

Different school designs present different access problems. A large number of districts have such portable classrooms as trailers or single-story houses that can be moved around on school grounds or from school to school. Whereas portable classrooms meet overcrowding needs of the district, they also create a significant security concern about unlocked doors, no communications link to the main building, and the need to have students walking from portables to main buildings during the school day.

One school district had a very serious access problem related to student restrooms at several elementary and middle school buildings. Many student restrooms were scattered throughout the campus and were only accessible from the outside of the building. This meant that students had to exit their classrooms and enter restrooms from the outside of the building. At the time of a security assessment, these restrooms were unlocked and accessible to anyone who gained access to school grounds.

Obviously, this presented a serious security risk because trespassers, child molesters, kidnappers, or just about any other person wanting to hide inside the restrooms could do so. Of course, the security assessment report included strong recommendations related to locking the restroom doors and having students escorted by adults. The ideal recommendation, although costly, was to have these restrooms relocated and accessible from inside the building.

Persistent individuals will likely gain access to the school if they really want to do so. Doors will be left partially open by legitimate users, and in larger schools, students will inevitably open doors for individuals coming in. Still, an aggressive effort to control access points should be maintained and signs should be posted on all doors directing visitors to the main office, along with signs posted throughout the building indicating the actual location of the main office.

Regardless of the number of secured doors or signs, school staff must assertively challenge visitors and strangers observed in their building. Security assessments of various schools have found staff to be extremely friendly and blatantly indifferent to the presence of strangers in their school. Staff awareness programs must be implemented in concert with other access control measures.

Basic visitor control should include the following steps:

1. Limit access points.

2. Post signs, directions, and/or floor plans.

3. Greet, question, identify, and log visitors.

4. Provide identification badges and escorts for visitors.

5. Sign out visitors in a logbook when they leave.

6. Train staff to challenge visitors and students to report strangers.

7. Maintain and upkeep doors, door hardware, and so on.

Many schools in the post-Columbine era have also invested in visitor management systems. One of the more popular types of systems operates by scanning a driver's license into a reader, and the visitor's information is processed via computer to compare the visitor's information against sexual offender databases. An identification (ID) badge for the visitor can be printed out if the person comes up clean after the check.

These and other measures such as maintaining closed campuses at student lunchtime should be included in this area of physical security.

A number of schools around the nation also remodeled their main entranceways or, in new construction cases, built the entrance and main office a bit more with security in mind. These schools have built a second set of inner doors that can be locked after students enter in the morning. Parents and other visitors coming into the first set of doors are then funneled into the main office where they can sign in and then, if necessary, get a visitor's pass before entering the rest of the building.

Communications

Many schools have antiquated communication systems, if any at all. Basic questions to be asked in the assessment of this area include the following:

- Can teachers contact the office through in-house phones or by use of a panic button in each classroom?
- Is there a PA system that can be used to broadcast emergency messages through the school? It is also helpful to have two-way public address systems by which broadcasts can be made and individual rooms can be monitored on the same system. Does the school have two-way portable walkie-talkie or radio units for use in routine and emergency situations?
- Can pay phones be removed from the hallways and school grounds, to reduce loitering, rumor control, false 911 calls, and related misuse?
- How do school officials dial "9-1-1" from school phones? Must they dial a "9" or other number in order to first get an outside line from which they can then dial 9-1-1? Are all school officials aware of this procedure? Can phones be programmed to allow direct dial of 9-1-1 since many people, when their adrenaline is flowing, may get tunnel vision and forget to dial the number required to get an outside line?

School officials should have cellular phones for crisis team members to use in crisis situations when mobility is needed or when regular phone systems are down. Some districts have been able to get the business community to donate cellular services for such purposes.

Identification Systems

School officials have debated the value of ID cards at the secondary school level for years, and they still appear to have no conclusive position on whether the benefits outweigh the costs.

Adult ID cards are helpful in identifying central office staff, employees from other schools, contract employees, substitute staff, and other individuals not normally assigned to a particular school. Student ID cards are also helpful in controlling school bus riders and identifying trespassers in buildings, but they are not foolproof. Adult and student ID systems require regular and consistent enforcement, with clear consequences and costs for those who fail to wear the cards.

Yes, wear them. What good is an ID card if it is tucked away in a wallet or pocket? The time consumed in repeatedly requesting ID cards, and replacing them, seems to be a major factor in the demise of most well-intentioned ID programs. Costs of implementing and maintaining such programs are another strong factor influencing decisions not to implement or to cease continuation of ID programs.

Schools with a large staff and student body are also likely to run into parking problems. A vehicle ID program for all cars parked on school property should be maintained. Cars should be registered with security personnel, the main office, or both, with vehicle description, license number, and related ID information for staff and student vehicles. Here again, information security is important to keep staff ID information out of the hands of students.

Regardless of whether student and staff ID systems are in place, visitor ID should be mandatory in all schools. In addition to the recommendations related to access control, visitors should be issued a clearly visible ID tag to be worn at all times that they are on school premises. Time-lapse visitor badges are now available from security product vendors that change colors or are otherwise altered after a predetermined time or following exposure to outside light. These disposable badges help maintain the integrity of the visitor ID program without creating excessive worries about walk-away badges. And as noted earlier in the book, some commercially solid visitor management systems operate by scanning a driver's license into a reader, and the visitor's information is processed via computer to compare the visitor's information against sexual offender databases. An ID badge for the visitor can be printed out if the person comes up clean after the check.

The bottom line for ID systems is simple: If you are going to do it, do it consistently and properly. Operational and enforcement logistics should be thoroughly discussed before seriously taking steps to implement such programs.

Intrusion Detection Systems

Intrusion detection systems, or alarms, vary from district to district and even from school to school. Generally, school districts have antiquated, fragmented, or nonexistent intrusion detection systems. Poor maintenance, irregular inspections, employee abuse of systems, and related factors contribute to their reduced effectiveness.

This area should receive increased attention, particularly when considering the infusion of high-tech computers and other technology into classrooms. It is not surprising to find schools with several million dollars worth of computer technology in one wing of a high school, and even one classroom with a million dollars worth of equipment inside. Yet we fail to find adequate security systems associated with this equipment and their storage areas.

Are systems antiquated or adequate? Are the systems fragmented or do multiple systems (and even multiple alarm companies) cover the same school, causing duplication, confusion, or ineffective coverage? Security assessments should address these and other questions related to intrusion detection systems.

It may be appropriate to have a technical consultant with expertise in this specific area assist with the assessment. Larger districts with internal security departments may find it valuable to have a dedicated staff member(s) to deal solely with intrusion detection systems and related alarms. The importance of maintaining alarm systems, making the appropriate system adjustments when high-value items are moved, and planning for future needs cannot be overstated.

Inventory Control

Inventory control is sorely lacking in most school systems. The larger the district, the greater the chance that this is the case. Yet thousands, and in many districts millions, of dollars in equipment are floating around school systems and out the doors of school systems, with no accountability.

ID mechanisms should be permanently affixed onto or engraved in the property, along with a clear ID of the school district to which it belongs. Most districts set a dollar limit on items requiring inventory tags or labels. Unfortunately, some districts set an exceptionally high limit on the dollar amount to avoid difficulties in finding items at the time of an audit.

Again, technology has helped address security concerns. Bar codes offer a tool for inventory control. Outside agencies are available to contract with schools to inventory all property. Although some school officials argue that it costs too much to perform such a service, would it not cost more to replace stolen or lost property?

Key and Lock Control

Most schools have terrible key control. In some schools, keys that have been duplicated, lost, or stolen are often more accessible to students than to staff. A high school in one city had its own key duplication machine in an assistant principal's office with boxes of blank keys openly available.

The user-friendly mentality can create other problems, even when all doors have locks. Crime prevention awareness must be ingrained in the school culture to make locking cabinets and doors routine behavior. A number of cases have occurred across the country where trespassers will slip into a school and go classroom to classroom where classroom doors are open, students and the teacher are gone, and teachers wallets can easily be stolen from unlocked desk drawers.

Card readers with swipe cards or proximity cards are more common today than a decade ago. These systems eliminate the need for keys and allow for cards to be programmed (and when necessary, deactivated) relatively easily. However, they do have a cost attached, and most schools still do not have this type of technology because they cannot afford such systems. When schools do use card readers, they are typically strategically located at a half dozen or so doors that are most used such as near teacher parking lots, doors used for physical education classes, recess doors to play areas at elementary schools, and so on.

Locks and other security devices need to be purchased for computer and other high-tech equipment placed in schools today. It should not be surprising to see a shift in after-hour entry suspects from juveniles to young adults, considering the amount of equipment in many schools today. Traditionally, juveniles broke into schools to vandalize property. Today older thieves also target schools for expensive equipment that they can easily fence on the streets, particularly in the absence of inventory control records, police reports, or both, to identify missing items accurately.

Assessments should include a review of key control, presence and use of locks, and related issues.

Perimeter and Outside Security

Many schools have poorly defined perimeters, transition markers, or barriers from street traffic. Playground equipment, poles, and other structures often provide easy access to fire escapes, roofs, and other potential entry points. Trees, shrubs, and related greenery frequently offer perfect concealment for juvenile parties, vandalism, or entry into schools at night.

Inspections of perimeter and outside security should be conducted during the school day and at night. This is especially true for buildings where night school programs are conducted. Schools have as much responsibility for security at night as they do during the day.

Protective Lighting

Protective lighting continues to be debated in some circles. Some advocates of a "lights out" policy unquestionably hold that this is the only way to go. They argue that by turning out all lights and requiring school neighbors and others in the area to report any signs of light to police, thieves will be caught much faster because they need light to do their dirty work.

Many security professionals still question this practice. The lights-out philosophy is frequently supported and advocated more from an energy (and dollar) conservation perspective than from a professional security perspective. Whereas it may work in some areas, particularly in rural or smaller suburban communities, security professionals working with larger, urban districts question whether lights-out is the best approach.

Most such lights as individual classroom lights, inside a school, should be turned off. The efficiency and logic of having a school completely lit up are questionable. Nevertheless, good lighting outside the building deters the amateur vandal or burglar who might otherwise commit an offense under the protection of darkness. It is logical to follow lights-out on the inside and lights-on on the outside as a general recommendation, recognizing that schools and districts are unique and may require individualized recommendations.

Bigger lighting problems exist in many schools with timer adjustments, inadequate maintenance, and infrequent inspections of lighting conditions. Some school lots and grounds have been found to have timers that turn on the lights during the day and off at dark. Security assessments have also turned up reports of burned-out or damaged lights that have gone unrepaired for months prior to the inspection, even though the facility had been used on a daily basis.

Like other physical security issues, lighting generally requires financial commitments. This includes costs associated with repairs, replacement, and labor. Costs, however, should not automatically disqualify corrective action. It is better to pay smaller amounts for prevention than larger amounts for damage awards in court.

Signage

Most schools make poor use of signs outside and inside schools. Outside signs should include notices prohibiting trespassing, identifying drug-free and weapon-free zones, providing directions to visitors, and identifying specific entrances by number on the inside and outside of each entranceway. Signs inside the school should include clear directions to the office and identification of different wings, program areas, or facilities.

One of the most disturbing practices is the posting of signs directing visitors to report to the main office; yet there are no signs or indicators of where the main office is located. Some schools have posted signs throughout the building pointing to the main office or nearest administrative office.

PRIVATE, INDEPENDENT, AND CHARTER SCHOOLS

Heads of private and independent schools are often hesitant to embark upon an assessment of their security as they fear an adverse impact on their school's culture. Image and school-community political concerns can also come into play. I have seen some of the best independent schools with excellent security, and I have also seen some very high-profile, affluent independent schools with grossly inadequate supervision and security.

Private schools are not immune from threats, where the threats come from inside or outside of the school. Oftentimes, because of their financial resources for student support services as well as the ability to withdraw students at their discretion, some of the more affluent schools tend to look more at outside than inside threats. Although a professional security assessment will find the proper mix of recommended strategies, the key to success will result from a mindset by private school officials that is open to reasonable and balanced security and preparedness measures.

Charter schools can also pose some unique positive features as well as some unique challenges. I have worked with a number of charter schools located in former office buildings and facilities, and in other older facilities. Oftentimes for charter schools their biggest challenge rests with physical security issues to the facilities in which they must operate.

Just because a school is not a public school per se does not mean it should not have reasonable school security and emergency preparedness measures. Too often we find the biggest hurdle to overcome, especially in private and independent schools, is the mindset of "It can't happen here." Unfortunately, yes it can, and like any other schools, they must be prepared.

PROBATION OFFICERS IN SCHOOLS

Some officials find it helpful to have court probation officers operate directly from their schools. An administrator from one large urban area claimed that more than one third of his entire high school study body was on probation at the same time. In that situation, it was easier to bring the services to the client, rather than the client to the services.

Benefits of such a program include the following:

- Easier and more timely communication between the probation officer and school officials (assuming that they form good relationships)
- Earlier intervention with students in school conflicts that often lead to suspension and/or probation violations

- Reinforcement of school rules and court orders that provide order, structure, and discipline for the youth

Difficulties that may arise include such travel logistics as required court appearances of the probation officer, access to a private office and operational equipment, and potential confidentiality issues that can arise if these issues are not planned for in advance. Still, it is a unique approach to providing collaborative services for at-risk and troubled youths. Although this approach seems to have been seen and heard more of in the late 1990s and early 2000s, we still hear about it in certain regions today. The problem is that with declining budgets, such programs may be much less of an option today than they were following the 1999 Columbine attack.

SCHOOL RESOURCE OFFICERS, SCHOOL POLICE DEPARTMENTS, AND SCHOOL SECURITY DEPARTMENTS

The placement of law enforcement officers, typically known as SROs, in schools grew dramatically following the school shootings of the late 1990s. More than a decade later, many of these programs are still operational and successful in many school communities. But because of budget cuts, the overall growth slowed dramatically, and a number of programs were eliminated in the late 2000's.

Various forms of security staffing are used across the country, and no single staffing method is the only and absolute approach for all schools, as each has its own set of pros and cons. In fact, it is not uncommon to use a combination of approaches, such as SROs and school security officials working side-by-side in a school.

SROs are typically city or county law enforcement officers assigned by their departments to work in the schools within their jurisdiction. The schools benefit by having trained, certified peace officers available to focus on law enforcement, counseling, and education programs related to the law and law enforcement. Funding, personnel selection, supervision, and other operational logistics should be addressed in the early stages of an SRO program.

The SRO model can be a win-win arrangement for schools, law enforcement agencies, and the community when selection, supervision, financial, and other logistics are worked out on the front end of a program. An SRO program can provide quality, cost-effective service for schools and police departments alike. It also typically improves school crime reporting procedures and the sharing of information on school and community juvenile crime activity between the district and the police.

Contrary to the perception that SRO programs simply mean having a cuff-and-stuff officer only focused on arresting students, an appropriately selected, trained, and qualified SRO performs many more tasks associated with prevention than with arrest and prosecution in schools. A successful SRO program depends on its design from the onset.

School police departments are regular law enforcement entities comparable with city or county police agencies. Many colleges and universities already have such departments in place. Officers from these departments usually have full arrest authority but work full-time for the school district. K–12 school police departments tend to be found more often in southern and western states, although there are certainly school police departments elsewhere around the nation.

Positive features of school police departments include full ownership over the department, with personnel selection and supervision. As full-time school employees, the officers' commitment is fully to school policing for that district. If the pay and benefits for school police officers are comparable with those of other police departments, then the school system could reasonably enjoy a full career of service from many such officers. Unfortunately, too often school systems pay their in-house school police at lower levels than other area law enforcement agencies, and when this happens, young officers often use the school police to get the police training, certification, and experience, and then move on to other area law enforcement agencies.

Another issue when considering school police departments involves finances. Police departments have significant budgetary expenses, including costs for ongoing training, equipment, vehicles, and other operational expenses. On the flip side of this issue, any professional security personnel option must have similar costs, especially ongoing training and necessary equipment.

Many states currently do not have legislation to authorize such departments. This can be overcome with proper leadership by state legislators, in cooperation with law enforcement and education officials. A handful of states have had school police departments in operation for many years, and there are many lessons learned to be shared by these districts.

School security departments generally consist of in-house personnel with varying levels of authority, depending on the school system or state and local laws. They also perform a wide range of functions, varying not only from district to district but also within the same district. The size of these departments can range from one person to hundreds, depending on the size and needs of the school systems.

One positive feature associated with school security departments, provided that they are properly supervised and operated, is the element of school district control over personnel selection and assignments.

School security personnel in many districts have a lengthy employment history, offering strong backgrounds, knowledge, and skills in handling school disruptions and crimes. It is also helpful that school security personnel are experienced in dealing with school discipline systems, politics, and bureaucracies that can be challenging for those unfamiliar with these operations.

Negative aspects of school security departments frequently include poor pay, lack of training, and frequent requirements to perform non-security-related duties that are more appropriate for administrative aides than for security professionals. School security departments often have low status in the district's organizational structure, placing them in frequent power-control struggles with other school administrators over professional security procedures and issues. Many times, these departments also lack experienced or long-term, sustained leadership to provide professional school security services.

Whereas these three personnel options are the most popular, they are not the only options, nor is this a detailed analysis of the pros and cons of each model. Some schools may use the traditional hall monitor approach for their security. A smaller number use contract security, although many security professionals have concerns about this option because of their history for high turnover rates, low pay, poor training, and lack of control over personnel assignments. Others may use a combination of approaches, such as SROs, in-house security, and periodic contract security for special projects such as construction or special events.

Many issues need to be evaluated when assessing which form best suits a specific school or district. These include local and state legal parameters, budgetary effect and constraints, school and community standards, and, most important, current and future security threats and service needs. When conducting an assessment, it is important to look not only at current needs but also at what will likely be needed in future years so that assessment recommendations reflect steps to prepare for, and it is hoped, to prevent increased security threats.

Equally important is the need to ensure that, despite the staffing method, duties and responsibilities of security personnel must be clearly focused on performing security functions on a regular and professional basis. One of the biggest problems identified in many security assessments is that individuals hired to perform security functions are often assigned duties and tasks not directly related to security. To have security personnel perform administrative support roles or other nonsecurity tasks routinely subjects the school to significant liability should an incident occur that could have been prevented, or potentially prevented, if the security official had been doing his or her proper job.

Which security staffing form best suits the current and future needs of the school or district? Are security personnel properly trained and deployed? Are security personnel performing official security functions on a regular basis? Does the security department have adequate policies and procedures to guide their personnel? Is there supervision and leadership by a trained, experienced school security profession or by someone with no experience in this area who also supervises other school services? All these, and much more, should be asked when assessing school security staffing and operations.

SCHOOL SECURITY EQUIPMENT: METAL DETECTORS, CAMERAS, AND OTHER TECHNOLOGY

Unfortunately, a number of school districts have created a false sense of security in response to high-profile school violence tragedies by moving quickly to install equipment and other physical and tangible measures, often for the sake of having something concrete to show students, staff, parents, the media, and the overall school community as evidence that they have worked on improving school safety. Educators need to ensure that they do not use equipment and technology in school safety programs as a panacea for solving safety concerns.

Conversely, when effectively utilized and employed under the appropriate circumstances, equipment can contribute to reducing school safety risks. Rather than simply having equipment for the sake of having equipment, however, school officials should focus on answering the following questions:

- What specific security threats are we attempting to address?
- How will the equipment be used on a day-to-day basis to help address these threats?
- What are the plans for maintenance, repair, and replacement?

Educators who can answer these questions in detail will likely be in a much better position to receive the maximum benefits from the use of school security equipment and technology.

School officials who face a high-profile incident or crisis frequently turn to security-related equipment as a quick fix to illustrate to staff, students, parents, and the community that they are taking action to deal with security concerns. Unfortunately, many equipment-related measures are undertaken without full consideration of the implications and operational issues associated with such ventures. Equipment should be a supplement to, not a substitute for, professional security personnel, policies, procedures, and programs. Any security equipment is only as strong as the weakest human link behind it.

Surveillance cameras and metal detectors are used to varying extents in a number of our nation's school districts. Cameras are in place in many urban, suburban, and rural districts. Metal detectors tend to be used regularly in a smaller number of districts, often larger districts with a chronic history of weapons incidents.

Parents, the media, and some in the community often have unrealistic expectations of security when cameras or metal detectors are in place. Many mistakenly believe anything occurring within or outside of the school at any point in time will be clearly captured if a school uses cameras, regardless of how many cameras or how large the school. If a school regularly uses metal detectors, some often believe a school will be weapons-free.

These unrealistic expectations can be attributed, in part, to modern television and movies. The *CSI effect*, as some in the security profession call it, refers to the false belief that cameras in a school will capture anything and everything at any point in time as shown in some TV dramas and movies. Even if a school has invested a large sum of money and has a well-designed camera system, every single inch of the building and grounds will not likely be covered on a 24/7 basis.

Likewise the *TSA effect* (Transportation Security Administration airport weapons screening operation), as I call it, leaves some parents and media falsely believing that because a school (or other facility) uses metal detectors, there is a guarantee that no weapons will ever be in the school. Most school security operations using metal detectors do not have the number of staff or the training for weapons screening comparable to a large TSA airport. And the reality is that, like TSA and airports, even if they did, there is a still a chance that weapons can and will get into the facility, not to mention that items already in the school can be used as weapons even if not designed for that purpose.

Educators should not create unrealistic expectations for students, parents, staff, and the community when they are using school security technology. Cameras are a deterrent to those who are deterrable and *may* serve as evidence for those who cannot be deterred. Metal detectors may serve as a deterrent and will likely detect weapons in some cases, but they cannot account for all cases or cases in which something else already in the school will be used as a weapon.

The largest amount of security technology, and the best quality of technology, will still not give the 100% guarantee of security that some parents, media, and others expect when these measures are in place.

Setting realistic expectations when security technology is used in a school is important. The first and best line of defense is a well-trained, highly alert staff and student body. Any security technology is only as good as the weakest human link behind it. And even the best of security technology will still not create a guarantee of 100% safety.

Students smuggle weapons through or around metal detectors. Some students have climbed into the building through windows or used other entrance points to avoid inspections conducted at the so-called single point of entry. Others have passed weapons through windows or under doors or used other methods for getting them into the building.

Anecdotal information suggests that administrators are more receptive to the random use of handheld metal detectors than to the use of stationary detectors. Random inspections of students boarding or exiting school buses, students taken from a random number of classrooms or periodic use at special events have reportedly kept students off guard about when they can expect to be checked. Keeping students off balance by the potential for inspection at any time seems to be critical in effectively using metal detectors.

Issues regarding notice are similar to those previously mentioned about drug-sniffing dogs, including, if you are going to do it, do it right. Many years ago, one school district canceled its metal detector inspections because it found *only* six weapons the previous year. How many more would have been brought to school without the inspections? Was *only* six an acceptable number of guns?

Likewise, thought should be given to all of the issues prior to implementing surveillance camera equipment. Many times, cameras are purchased and installed because of the availability of funds or the need to meet a public relations crisis. Administrators must also consider underlying issues such as installing cameras where they will be most effective, determining who will monitor the cameras, and identifying funding sources for the necessary repairs and replacement of equipment.

Digital technology has resulted in newer and newer surveillance camera products on the market. Cost is always a factor for schools. But digital technology brings a number of other issues requiring school security administrators to work with technology administrators to discuss issues such as the capacity of the district's technology system to store images for camera districtwide.

Good common sense is especially important when setting up cameras. Cameras should not be placed in a location where there are such reasonable expectations of privacy as restrooms or locker rooms. Although such locations may be priority areas in terms of security problems, other liability concerns will be equally high if an administrator chooses to place cameras in locations such as these.

Another issue frequently ignored is whether a reasonable expectation exists for a response to problems that occur in the view of surveillance cameras. If a student or staff member is attacked and beaten in front of a camera, does that person have a reasonable expectation that security or administrative personnel will respond to assist? Likewise, what are the implications of using dummy cameras in which there may be a dozen camera boxes, but only two functional cameras are rotated among the boxes?

Many schools have purchased camcorders for use by their security, administrative personnel, or both. These have come in quite handy for taping trespassers, fights, or other criminal or disruptive behavior. Not only does the tape provide a good record to support disciplinary or criminal action, it also serves as a nice tool for disarming parents when they start to tell officials how their lovely children would never do what they are accused of doing.

School officials should consult with their legal counsels, develop appropriate policies and procedures, and train their personnel before implementing metal detectors, surveillance cameras, or similar programs.

SEX OFFENSES

There is a strong possibility that administrators will encounter an incident of inappropriate touching early in their administrative careers. By waiting one school day to further investigate such cases, some administrators have received negative publicity, lawsuits, and threats of criminal charges by law enforcement officials.

Incidents of rape, sexual imposition, molestation, and related offenses can and do occur in school classrooms, hallways, buildings, and on school grounds. A review of state laws and local ordinances on sex-related crimes is a must for all school administrators and should be incorporated into annual administrator training programs. Policies, developed to be consistent with the laws, should be used to create clear guidelines on what, when, and how administrators report sex offenses to law enforcers and parents.

Any time a school official questions whether to call police on sex-related cases, the administrator should err on the side of caution and notify law enforcement authorities. Law enforcement officials have much more expertise than an average school administrator in handling such offenses. By involving law enforcement, administrators are operating in the best interests of the child and in their own best interests.

STUDENT INVOLVEMENT IN SCHOOL SAFETY PLANNING

One of the most common missing components in school safety planning is student involvement. Too often, adults talk about and plan for student safety, but they do not fully engage students in planning and training for their own safety. Although many aspects of security and emergency planning are adult responsibilities, students can, and should, be more involved in many ways in school safety.

Some of the more common ways of involving students include using student focus groups, student climate surveys, and student-led organizations in a school's safety program. A key factor is to also engage students who are not part of the formal student governing groups, athletes, or other highly active students in the school. Picking out students who are not extremely active in social, athletic, or other official groups can give educators a better feel for what the average student sees, hears, and feels.

One of my favorite questions to students is quite simple: If I put you in charge of school safety and gave you all the authority, money, and support to do whatever you want to do, what would you do to make this school safer? It is amazing how they come back with so many practical, common-sense suggestions. And many times, these suggestions are ones that are not even on the radar of the adults responsible for school safety.

STUDENT SEARCHES

Most school officials are well-informed about their legal rights regarding when they may conduct a search if a student violates a law or the school rule. Few officials, however, have received training in how to perform an effective student search. All administrators and security personnel should receive training on the legal aspects of student searches and how to conduct a search.

Some basic tips on searching students include the following:

• If there is any suspicion of a weapon or potential safety risk to a school staff member, including the administrator leading the search process, engage the support of security and police personnel. School administrators are not superheroes and should exercise caution in every search situation.

- Personally escort the students to be searched to the office. Maintain visible contact with the students from the time they are retrieved from the classroom to the time they reach the predetermined destination. It would be prudent to have at least two staff members escort students to provide extra support in monitoring students so they do not throw away any contraband, run, or attempt to assault or resist the escorting adults.

- Always watch the students' hands. If a student is suspected of having a weapon or drugs, it is likely that he or she will try to ditch it if an opportunity arises. This can occur from the time the student is told to accompany a security or administrative official to the office up to and including the time when the student is in the office and searched. Never allow a student to follow behind a staff member where the student cannot be observed. It can be prudent to conduct the search under these circumstances where students are believed to have weapons, drugs, and so on, in the actual location, or one as close as possible to it, where the student suspected of having the items is taken into custody.

- Before beginning the search, when appropriate ask the students if they have anything in their possession, in a locker, or in anyone else's possession that violates the school rules or the law. If they hesitate, tactfully advise them that you have reasonable suspicion that they do, that you plan to conduct a search, and that it would save everyone time and unnecessary embarrassment if students cooperate on the front end. As strange as it sounds, students often acknowledge that they do, with minimal hassles.

- Remove outer clothing such as heavy jackets. It is difficult to effectively pat down a student wearing three layers of jackets. This note is about jackets and is not to suggest, however, removing students' clothing, which would constitute a strip search.

- Remember that concealment places are not limited to pockets. Determine, within legal and procedural parameters, how far you may search, but never assume that the absence of the item means that it is totally absent from the school.

- Secure confiscated contraband and document the incident as soon as possible. If it is a criminal offense, notify police and maintain a clear chain of evidence until they arrive.

Administrators, teachers, and staff must remember that strip searches by school personnel are frowned on by the legal system, not to mention parents and the media. Unfortunately, cases continue to arise in which school officials conduct questionable searches, most often to look for money stolen from class fund-raising projects, the desks of teachers or students, and related areas. Generally, students will tell who took the money if timely and effective investigations are conducted. School officials must ask themselves if a strip search to find $30 is worth losing their job, personal valuables, and public reputation.

These are only points for discussion and consideration, not formal advice or training on conducting searches. Administrators and school safety personnel should consult with local law enforcement, school security specialists, or both for training and establishing detailed procedures for conducting student searches.

SPECIAL EDUCATION AND SCHOOL SAFETY

Special education students are often a source of challenge for school administrators responsible for discipline and safety. Individualized Education Plans (IEPs) and legal limitations associated with special education students influence disciplinary decisions and parameters. This often leaves administrators feeling frustrated and handcuffed in managing discipline and safety issues.

School leaders should establish training for principals, assistant principals, and deans (at a minimum) on special education issues related to school discipline. If this is not done, there is a risk of misinformation adversely impacting school discipline decisions. Administrators need to know what they can and cannot do in incidents involving the discipline of special needs students.

One thing school administrators must keep in mind is that whether or not an individual is a special education student is irrelevant when a crime has been committed—at least at the time of the investigation and arrest. A suspect's special needs may be taken into consideration during sentencing if he or she is found guilty of committing a crime. But having the academic classification of *special education* student does not prohibit a student from being arrested if police have probable cause to effect an arrest for a crime.

I am not advocating targeting special education students for arrest. However, I am pointing out that limitations in administering discipline for special education students do not prohibit the criminal justice process from proceeding forward if and when appropriate. Too often I believe people in education may falsely be under the impression that special education status limits both discipline and potential law enforcement involvement, which is not the case.

SUICIDE

Suicide and other self-harm threats and attempts have been made in schools long before recent high-profile school violence incidents. Today, media, parents, and special interest groups are looking at suicides to determine if there is a connection with bullying and the suicide. As such, eyes will be focused upon the schools should a student complete suicide, regardless of whether it is on school property or somewhere out in the community.

School administrators should work with their counselors, psychologists, and related mental health experts to identify protocols for assessing and managing suicide threats, managing incidents where students or school staff have completed suicide, and for heightening student and staff awareness on suicide issues and resources.

For additional information on teen suicide and schools, see the work of Dr. Scott Poland, an international expert on teen suicide and school violence, who also authored the foreword to this book.

TASERS AND SCHOOL-BASED POLICE OFFICERS

School-based police officers (certified, sworn police officers) armed with Tasers in schools can become a highly emotional and debated school safety issue, especially when an officer uses one on a student.

Tasers are hand-held devices used by law enforcement personnel that deliver a jolt of electricity. The jolt stuns the target by causing an uncontrollable contraction of the muscle tissue. The target is immobilized and falls to the ground.

A handful of anecdotal incidents occurred over the years suggesting questionable judgment in the use of Tasers on juveniles by a small number of officers whose actions received a large amount of media and public attention. Unfortunately, inappropriate uses of Tasers generally reflect situations involving poor individual judgment. Fortunately, they do not characterize the vast majority of police officers carrying Tasers in our schools. Although one inappropriate use is one too many, caution should be exercised to not characterize all police officers carrying Tasers in the category of those making poor judgments in anecdotal cases that capture high-profile media and public attention.

It is important for parents and the general public to also realize that many police officers are not equipped with Tasers. Many, if not most, school-based police officers are also not equipped with Tasers, especially if their respective law enforcement agencies have not so equipped their entire departments. For those school-based officers who are equipped with a Taser, it is important for school and public officials to recognize that these officers are typically certified police officers who are equipped with the same tools as any other police officer in their department.

Many law enforcement officers report that Tasers are useful tools for police officers and that they add a new step in the *use of force continuum* used by police to counter threats against them and others. They point out that the Tasers add an additional intervention tool that falls between the ultimate use of deadly force (the use of a firearm) and other less than lethal interventions. It has been noted by officers that the Taser may be more appropriate under some conditions than the use of chemical agents (mace, pepper spray) or the baton, and that it is less dangerous to bystanders when used in a crowd than chemical spray. A number of police departments have also credited Tasers as a contributing factor to major decreases in suspect and officer injuries, and decreases in police officer firearm shootings.

School-based police officers have noted that the Taser can potentially be helpful to officers working in schools if a threat is posed by an adult nonstudent intruder threatening harm to himself or others. They also report that the Taser can be a useful tool in situations where students who pose a serious threat to themselves or others, or when no other intervention beyond the use of a firearm is an option. Questions have arisen in school communities and particularly in the media, however, when the Taser has been used on younger children, especially elementary and middle school aged youth.

I recommend that age and developmental stages be given serious consideration in discussions between law enforcement officers and educators about using Tasers in school settings with all children, particularly younger children. I acknowledge, however, that there could be life and death situations, and situations with threats of serious harm, where a Taser may be a necessary option and a better alternative than the use of a firearm. Although such situations are rare, society must acknowledge that they can and do occur.

On a day-to-day basis, however, I strongly advise school officers to take a very *conservative* approach to the use of Tasers in a school setting—and most do. The use of such a device, or even the displaying of such a device in a crowd of students, will likely draw a great deal of emotional and political responses in a school community. School-based officers should consider all options before using a Taser on a student, including what they would have done in a similar situation in the past before they were trained and equipped with a Taser, and if that course of action is an option in lieu of using the Taser on a student.

Fortunately, most school-based police officers have long understood the seriousness of weapons retention issues because of their having a firearm in large groups of students. The vast majority of school-based police officers are highly sensitive to the need for caution, consideration, and conservatism in the use of Tasers or firearms in a school setting. School-based officers are also typically better experienced, trained, and skilled in dealing with students and large groups of juveniles than the regular street officer who has not had a daily exposure to school settings.

Some chatter occurs regarding having school administrators carry Tasers. I *strongly* believe that if Tasers are used in schools, only sworn, certified, and trained police officers should be allowed to carry them, not educators, without exception. I do *not* believe that non-law enforcement personnel should be armed with Tasers in school settings.

Although arming officers with Tasers is much more common on the streets, it is an issue drawing increased attention as more and more SROs become provided with these tools. There appears to be much less debate and controversy over the use of Tasers on adults than on juveniles, although there has been debate on the use of the devices on adult suspects who have died in the broader community. In general, it appears that Taser advocates say deaths are often caused by other factors such as suspects being under the influence of drugs or alcohol, and that the devices are safe for use on adults over a designated physical weight. Opponents still question such use.

Some questions we advise school administrators and public safety officials to expect that the community and media will ask, and issues to be prepared to consider if a Taser is used on a student, include the following:

• What policies, procedures, or joint memoranda of understanding are in place with the law enforcement agency and the school district regarding use of force issues followed by the police department that could surface in use of force by school-based police officers?

Note: This is not to suggest that school districts can, should, or even could negotiate a separate or lower standard use-of-force policy by the police department for officers who are working in a school setting. School and police leaders should discuss what policies and use-of-force continuum guidelines are in existence by the police department, how they may surface in various types of scenarios in a school setting, what supportive measures can be put in place in consideration that an officer may use a Taser on a student, how schools and police will issue joint communications on the incident to the media and community, and so on.

One supportive measure that could be incorporated into procedures, for example, is to take to the hospital any student upon whom a Taser has been used in school prior to the student being booked/processed by police.

Another procedure could focus on protocols for the joint release of information on the incident to parents and the media by the school district and police department.

The school district should attempt to negotiate a lower-standard of police use-of-force policy in reaction to high-profile, emotional, or political considerations in the school-community.

• What research and data exist on the use of Tasers specifically on juvenile-aged offenders versus adult offenders? This may be hard to find as there probably are not a lot of parents willing to volunteer up their children to be tested with jolts of electrical shock. It is also a point of contention by those who advocate against Tasers.

• What liability issues may exist for school and law enforcement officials if a Taser is used on a student?

• What if a Taser is used on a student with special needs or one who has a known or unknown medical condition (heart problems, for example)?

• How will school and police officials handle the school-community relations aspect of an officer using a Taser on a student?

Being prepared for these questions and issues is a prudent step in planning. School and public safety administrators should implement a strong education and awareness effort with school staff, PTA, parents, students, and the school community on the purpose, impact, and use of the Taser on the front end, rather than waiting until after it may be used to try to educate members of the school community. A lot of front-end homework and serious discussions should occur, and it is unclear as to whether or not these discussions are currently taking place in many school communities.

Law enforcement agencies should already have policies in place before arming officers with Tasers. School and police officials should discuss legal and policy implications regarding officers carrying Tasers in schools. Police departmental policy, officer training, advance communications between school and police officials, officer judgment skills and common sense, and parent/community education will play big roles in determining the direction this issue takes in a school community.

THEFT

Thefts of property belonging to the school district, its staff, and its students are fairly common. Perpetrators are not only students. Internal theft by school employees occurs in school buildings, office sites, warehouses, and other school facilities.

School systems often have inadequate inventory control and property transfer procedures, making it relatively easy for equipment and supplies to disappear without someone noticing. Schools generally have inadequate or nonexistent key control, as reflected in one security officer's comment that "The students have more keys to this building than I do." Unfortunately, the trusting nature of educators also contributes to the problem, especially opportunity thefts created by individuals not securing valuable equipment, leaving purses and other properties accessible, failing to lock doors, and being overly friendly and not questioning unknown visitors.

What should administrators do to reduce thefts? Steps should include the following:

1. Establish key control procedures.

2. Institute and maintain an effective inventory control and property removal or transfer procedure.

3. Create an increased awareness between faculty and staff to reduce opportunity thefts. Encourage them to lock doors, secure keys and personal property, and question strangers observed in the school.

4. Report thefts of school and personal property to law enforcement. If suspects are identified, prosecute them and pursue restitution.

5. Establish an anonymous reporting system for students and staff, to provide tips on theft suspects and incidents.

Thefts are crimes and should be treated as such. If administrators place a strong emphasis on respect for school property and the property of individuals, and aggressively pursue those found stealing, thefts may decrease.

TRAINING STAFF ON SCHOOL SECURITY AND EMERGENCY PREPAREDNESS

Training time for school violence prevention, security, and emergency preparedness issues is in direct competition with training time to cover the latest in curriculum, brain research, new learning models, and other topics related to improving test scores. Yet one of the first areas attorneys will look at in their lawsuits against school employees for negligent security claims is the amount, type, and quality of training provided to administrators, teachers, and support staff related to school safety and emergency preparedness.

When we ask school administrators to describe the training their staff has received on school safety issues, they often refer to having gone over a portion of their crisis plan at the first faculty meeting or in-service meeting at the beginning of the school year. Too often this means they spent a very brief time or did minimal in-depth actual training. A difference exists between training and reviewing a manual, and it is likely many school officials would have a hard time pinpointing professional training in school safety as a part of their staff's ongoing staff development offerings.

There is an increasing recognition of the need to better train school support staff in school safety, in particular in the area of school emergency planning. One goal in engaging school support staff in emergency planning is to generate new conversations and perspectives into school-level and district-level emergency planning processes. Some issues we address and encourage all schools to cover with these valued nonteaching employee groups include the following:

- Secretary/office support staff safety and crisis issues typically include managing angry and threatening persons, role in access control, parent-student reunification roles, managing bomb threat calls, role on crisis team, and so on.
- Custodian and maintenance staff training and planning sessions focus on roles of day and night custodial staff related to security and emergency response, roles on crisis teams for planning, facility information needed in tactical response, procedures for specific emergencies, after-hours emergencies, and related topics.
- Food services conversations tend to include cafeteria security procedures, impact of drills (lockdowns) during breakfast and lunch periods, emergency food supplies, food security and protection measures, access to food service vendors, role on school and district crisis teams, and related topics.
- Transportation staff discussions often focus on the role of transportation services in school emergencies, preventing and managing violence incidents on the bus, verbal intervention techniques, what to expect if police respond to your bus, bus emergency plans and exercises, and related topics.

School security and emergency training for school support staff is more than providing them with a 20-minute video purchased for the purpose of satisfying minimal training requirements or the desire to say some type of training was provided by referring to a quick review of the school's crisis plan as training. We would not give teachers a 20-minute video on brain research or how to improve test scores as their only in-service, but we often see schools doing this with school safety training for support staff and other school employees.

TRANSPORTATION SECURITY

My colleague, Chuck Hibbert, has long said that school districts do a great job of training drivers how to drive the bus, but they do a poor job of training drivers how to manage behavior on the bus. We can add to the lack of behavior management training an additional lack of training in security and emergency preparedness issues. Our bus drivers have one of the most high-risk areas for potential danger and conduct their jobs with their backs to dozens of students in attempting to prevent such dangers from occurring.

Many districts cannot afford to hire adult monitors to supervise student behavior, leaving drivers to single-handedly manage traffic and student safety aboard the units. What can be done to improve security on buses?

Some practical strategies for managing school transportation security and emergency preparedness include the following:

• Install video surveillance cameras to monitor student behavior. Follow the guidelines previously referenced regarding notice and the legal concerns. Cameras serve as a deterrent to many students, and for those who are not deterred, the video serves as good evidence for administrators and parents to use to determine disciplinary or criminal charges or both.

• Establish pre-employment screening and interviewing protocols for new bus drivers.

• Provide comprehensive training on student behavior management, discipline procedures, working with students who have special needs, dealing with irate parents, security and emergency preparedness, applicable state and local laws, and associated issues for all transportation staff, including newly hired drivers.

• Conduct school security assessments, including physical security assessments, of school bus depots and associated school transportation facilities. Also train drivers on physical security issues related to bus units.

• Employ the effective use of technology, such as two-way communications capabilities and surveillance cameras, on school buses.

• Establish guidelines related to safety and emergency planning, including emergency communications procedures, for all field trips.

• Establish emergency preparedness guidelines from an all hazards approach, covering both natural disasters (weather related, for example) and man-made acts of crime and violence.

• Develop emergency plans with your school district, neighboring districts, and the broader community in mind. Do you have mutual aid agreements with other school districts for backup bus support if needed in an emergency? How would you mobilize buses in a major community emergency? What role do school buses have in emergency management for cities and counties? What happens if public safety and emergency management officials commandeer your buses? How would an emergency impact gas supplies? Who could and would be able to drive school buses if regular drivers were not available?

• Create guidelines and train school bus drivers on dealing with intervening in student fights and conflicts on buses, irate parents, potential trespassers aboard buses, student threat assessment, early warning signs of potential violence, and related threats.

• Train school bus drivers and transportation supervisors on terrorism-related issues, bomb threat and suspicious devices, inspecting buses, heightened awareness at bus stops and while driving, increased observations skills while coming and going at schools, sharpening skills in reporting incidents, and so on.

• Include school transportation supervisors and school bus drivers in district and building emergency planning processes and meetings.

• Establish mechanisms for mobilizing transportation services during irregular transportation department operations times, such as midday when drivers are not normally scheduled to work. Consider establishing mutual aid agreements with neighboring school districts for mass, rapid mobilization in an emergency.

• Train school bus drivers on interacting with public safety officials aboard buses, at accident scenes, in on-road emergencies, and when emergency situations exist at schools. Include protocols for dealing with school evacuations, student release procedures, family reunification issues, and associated matters.

• Have student rosters, emergency contact numbers, first-aid kits, and other necessary emergency information and equipment aboard all buses.

• Make school buses available to local law enforcement, SWAT teams, and other public safety officials for their training exercises.

- Put identifiers (numbers, district initials) on top of all school buses that could be used to identify specific buses from police helicopters overhead in an emergency.

- Hold periodic meetings during the school year between bus drivers and school administrators to discuss discipline procedures, safety practices, and associated issues.

- Provide a method for parents to identify substitute bus drivers as district employees prior to putting children on a school bus with an unfamiliar driver.

- Practice emergency exercises to evaluate and refine written emergency plans to make sure that what is in writing could work in a real emergency. Drivers, like personnel working in a school, need to be prepared for quick thinking on their feet in an emergency, such as having to reroute because of adverse weather or because of an emerging emergency situation at a school or bus stop.

Discipline on buses should be a top priority for administrators. Regular communication and strong relationships between drivers and school administrators will go a long way toward creating a safe environment on school buses. If drivers are considered part of the school staff, students are likely to think twice before victimizing them than if the drivers have weak links to school authorities. The same applies for making drivers part of the district's school emergency planning and preparedness efforts.

TRESPASSING

Former students, suspended or expelled students, truants, and strangers present problems for school administrators as trespassers on school property. Some basic suggestions for managing trespassing include the following:

- Use effective access control procedures as previously mentioned.

- Include trespassing as an offense in the student handbooks. Pursue trespassing cases with disciplinary and criminal action.

- Communicate to students, early in the school year and periodically during the year, that they are not to have friends or relatives come to school grounds to meet with them before, during, or after school. Students who support and encourage trespassers should face disciplinary consequences.

• Use a camcorder, camera, or similar device to record trespassers or nonstudents in the area of buses and school property at school dismissal. Often, these individuals are unknown to the staff of the school where they are trespassing, but they may be quickly identified by administrators of other schools in the area. Once trespassers or loiterers are identified, their home school administrators should pursue the appropriate disciplinary action.

Trespassing can lead to other incidents of violence and should be treated as a priority concern by school administrators, teachers, and staff.

TRUANCY

For many years, truancy has ranked on the low end of priorities of school and law enforcement. An increase in truant students' involvement in daytime burglaries, auto thefts, trespassing for criminal purposes at schools other than their own, and other disruptive and illegal behavior often triggers new efforts to deal with truancy.

Police sweeps for truants were conducted in many cities during the 1990s, although we have not heard of them as often in recent years. In many communities, this process has been taken one step further by collaborating with multiple agencies in an attempt to deal with the broader issues that motivate students to be truant. The purpose is to provide earlier identification and intervention for youths at risk for abuse, neglect, and delinquent behavior.

For example, collaborative partnerships can involve schools, public safety forces, prosecutor's office, county administration and human service offices, adult and juvenile courts, and other nonprofit and private sector agencies. Police and school sweeps are immediately followed up with on-site assessments by court and social service representatives in an effort to better coordinate intervention and prevention services to children and their families. Many truants are already active with multiple criminal justice and social service agencies, and uniting these agencies can better serve their mutual clients.

UNIFORMS AND DRESS CODES

Some schools turn to uniforms and dress codes as an added tool in their safe and secure school initiatives. As with the issues of equipment, drug-sniffing dogs, and other security strategies, research and professional opinions differ on the actual effect of this strategy on school security. On the front lines, however, some agreement exists among school officials that student uniforms, dress codes, or both at least contribute to a more orderly educational environment.

A uniform, or standard form of dress, provides several positive contributions toward safer schools, including to

- reduce student competition for status based on who has the most expensive clothing;
- reduce (but not eliminate) methods for gang identification in school;
- reduce opportunities for robberies of expensive clothing items often worn by students in school and to and from school;
- help school staff more quickly identify trespassers and visitors who enter school buildings.

Uniforms and dress codes are not a panacea for solving discipline and school security concerns. They do, however, provide another tool for addressing these issues and for setting an improved tone and climate in the school.

School officials who consider uniforms should promote and encourage them but not necessarily mandate them without first getting input from staff, parents, and students. Many schools voluntarily adopt uniforms with minimal resistance by involving students and parents on the front end of the process. Even parents who initially balked at the idea have changed their positions, once they discovered that clothing associated with school uniforms usually will be less expensive than other popular clothing. This saves parents money and arguments with their children over what to wear each day.

VANDALISM

Some administrators ignore or downplay the seriousness of vandalism and other property crimes compared with such crimes against persons as assault and robbery. Although assaults and robberies cannot be treated lightly, the importance of dealing with small problems cannot be overlooked. If students perceive vandalism as minor offenses, they are likely to progress to more serious crimes once they get away with the others.

A few practical measures to reduce the risk of school vandalism include the following:

- Distinguish vandalism from such crimes as burglaries and thefts. Whereas the latter generally involve unlawful entry, stealing property, or both, vandalism usually involves destroying or defacing property.

• Document all vandalism incidents in internal incident reports and report crimes of vandalism to police. Vandalism costs are very high in many districts and cannot be written off as a part of doing business.

• Identify high risk areas for vandalism as a part of your school security assessment. Ensure that staff lock windows, doors, and roof hatches to reduce entry points after hours.

• Ensure that intrusion detection systems adequately cover school facilities.

• Post warning signs that trespassers and vandals will be prosecuted. Seek restitution from prosecuted offenders.

• Assess the layout and design of the school, inside and outside. Increase visibility of potential entry points by keeping trees, bushes, and shrubs cut and trimmed so they cannot conceal vandalism or cover unlawful entry points. Assess night lighting needs on a regular basis.

• Have aggressive canvassing of the neighborhood by administrators and school security officials to encourage neighbors to monitor schools after hours and to call police officials, school officials, or both when they observe vandalism, burglaries, trespassing, and other suspicious activity.

• Repair or replace damaged property quickly. One broken window or graffiti-sprayed word will lead to a dozen more shortly thereafter if it is not fixed.

• Consider employing a mobile security patrol for nights and weekends in larger school districts with high vandalism rates.

Finally, school officials should create a school culture and climate of ownership and responsibility. Students and staff who feel connected to the school are less likely to vandalize property and take out their anger against the building.

ZERO TOLERANCE AND SCHOOL DISCIPLINE

Zero tolerance has been a political buzzword for so many years now that it has more meaning in the minds of academicians and politicians than it does in day-to-day practice by school administrators.

The vast majority of school administrators strive for firm, fair, and consistent discipline applied with good common sense. Unfortunately, anecdotal incidents occur from time to time that lack the latter part of the equation. It is these cases that get labeled as *zero tolerance* by critics who falsely try to create a perception that there is some type of mass conspiracy by educators to unfairly discipline children. Contrary to suggestions by the media, politicians, and Ivory-Tower theorists, the real problem is the absence of common sense and questionable implementation of disciplinary policies, not the presence of intentionally harsh actions committed to fuel a master nationwide conspiracy plan called zero tolerance.

Schools have also developed tunnel vision focus in training school administrators on how to improve test scores but often fail to provide adequate training on discipline and school safety issues. Proper training of school administrators on school board policies, disciplinary procedures, and overall school safety issues can reduce the risks of questionable actions by school administrators.

Many educators tend to bend over backward to give students more breaks than they will ever receive out on the streets of our society and in the workplace, where we are supposed to be preparing them to function. We can count many more instances where we have seen far too lax discipline in our schools than we can count cases where the discipline administered was overly harsh and abusively punitive, as some critics want to suggest. In the end, those kids who receive less than firm, fair, and consistent discipline end up being taught that there are no consequences for inappropriate—and sometimes illegal—behavior when it occurs within the grounds of those schools having administrators who are often more worried about keeping their disciplinary and criminal incident reports down for the sake of their own career advancement.

Perhaps most alarming is how the zero tolerance phrase has taken on a life of its own and how it has been exaggerated for the purpose of either supporting or opposing other school safety strategies. For example, academic and think-tank theorists use zero tolerance as a backdrop to promote prevention programs while discrediting school security practices. These arguments typically err, however, by inaccurately and narrowly defining school security to mean metal detectors, surveillance cameras, school security personnel, SROs or other police in schools, locker searches, or school uniforms. Most school security specialists agree that professional school security programs are much more comprehensive and include security policies and procedures, crime prevention training, crisis preparedness planning, physical design evaluation, coordination with public safety officials, and numerous other components. Although these other tools and strategies may be a necessary and appropriate part of many school safety plans, truly professional school security programs are much more encompassing than one or two single approaches.

It is also particularly interesting that the primary basis for many of the reports and antisecurity and antipolice arguments rest upon the absence of formal academic studies of school security and school policing programs. Ironically, these reports typically fail to also point out that a number of academic evaluations have identified major weaknesses in many prevention and intervention programs, too, and in some cases have indicated that a number of those programs evaluated are simply ineffective. Yet the authors of these reports condemn school security programs (under the guise of zero tolerance) while continuing to promote prevention programs simply because there have indeed been formal evaluations of prevention programs—regardless of the mixed evaluation findings. Some academicians have also slapped the label of zero tolerance broadly upon discipline and security measures to suggest they contribute to disproportionate suspensions, expulsions, and arrests of minority students.

Practical experience repeatedly demonstrates that school safety plans need to reflect a balance of strategies focused on prevention, intervention, school climate, firm and fair discipline, mental health support, proactive security measures, crisis preparedness planning, and community networking. Reasonable security and discipline measures must be a part of these plans so that educators can maintain a secure environment in the here-and-now in order for education and prevention programs to have their longer term impact in the future. Furthermore, professionally utilized SRO and security personnel, security technology, and related measures can and do, in many cases, reduce risks and prevent school violence.

The phrase zero tolerance has taken on a life of its own, but primarily by politicians, academicians, and in some cases the media. We owe it to our students, school staff, and parents to get beyond the political and academic rhetoric of the zero tolerance debate. Improve training for school administrators on board discipline policies, implement student code of conducts fairly and consistently with common sense, and improve school safety in a balanced and rational manner. Deal with each individual case of questionable discipline, but move on to the real work of implementing meaningful, balanced school safety programs such as those enacted by the majority of educators across the nation (Trump, 2010i).

Too often, school leaders look for the one-shot program or strategy that will enhance school security so they can move ahead with the many other tasks on their agenda. No one such program or strategy exists. Each school and each district must assess its own security posture and evaluate potential strategies based on the unique conditions prevailing at the particular point in time when security concerns are reviewed. They must then build on existing strategies to meet the new threats and demands.

6 Managing Bullying

Focusing on Supervision, Conduct Codes, School Climate, and Mental Health Strategies

Bullying has received a significant amount of attention following a number of high-profile school shootings and related incidents of violence in the late 1990 and early 2000 school years. As this book heads to press in 2011, a media and public craze exists around bullying, with almost daily news stories of violent acts, teen suicides, and other high-profile incidents attributed to bullying. The hype is fueled by special-interest advocacy groups pushing anti-bullying state and federal laws, and elected officials capitalizing on the frenzy by focusing on anti-bullying legislation and political posturing.

Bullying is a serious issue worthy of reasonable attention, awareness, and action. It is one component of a comprehensive and balanced approach to school safety. Schools have been working on bullying issues for many years, with an added emphasis on school climate after the 1999 Columbine High School attack.

The focus on dealing with bullying is missing its target with demands for more anti-bullying policies, programs, and laws. Schools do not need new laws, unfunded mandates, or an array of vendor-driven programs and products to meaningfully address bullying. Much of what they need is either already in place or readily available if they choose to use it.

School administrators can manage bullying issues using a practical, coordinated approach consisting of the following strategies:

- Supervision and security.
- School discipline and classroom management.
- Criminal and civil law (when appropriate).
- School climate strategies.

- Mental health support for students.
- Effective communications plans.

Many of these practices are already in place in schools across the country, and except for the mental health component, most are readily available to school administrators who are currently not using such strategies. Many schools are already addressing bullying, but often are not viewing all of the components as related to a broader, coordinated anti-bullying effort in their school. And most schools fail to proactively and effectively communicate to parents those efforts they do have in place.

DEFINING BULLYING

Ask 100 people to define *bullying,* and you will get 100 different answers. This is exactly what I have done in recent years in school safety workshops. Invariably, our nation's brightest school administrators, counselors, teachers, and safety officials often do not have the same answer to define bullying.

The most commonly used words include *aggression* and *harassment.* Occasionally, people use *repeated* in their descriptions, such as *repeated aggression* or *repeated harassment.*

The difficulty is that the words aggression and word harassment are very broad terms. Harassment can mean many different things to different people. Creating school district legal policies and state or federal laws using such generic language is a challenging, and somewhat dangerous, thing to do given the broad range for interpretation of the definitions.

Bullying often refers to verbal, physical, or other acts committed by a student to harass, intimidate, or cause harm to another student. The behaviors attributed to bullying in school settings may include, but are not necessarily limited to, verbal threats, intimidation, assaults, sexual harassment, sexual assault, extortion, disruption of the school environment, and related behaviors. When discussing bullying, the focus should be on the specific inappropriate *behaviors* rather than a generic, less specific label of *bullying, aggression,* or *harassment.*

The vast majority of schools in the nation, if not all schools, already have disciplinary policies to address these and related types of behavioral misconduct. The policies may not include the word bullying, but the behavior we refer to as bullying is typically addressed in school policies and student codes of conduct, and in many cases in criminal laws (assaults, threats, intimidation, extortion). The goal should be to zero in on specific inappropriate behaviors, rather than to create new policies and laws that use generic terminology to describe the behaviors.

BULLYING: ONE THREAT ON A BROAD THREAT CONTINUUM

Bullying is one threat of many on a broad continuum of potential school safety threats, and it should be part of a comprehensive approach to school safety. Bullying is one of many factors that must be taken into consideration in developing safe schools prevention, intervention, and enforcement plans.

But bullying prevention efforts and initiatives are just part of a larger strategy that should be included in a comprehensive school safety program. Bullying is neither a stand-alone, single cause for all school violence, nor is bullying prevention alone a panacea or cure-all for school violence. Skewed policy and funding focused on bullying is no more logical and appropriate than skewed policy and funding focused on school police or security equipment.

Although bullying is an important issue that adversely impacts school safety, many other issues contribute to interpersonal conflicts, violence, and crime in schools. He said, she said rumors, boyfriend/girlfriend issues, disrespect, gang conflicts, and other factors can lead to school violence. Whittling all of these down to just *bullying* is a far stretch and an overemphasis on bullying, which is an extreme and inappropriate approach to school safety. Schools must view threats on a continuum, as described in Chapter 1, and the continuum is not a one-topic line.

THE MYTHICAL ATTRIBUTION OF BULLYING AS THE CAUSE OF SCHOOL SHOOTINGS

For nearly a decade, bullying was attributed as a significant contributor to why shooters killed students in schools. Bullying was frequently cited as the reason the Columbine killers performed their attack. Bullying was also referenced in a number of other school shootings.

It was not until 2009 that this myth of bullying as the cause of school shootings received highly publicized challenges. The research of Dave Cullen and Dr. Peter Langman, who authored two unrelated books on school shootings, challenged the assertions that bullying was responsible for Columbine and other school shootings. Cullen's book, *Columbine*, is based on his extensive research of the Columbine High School attack in 1999, and Langman's book is based upon his research and experience as a Pennsylvania-based child psychologist who studies school shooters.

Both Cullen and Langman concluded that mental health issues, not bullying, are the primary factors behind the actions of school shooters.

Many school safety professionals, including myself, have long stressed the role undiagnosed, misdiagnosed, or untreated mental health issues play in so many incidences of school violence including shootings. It is much easier to attribute bullying as the motivating factor of the shooters than it is to go outside of the bullying sound bite and discuss the complex causes of, and strategies for addressing, teen mental health issues.

In his chapter "Media Crime," Cullen (2009; pp. 158–159) describes the media atmosphere at Columbine after the attack: "The 'bullying' idea began to pepper motive stories. The concept touched a national nerve, and soon the anti-bullying movement took on a force of its own. Everyone who had been to high school understood what a horrible problem it could be. Many believed that addressing it might be the one good thing to come out of this tragedy. All the talk of bullying alienation provided an easy motive. . . . The details were accurate, the conclusions wrong. Most of the media followed. It was accepted as fact."

Cullen went on to explore in-depth the mental health issues of the Columbine killers, building a case that mental health issues, not bullying, was a causal factor leading the killers to attack.

Langman counters claims of bullying as a cause of school shootings in *Chapter 1, School Shooters: Beyond the Sound Bite* (2009; pp. 11–16). Langman states: "The issue that has received the most attention as a factor in school shootings is bullying. According to this sound bite, school shooters are victims of bullying who seek revenge for their mistreatment. It is understandable that this idea would take hold in the minds of many people. We can easily grasp and relate to the concept of being hurt and wanting to retaliate. If a student attacks his peers, it seems logical to think the he must have been driven to such an act. In reality, however, this sound bite is not accurate. The situation is much more complex."

Langman studied 10 shooters and classified them into three different types: psychopathic, psychotic, and traumatized. The causes were mental health driven, not by being bullied to the point of killing people. Langman states: "[T]he idea that school shootings are retaliation for bullying is highly problematic. This is not to say the peer relationships are irrelevant. . . . To be teased is normal; to be turned down for a date is normal. The shooters, however, were often so emotionally unstable or had such vulnerable identities that normal events triggered highly abnormal responses."

So after a decade of educators, legislators, and advocates crying *bullying* after every school shooting, a deeper look suggests this simply was not the case. Their explanations of mental health issues is much more plausible, although perhaps not as easy to digest in a media sound bite or as a way to justify other agendas for which people are using bullying as a cause.

BULLYCIDE, THE MEDIA, AND THE CONTAGION EFFECT

The media frenzy on teen suicides has lead to the creation of a new buzzword: *Bullycide*. Bullycide in essence refers to kids being bullied to death. It is now frequently used to refer to cases where there are alleged repeated bullying incidents of a victim who eventually completes suicide.

But is bullying the cause of suicide? The American Foundation for Suicide Prevention (AFSP), www.afsp.org, cites figures indicating that 90 percent of all people who die by suicide have a diagnosable psychiatric disorder at the time of their death (AFSP, 2011). Many professionals also agree that there is no single cause for suicide, often a number of factors come into play, and that kids' coping skills and support for dealing with bullying and other stressors vary.

Bullying is a serious issue. There is no doubt chronic bullying would be a stressor, especially to youth who are already vulnerable because of mental health or other pre-existing conditions making the youth at higher risk for suicide. But the casual attribution by media, anti-bullying, and gay rights advocates, and others who state or imply that bullying directly causes suicide, warrants a deeper analysis.

Psychology experts refer to increases in suicide that are suspected as being attributable to increased media attention as the *contagion effect*. The media frenzy surrounding a recent spate of teen suicides in the second half of 2010 caused some experts to raise concerns of a contagion effect. Could traditional and social media buzz, along with anti-bullying and gay rights advocates repeatedly claiming bullying caused the suicides, have contributed to the increased number of incidents in such a short period of time?

The American Foundation for Suicide Prevention, American Association of Suicidology, and Annenberg Public Policy Center (n.d.) developed *Reporting on Suicide: Recommendations for the Media* in cooperation with the Office of Surgeon General, Centers for Disease Control and Prevention, National Institute of Mental Health, and other organizations.

Their Recommendations to the Media report read as follows:

Research finds an increase in suicide by readers or viewers when:

1. The number of stories about individual suicides increases

2. A particular death is reported at length or in many stories

3. The story of an individual death by suicide is placed on the front page or at the beginning of a broadcast

4. The headlines about specific suicide deaths are dramatic

Their recommendations also note:

1. Research suggests that inadvertently romanticizing suicide or idealizing those who take their own lives by portraying suicide as a heroic or romantic act may encourage others to identify with the victim.

2. Exposure to suicide method through media reports can encourage vulnerable individuals to imitate it.

3. Clinicians believe the danger is even greater if there is a detailed description of the method. Research indicates that detailed descriptions or pictures of the location or site of a suicide encourage imitation.

4. Presenting suicide as the inexplicable act of an otherwise healthy or high-achieving person may encourage identification with the victim.

Media leaders should review their ethical and professional guidelines when addressing bullying and, in particular, suicides being attributed to bullying. It would also be advisable for advocacy special interest groups to research the contagion effect concept to make sure they are not inadvertently contributing to the risk of the contagion effect when publicly spotlighting and holding events around higher profile teen suicide incidents. This is not to suggest the incidents be ignored; but instead to recommend responsible communications and actions so as not to contribute to a contagion effect resulting in further deaths.

When the dust settles, we will likely reach similar findings on teen suicides labeled bullycides as to that which Cullen and Langman found regarding the bullying myth about Columbine: That the true factors responsible for the behavior of the individuals will be attributable to mental health issues, not bullying—or at least not bullying as a sole or primary causal factor.

PRACTICAL ANTI-BULLYING STRATEGIES: SUPERVISION, SECURITY, DISCIPLINE, AND CRIMINAL LAW

Supervision and Security

In one bullying study (Martin, 2006), Ronald Pitner, PhD, assistant professor of social work at Washington University in Saint Louis, concluded that schools must focus on the physical context of the school in addressing bullying. Dr. Pitner noted that bullying and school violence in general typically occur in predictable locations within schools, specifically unmonitored areas such as hallways, restrooms, stairwells, and playgrounds. He stated that schools can cut down on violence if they identify the specific *hotspots* within the school where students feel violence is likely to occur.

"Although this approach will not completely eliminate bullying, research has shown that it would at least cut down on the areas where violence is likely to occur," he said. His recommendation: "This focus underscores the importance of viewing school bullying as both an individual- and organizational-level phenomenon."

Dr. Pitner's study reinforces the importance of adult supervision and security measures. We know that hotspots like those referred to by Dr. Pitner include the following:

- Restrooms.
- Hallways.
- Stairwells.
- Playgrounds.
- Cafeterias.
- Bus drop-off and pick-up areas.

What is the common thread among these areas? Greater concentration or mobility of students and less adult supervision.

These specific areas, and others having a tendency toward less adult supervision, should be considered higher risk areas for bullying. If we want to reduce bullying, we should increase active adult supervision in these areas.

Ideally, all adults contribute to the supervision of children in our schools. The custodian who goes into the restroom to change a light fixture should also be engaged in supervision. The teacher who is in between assigned classes and walks down an isolated hallway on the way to the teacher's lounge should be engaged in supervision. All teachers should be at their doorways and monitoring the halls around their classrooms between periods, again being active participants in supervision.

Supervision duty assignments should also be formally assigned at all schools. This includes listing by name who is responsible for supervision duty at those higher risk areas and at what times they should be there. Thus, the creation of adult assignments for bus duty, cafeteria duty, hall duty, while not a favorite part of their job in the eyes of most educators and support staff, is clearly a critical one for maintaining safe and supportive schools.

School security officers and school-based police officers can play an important role in supervision and, in turn, in reducing bullying in schools. Their mobility on school grounds should allow them to enhance supervision of the common areas and hotspots that teachers and other school staff may get to less frequently. School surveillance cameras, when properly used, can also serve to enhance monitoring of hotspots or serving as a deterrent where human surveillance and supervision need to be augmented.

School Discipline and Classroom Management

Kids want a climate characterized by order, structure, and discipline. Discipline must be firm, fair, and consistent in its application. These elements are not only tools for effective classroom management, but also must be consistent throughout the school, including in the hotspots where bullying and violence tend to occur.

Discipline and structure should not be interpreted to mean punitive, abusive, or prisonlike in nature. It does need to be firm and consistent.

I have seen the difference in student behavior in side-by-side classrooms with elementary children in their first few years of school. In one classroom, a classroom management style produces an orderly, calm, attentive, and quiet climate. Next door, the classroom management style, or lack thereof, allows for yelling, screaming, kids pushing each other and turning over chairs, and a teacher yelling—and begging—for students to listen and comply with directives screamed at them.

Where should we expect a higher risk of bullying, assaultive behavior, and violations of school rules? Obviously, in the classroom where the teacher is lacking strong classroom management skills.

Criminal and Civil Law

Local and state laws have been used, including in higher profile bullying and harassment cases, to bring criminal charges against individuals alleged to have harassed other students. We see applicable statutes such those covering assaults, extortion, and hate crimes available for use, as appropriate.

In late 2010, the Obama administration began using federal civil rights laws via the U.S. Department of Education and the U.S. Department of Justice to investigate complaints filed against school districts that claimed districts were inadequately address bullying incidences that rose to the level of harassment and discrimination. (This is addressed in more detail later in the chapter.) School leaders should review with their legal counsel Title IX and other federal civil rights education laws to make sure their policies and procedures are consistent with federal guidance. School administrators and staff should be trained accordingly.

In addition to local, state, and federal law recourse, victims of harassment and discrimination also have the option to file lawsuits against school districts and individual offenders. This civil option is one more legal tool available.

Proposed anti-bullying laws at the state and federal levels provide no new resources for school administrators or for most victims of bullying behaviors.

At best, they provide a civil rights enhancement for a new special protected class of individuals, that is, those discriminated against because of sexual orientation or gender identification, depending upon how the law is written. And if that is the objective, then the laws should be labeled, introduced, and debated as civil rights bills, not under the guise of anti-bullying bills.

SCHOOL CLIMATE STRATEGIES

School climate is another elusive phrase. Again, ask 100 educators to define school climate, and you will get at least 100 different answers. Educators often know what it is when they see or feel it, but they struggle to define it in concrete, measureable terms.

Bullying behaviors, like other behaviors, are learned. Children will model the behaviors they see at home, in school, and elsewhere in their lives. Developing appropriate behaviors, and coping skills for managing inappropriate behaviors by others, is critical to addressing the bullying and incivility concerns cited by anti-bullying advocates.

Common agreement exists that the following issues fall under the umbrella of school climate and would address the underlying issues associated with what is referred to as bullying, incivility, and the fostering of positive learned behaviors. These include the following:

- Respect.
- Trust.
- Diversity.
- Belonging/connectedness.
- Pride and ownership.
- Involvement.
- Positive relational interactions.
- Peaceful resolution of conflicts.
- Support from adults and peers.
- Clean, orderly, and maintained facilities.

School assemblies and classroom and schoolwide reinforcement of positive behaviors can help reinforce efforts to minimize bullying behaviors.

Do school administrators need a separate program to address these issues, or can they be incorporated as a part of the school culture? If each school had a school climate improvement team to develop schoolwide strategies around these issues, all students would benefit as would the overall climate, and bullying behaviors would be reduced. Creating new programs for the sake of creating programs does not reflect the substantive change that may be needed to address the desired behavioral outcomes.

MENTAL HEALTH SUPPORT FOR STUDENTS

Cullen and Langman hit home runs with their respective books. Unlike the many anti-bullying advocates, legislators, media, and others who have jumped on the bullying bandwagon, they took the time to dig a little deeper to find the real factors behind school shooters.

The conversation and the funding need to shift from bullying to youth mental health support. It is easy to slap a label of bullying on just about any youth misbehavior that is somehow connected to bullying. It is much harder to dive into dissecting the complex issues associated with the mental health issues and needs of youth, and it is even more difficult to find funding for the scope and depth of services these children really need.

Some people hesitate to bring up mental health issues out of fear they will be accused of blaming the victims. Cullen and Langman do a great job in detailing the mental health issues of the Columbine and other school shooters, thereby dispelling the myths about bullying as the prime cause of them shooting. However, many, out of fear of being accused of blaming the victims, are reluctant to do so in cases of those who complete suicide.

So at best the issue gets a passing glance with code words and back-door innuendo. "We need to look at the coping skills of youth," or "Why do so many kids get bullied and do not take their lives while others get bullied and do kill themselves?" What many people want to say is that there are some kids who are victims of bullying and take their lives who may have had broader mental health issues beyond the bullying and slipped through the cracks without getting help.

Three groups of players are commonly discussed in the bullying debate: bullies, victims, and bystanders. Although there is, and should be, more conversation about changing the culture of the bystanders, when deaths are involved, the focus shifts to the shooters or the victims. I believe we are dodging the elephant in the living room by bantering around bullying while we should get the political courage to talk about, and tackle, youth mental health needs.

Putting the burden of solving youth mental health issues on the backs of schools is unfair and unrealistic. Should schools be a key player at the table in planning to improve youth mental health support? Absolutely! But some realities of operating our schools exist that are not considered or understood by people who want to set unrealistic expectations of our schools to solve this crisis alone:

• Schools do not, and will not in the foreseeable future, have the funds to provide the level of mental health services many students coming through the schoolhouse doors need. Given the nature of how schools are funded, it is unlikely we will see a point where such resources are available on a sustained basis.

• Even if schools did have the financial resources, they would not have the time during the course of a school day to provide the scope and depth of mental health services students need. There is a growing momentum for school reform, increased academic achievement, and a finite number of hours in which students are in school. I do not believe in making excuses for schools not doing their part, but I also will not be one who wants to put the whole burden on schools for solving complex problems that extend, and often originate, far beyond the school. We have to get real about the expectations we keep piling upon our schools.

• Even if school leaders had unlimited money and time, children with mental health issues eventually have to go home or back into the community. In many cases, the root cause of many students' mental health problems stems from the home or the community. We could have a perfect world at school, but what happens when the student walks back into the home filled with dysfunction and stressors that have contributed in some cases to the student's state of mental health? Simply put, the schools are an important player in addressing youth mental health issues, but they cannot solely own this fight.

So what do we do? Too often, the answer is nothing, which is why we continue to have the same problems. The first step is calling the problem what it is: mental health issues.

CYBERBULLYING AND SEXTING

Digital communications have added a force to be reckoned with. How do we police the Internet? How do we prevent cyberbullying before it happens? How do we figure out who the vulnerable next victim will be and get to them before they take their own lives?

Experts are supposed to have the answers to these types of questions. I do not. I do not know how to police the Internet, or, more precisely, I know we cannot police it to the extent people expect and in some cases want to demand of school principals and educators.

Cyberbullying challenges everyone, especially the victims, who are repeatedly victimized with mass exposure that goes far beyond the one-on-one or small group embarrassment of in-person bullying in a school hallway. Experts point to cyberbullying opportunities through the use of online gaming and in virtual game worlds.

The scope of opportunities for cyberbullying is so broad and the pool of potential victims so deep that I cannot look parents or educators in the face and tell them we stand a great chance of eliminating the problem. The likelihood of many overall good kids getting drawn into an episode of sexting—sending, receiving, or passing along inappropriate pictures of themselves or others—is high because of the nature and availability of today's technology and the culture in which even the most fortunate of children live.

The challenges of cyberbullying, sexting, and related issues are overwhelming if we look at the big picture perspective. But if we look at the smaller picture, what we can do as parents with our own children, and what we can do as school leaders with the kids for whom we are responsible, we have a chance of having an impact.

What can school leaders do? Some practical steps include the following:

1. *Educate the end users of the technology, the students, about issues of cyberbullying, sexting, and related issues.* Ultimately, as the users of the technology, they may likely be confronted with these situations. We must have candid conversations about the issues, what to do if it pops up on their cell phones, and what the implications are if they fail to make the proper choices.

2. *Set policies and enforce them to address cyberbullying, sexting, and related issues that occur during school hours and at school-sponsored events.* Confer with legal counsel to determine the scope of what school officials can and should do with other incidents outside the school but having a nexus to the school. Put procedures in place to investigate incidents and allegations. Make sure at least one computer can override school district filters so administrators or their security or police personnel can access websites and related points without delays caused by blocked sites.

3. *Have candid conversations with parents of your schoolchildren.* Let them know what school officials can and cannot do when it comes to cyberbullying and sexting. Review district policies and conduct codes. Inform them of educational opportunities such as parent workshops on these issues for them and their children. Set reasonable expectations so parents know up front the limitations of school officials' reach on these issues. And let them know this is a shared responsibility by schools, parents, and the children, not just something owned by the schools.

Is this an exhaustive or perfect list? Absolutely not. But it is a realistic place to start as we collectively work to figure out the ever-changing nuances and methods for tackling these challenges.

ANTI-BULLYING COMMUNICATION STRATEGIES

In Chapter 15, I discuss a number of ways school leaders can positively promote school safety efforts when there is not a high-profile incident or issue at hand. School leaders need to develop a strong communications program for educating students, staff, and parents about the school's efforts to address inappropriate behaviors, promote positive school climate, and hold students accountable for inappropriate behaviors. Too often, school officials do not communicate enough about safety until a crisis occurs. Behavior expectations need to be reinforced over time, and communications with all parties involved (students, parents, and staff) will help refocus attention to positive school climate efforts.

POLITICAL HIJACKING OF BULLYING FOR BROADER SOCIAL AND POLITICAL INTERESTS

School administrators need to be aware of the political dynamics associated with bullying. Gay rights advocates have been lobbying for anti-bullying laws that include the phrases *sexual orientation* and *gender identification* in the language of the law as a part of their advocacy for lesbian, gay, bisexual, and transgender students. Meanwhile, Christian conservatives have pushed back, saying gay rights groups are promoting an agenda of introducing homosexual issues into public school curriculum and that a broader approach needs to be taken to bullying policies.

In fall 2010, the Education Department under President Obama announced in a *Dear Colleague Letter: Harassment and Bullying* (2010a) that it will pursue, through its Office for Civil Rights, investigations of school bullying cases as violations of federal harassment laws, as it sees applicable. The U.S. Department of Justice has also interceded in local bullying/harassment cases.

Local school administrators now may face federal investigators coming to their office to investigate what traditionally has been handled as local discipline, crime, and climate issues. Many experts, including myself, believe this is a gross overreach of the role of the federal government. The National School Board Association's legal counsel filed an 11-page challenge and called for clarification from the Education Department in December 2010, expressing fear that the Department's action invites "misguided litigation" and "creates adversarial climates that distract schools from their educational mission." The letter calls the Education Department's attempt to apply federal civil rights laws to local bullying cases an "expansive reading of the law."

This reinforces the importance of school leaders reviewing with their legal counsel Title IX and other federal civil rights education laws to make sure their policies and procedures are consistent with federal guidance. School administrators and staff should be trained on the Education Department's guidance and applicable district policies and procedures.

School leaders must recognize that school safety in general, and presently the issue of bullying, is being hijacked for broader social and political interests. The Education Department's expansive role as an investigatory agency over local school bullying poses the potential to impact any school administrator against whom a complaint has been filed. All school administrators will be affected if state and federal laws are adopted with language and requirements driven by special interests and political agendas, rather than best practices in school safety.

Likewise, school administrators need to thoroughly examine programs, curricula, staff training, and other materials put forth to them for use in their schools for purported anti-bullying and other school safety reasons. Many credible programs are focused on anti-bullying strategies, but as bullying and school safety get increasingly politicized and a cottage industry of bullying program and product vendors grows, educators need to be tuned in to potential masked agendas and goals behind the programs, curricula, staff training, and other materials offered to them for use in their schools.

THE CASE AGAINST ANTI-BULLYING LAWS

A number of state legislatures have proposed and enacted laws requiring schools to have anti-bullying policies or programs. Federal legislation was proposed in 2010 and will likely appear in Congress again in 2011.

I am opposed to state and federal anti-bullying laws for a number of reasons, including the following:

• Proposed anti-bullying laws fail to focus on bullying behaviors, instead focusing on personal characteristics of the victims. These proposed laws would better be described as proposed civil rights laws, not anti-bullying laws. Masking broader civil rights agendas and bills under the guise of anti-bullying is not in the best interest of school safety; to the contrary, it politicizes school safety. If the goal is truly a civil rights bill, special interest groups should advocate for a civil rights bill that applies throughout society, not just one that targets schools, as their reported concerns logically would extend beyond the schoolhouse to other places where youth associate and encounter discrimination.

- If the goal is fairness and equality, which it should be, then we should focus on policies and practices that create safe schools for all kids, not by further dividing and creating special protected classes of one group over another group of students, and excluding (and thereby lessening the importance of) many other types of bullying, such as that against overweight kids, kids who have red hair and freckles, kids who wear glasses, and kids with physical disabilities or special learning needs.

- Federal and state school anti-bullying laws take the wrong, and unnecessary, approach. Local school policies that apply to behaviors that constitute bullying are in place in the vast majority of our nation's schools. Bullying typically refers to verbal, physical, or other acts committed by a student to harass, intimidate, or cause harm to another student. The behaviors attributed to bullying may include verbal threats, menacing, harassment, intimidation, assaults, extortion, sexual assault, sexual harassment, disruption of the school environment and associated disorderly conduct, and other related behaviors. The proposed federal laws, and many state laws, enumerate personal characteristics and not specific behaviors that constitute bullying. More importantly, this is a moot issue as there is not a need for more state or federal laws since behaviors that represent bullying are already outlined in school policies and student codes of conduct. The proposed laws provide frontline educators no tools to address bullying behaviors that they currently do not have available to them in local school policies, in criminal and civil law, and in the school climate strategies already available to schools.

- Laws that are too vague will open up the flood gates for frivolous lawsuits against school districts. Vague laws also beg the question of what such anti-bullying laws will accomplish that existing civil rights laws, education laws, criminal laws, and school policies/student codes of conduct do not already address.

- Existing school policies, along with criminal and civil laws, provide tools to address the safety of all students, including lesbian, gay, bisexual, and transgender students who, like all students, deserve to be safe in school. Whether or not those tools are used to their maximum effectiveness is a local, case-by-case issue, which can and should be addressed with each school district and their school community.

- Anti-bullying efforts should be *one* component of a comprehensive and balanced approach to school safety. It is not the *only* component, though, nor should it be skewed to be the only component. Overemphasizing laws, policies, and funding actions around bullying is no more appropriate than overemphasizing gangs, drugs, weapons, security equipment, school-based policing, or emergency planning.

• The legal tools are in place to initiate criminal and other investigations and charges on harassment-related offenses when warranted. State criminal charges exist, and have been used in high-profile harassment offenses. Federal hate-crime law exists to include crimes motivated by a victim's actual or perceived gender, sexual orientation, gender identity, or disability. Certainly local, state, and federal laws (civil rights and criminal) are in place that provide tools to redress inequalities, harassment, and behaviors that constitute a crime. And as previously noted, under the Obama Administration, both the Education and Justice Departments are now extending their reach into local school districts to investigate alleged bullying, harassment, and discrimination as civil rights violations.

• Anti-bullying policies and climate strategies need to be tailored school-by-school. School policies and practices are local control issues. Federal and state governments have traditionally addressed bullying and other school safety issues through advancing research and funding prevention and intervention programs. It is not the role of the federal government to become the bullying police. The Education Department's Office of Safe and Drug Free Schools has said multiple times that it failed in managing the Safe and Drug Free Schools grant program for more than 10 years, claiming themselves that the program they ran for a decade was "ineffective," which begs us to ask about the competence and ability of the federal government to run meaningful federal safe schools programs. The Department has a tough enough time and a lot of resistance defending its education proposals for local schools, much less taking a more hands-on approach with day-to-day local school safety. An overreaching federal hand in investigating local school bullying cases and skewing the bulk of federal school safety funding to "bullying, climate, and incivility" is not in the best interests of school safety.

• Special interest advocacy groups should put their full agenda on the table, call it what it is, debate it openly, propose a law reflecting the agenda if they so desire, and let legislators vote on it. I am not advocating against gay rights or civil rights, nor am I advocating for a political agenda opposing their interests. I am advocating against masking broader social/political agendas under the guise of bullying and politicizing school safety by special interests. I am also advocating against a skewed federal school safety public policy and funding approach for bullying and school climate surveys that is currently proposed by the Education Department.

• Special interest advocates advance their arguments by putting a human face on their cause. Gay rights and anti-bullying law advocates frequently refer to students who have completed suicide after being bullied by antigay taunts and harassment. Anti-bullying advocates often add the comment that they were bullied as students. Christian conservatives point to cases where parents have objected to the introduction of homosexual referencing curriculum introduced in local schools under safe schools and anti-bullying initiatives.

By no means do I minimize the seriousness of the individual losses by families of children who have committed suicide, nor do I minimize the importance of parents having a voice in what is and is not taught in their child's public schools. Many individuals, including myself and members of my family, have been the victims of bullying, so we also have personal experiences. As a parent and as a school safety professional, I never want to see the loss of life of a child and the harassment of kids in schools.

But I also don't believe in legislation by anecdote. Putting a human face on a cause touches the heart. But it also is a tool used by social and political advocates to advance their cause. When discussing and debating legislation, policy, and funding, the focus needs to be on facts, practicality, and usefulness of the policy and law, and the pros and cons of the law or policy.

We can all put a human face on school safety. Recently, a school resource officer in a Tennessee high school intervened when an armed intruder pointed a gun at the school's principal. By all accounts, the officer was a hero and likely saved the principal's life. Advocacy groups could easily exploit that incident and call for legislation and funding to put a School Resource Officer (SRO) in every school across the nation, resulting in a dramatically skewed policy and funding shift. However, although I strongly support SROs, I and others have not used that situation to make that type of proposed change. Instead, I continue to advocate for a balanced and comprehensive approach to school safety.

Legislative mandates requiring schools to have anti-bullying policies and programs create great election year hype around a topic that even the most rival of politicians would find hard to shoot down. But once one gets past the feel-good aspect of the proposal, more level heads should look at whether there is a need to generate new legislation specific to bullying or if the topic is already being adequately addressed. Anti-bullying specific legislation implies that schools are doing little at the present time to deal with bullying and that simply is not the case in schools nationwide.

Given this issue is evolving as this book goes to press in early 2011, persons interested in following new developments should visit my blog at www.schoolsecurityblog.com.

7 Preparing Schools for Terrorism

I f terrorists want to strike at the hearts of Americans, they could strike at our schools. The devastation of a terror attack upon our nation's schools would have both a huge emotional toll as well as significant financial impact on the *business* of education that would likely be shut down in the days and weeks following an attack.

The good news is there are steps we can take to reduce risks and better prepare for a catastrophic attack. The bad news is that our political and administrative leaders are hesitant to discuss the matter out of fear of creating panic among the parents of school children around the nation. Fortunately, schools in general have improved security and emergency preparedness in the decade following the 1999 Columbine High School attack, but the fact remains that especially for sophisticated individuals with ill intentions, our schools remain soft targets.

THE TERRORIST THREAT TO SCHOOLS: SOFT TARGETS

Although a terrorist attack upon a school in the United States may be *improbable,* the first step toward preparedness is admitting that it is at least *possible* that terrorists could strike a school or schools in our country. Even the U.S. Department of Education, a federal agency characterized for years by its denying and downplaying of the potential for a terror attack upon American schools, issued an advisory to schools in October of 2004 with recommendations for heightening security and emergency preparedness in light of the Beslan, Russia, school terror attack months earlier (U.S. Department of Education, 2004).

Terrorists attack their targets to accomplish the following:

- Attack a symbolic target.
- Send a message far beyond the actual target itself.
- Produce mass fear and panic.
- Alter the ways people live and do business, including having an adverse economic affect on the target's community.
- Instill a lack of confidence in the government.

By attacking a school, all of these objectives would be met.

According to the National Advisory Committee on Children and Terrorism (2003), "Every day 53 million young people attend more than 119,000 public and private schools where 6 million adults work as teachers or staff. Counting students and staff, on any given weekday more than one-fifth of the U.S. population can be found in schools." Hundreds of students and staff fill the same elementary schools each day, while several thousand may fill the high school just down the street. And each day, the same school buses pick up the same several dozen children at the same corner at the same time.

So the potential targets are in place 5 days a week and behave in a relatively predictable manner. It would only take a bit of surveillance on the part of the terrorists to figure out the routines and get a feel for a particular school or school bus.

DOMESTIC VS. INTERNATIONAL TERRORISM

From the perspective of the targeted school(s), whether an act of terrorism is domestic or international in origin likely would not matter. Either way, the threat of harm and actual harm to children and school staff would have a devastating impact.

Educators and safety officials increasingly recognize that the threat of terrorism—domestic or international—is real. We now know from 9/11 that international terrorists have been, and some likely still are, among us here in the United States. Likewise, we know the evolving face of terrorism has introduced the possibility of homegrown terrorists, that is, American citizens recruited by foreign nationals to perform terrorist activities. And the threat of domestic terrorism, whether hate, social, political, or other motivated extremists, continues to pose a threat to not only our society, but also our schools.

Education and school safety leaders, therefore, cannot assume that a potential terrorist would only be someone who is of Middle Eastern descent, speaks with an accent, or otherwise appears to be of international origin. A female having blonde hair, blue eyes, and an American dialect as easily poses a threat. The key is to focus on behavior, not on appearance or related characteristics.

In examining school safety threats, we must therefore recognize that schools, school buses, and our children in general are potential targets for terror. September 11 brought the focus on the airlines and terrorists, and the 2004 Beslan, Russia, school siege brought the focus briefly on schools. But America never really took the Beslan incident to its full level of meaning for schools in the United States, largely because of denial and due to the perceived adverse political and public panic implications if our leaders did so.

OVERCOMING THE DENIAL, FEAR, POLITICS, AND NAYSAYERS

The difference between a target of opportunity and a target not selected can be good security and preparedness. The key to successfully preparing school communities without creating panic is for school and public safety officials to be candid about the possibility that schools can be impacted by terrorism. Success in managing the issue also requires that officials communicate terrorism issues in a balanced and rational context, and that they educate their school communities on the roles that everyone plays in keeping schools and communities safe.

Denial (or the Ostrich Syndrome) and inconsistent messages exacerbate, not reduce, fear and panic. We frequently used weak arguments from the naysayers who misguidedly attempt to downplay the possibility of a terrorist attack on U.S. schools. Some of these arguments, and my response, include the following:

Naysayers: "Terrorist attacks upon schools in the United States and abroad are statistically rare events. It has been an extremely rare event when terrorists attack a school."

Reality: The Columbine High School attack in 1999 was an extremely rare event that no one anticipated. It was an attack in an American school at a level for which no prior precedent had been established. The impact of Columbine changed the landscape of the school safety profession forever, causing many schools to play catch-up with decades of neglect in security and emergency planning, while setting a new threshold for best practices in school safety.

The 9/11 terror attacks on America were extremely rare events that no one anticipated. These were attacks on the United States at a level for which no prior precedent had been established. The impact of 9/11 changed the landscape of American homeland security forever, setting an unprecedented focus on heightened security and emergency preparedness measures comparable with no other time in American history.

To state or imply that we should ignore or downplay the possibility that terrorists would strike American schools defies logic and is contrary to the lessons learned on 9/11, at Columbine, in Beslan, Russia, and elsewhere. It is this mindset of denial and Ostrich Syndrome that makes us most vulnerable. It is also a mindset contrary to the overall goals of our U.S. Homeland Security policy that encourages thinking outside of the box and being proactive to prevent a future terrorist attack, rather than looking for ways to rationalize that "It can't happen here" until such an attack occurs again.

Naysayers: "Talking about the possibility of terrorist attacks upon schools only furthers the terrorists' goals of creating fear."

Reality: Talking about terrorists possibly using airplanes to attack American buildings did not instill the fear that occurred on and after 9/11. In fact, our failure to talk about the possibility of such an event before it occurred has been identified by many professionals as creating a climate that made us more vulnerable.

School and public safety officials nationwide now proactively pursue prevention programs, security measures, and emergency preparedness measures to prevent a future Columbine-like attack in their schools. The failure to talk about the possibility of such an incident occurring and the failure to take steps to prevent such an occurrence would be considered as negligence in the eyes of most educators, public safety officials, parents, media, and courts. Talking about the possibility in a balanced and rational way does not create fear, but instead it reduces fear, improves preparedness, and has resulted in many death plots being foiled thanks to a heightened awareness.

The naysayer mind-set that talking about the possibility of terror attacks upon our schools furthers terrorist goals of creating fears is contrary to our overall national approach to homeland security. Our President, Congress, military, homeland security, and other federal officials talk regularly and openly about the potential for terrorists to strike our airlines, military facilities, government offices, and other American interests right here in the United States, and in turn our need to be appropriately prepared. If we followed the logic of the naysayers who claim we should not talk about terrorism and schools, we would also not be talking about the possibility of terror attacks on our airlines and other government facilities. In fact, using their logic, there would be no need for a Homeland Security Department . . . and it is this mindset that makes us the most vulnerable.

Fear is best managed by education, communication, and preparation—not denial. Educate school community members to define the issues and appropriate context. Communicate with school community members to discuss risk reduction, heightened security, and emergency preparedness strategies. Be prepared for both natural disasters and man-made acts of crime and violence by taking an all-hazards approach to school emergency planning.

Naysayers: "Money spent on preparing schools for terrorism is wasted money that could be better spent elsewhere. Just prepare our first-responders in the community and they will take care of the schools if something happens."

Reality: Teachers, administrators, school support staff, School Resource Officers (SROs), school security personnel, and other professionals on the front lines of our nation's school *are* the first-responders to any emergency that occurs in their schools. Although we value our community public safety partners and we encourage our schools to work hand-in-hand with them in emergency planning, the reality is that those working inside a school will be the ones immediately responding to and managing an emergency incident while police, fire, emergency medical services, and other community first-responders are en route. School officials will also be the individuals working with community first-responders once they arrive and throughout the emergency incident. In fact, if an event occurs on the scale of the 9/11 terror attacks, school officials may be forced to manage a school-based emergency with minimal support from community first-responders if these responders are tied up managing other aspects of the emergency elsewhere in the community or if they cannot get to the school. School officials will also be the individuals left to carry the school a long way through the recovery phase after an emergency.

Although no public budgets are unlimited and no blank checks exist for school security and emergency preparedness efforts, the trend in recent years to cut school safety budgets is disturbing. It is also counter to the direction America is going in heightening security and emergency preparedness efforts at other public and private facilities. It makes no sense that at a time when our nation's leaders have pushed to increase funding for protecting airlines, bridges, monuments, and even the hallways of Capitol Hill that they simultaneously cut funding to protect the children and teachers in the soft target hallways of America's schools.

Funding for school security and emergency planning should not only be spared from cuts, but should also be incrementally increased as we continue to increase our national defense and antiterrorism preparedness in other public sectors.

A terror attack upon American schools would create fear and panic, disrupt the economy if the business side of school operations were shut down on a large scale, and instill a lack of confidence in our school and community leadership. Such terror tactics have already been employed elsewhere, including attacks upon schools and school buses in the Middle East, and most recently the Beslan, Russia, school terror attack. Although it may not be a *probability* that terrorists will strike our schools, we must acknowledge that it is a *possibility* and take reasonable steps to prevent and prepare for such an incident.

HEIGHTENED SECURITY PROCEDURES FOR SCHOOLS

A terror threat to our schools would trigger immediate calls for parents for heightened security. But most school administrators would likely not have a good sense of exactly what heightened security might look like in real terms in a school setting.

Before schools can heighten security, they need to have their fundamentals in order. The fundamentals include issues discussed in Chapters 4 and 5, in particular. And as I have so often said, the first and best line of defense is always a well-trained and highly alert school safety and student body.

What constitutes heightening security at school? Some examples of what school leader can do include the following:

• Train teachers and support staff, evaluate and refine security plans, and test/exercise school emergency plans.

• Encourage school personnel to maintain a heightened awareness for suspicious activity and to report same. This may include suspicious vehicles on and around campus, suspicious persons in and around school buildings, including those taking photographs or videotaping, suspicious packages around the building perimeter or in the school, and suspicious information-seeking efforts by phone or by unknown visitors.

• Provide special attention to perimeter security and access control issues. Have clearly defined perimeters for schools through the use of fences, gates, environmental design, signage, and other professional security measures. Use designated parking areas especially for visitors and register staff and student vehicles. Provide supervision and monitoring of parking lots and outside areas as appropriate. Train custodial, maintenance, and grounds personnel on identifying and handling suspicious packages and items found on campus. Establish routine inspections of the building and grounds by trained facility personnel. Secure roof hatches and eliminate structural items that facilitate easy access to school roofs. Make sure that classroom windows are secured at the end of the school day. Utilize security technology and devices for monitoring and controlling exterior facilities as defined by professional security assessments.

• Review staffing and supervision plans. Stress the importance of adult supervision before, during, and after school, both inside school buildings and on campus, and in common areas such as hallways, stairwells, restrooms, cafeterias, bus areas, and other high-traffic areas. Encourage staff to maintain a heightened awareness during recess, physical education classes, drop-off and dismissal, and other outside activities. Examine staffing levels and procedures for security personnel, school resource officers and other police personnel, and associated protection personnel.

• Maintain a proactive effort of visitor access and control. Reduce the number of doors accessible from the outside to one designated entrance. Stress the importance of staff greeting and challenging strangers, and reporting suspicious individuals. Review security procedures for after-school and evening activities and building use. Utilize security technology and devices for monitoring and controlling interior facility access as defined by professional security assessments.

• Verify the identity of service personnel and vendors visiting the school, including those seeking access to utilities, alarm systems, communications systems, maintenance areas, and related locations. Do not permit access and report suspicious individuals representing themselves as service or delivery personnel who cannot be verified. Maintain detailed and accurate records of service and delivery personnel including a log (signed in by school personnel) of the full names, organization name, vehicle information (as appropriate), and other identification information.

• Evaluate security measures at school transportation facilities. Assess emergency plans involving buses and other transportation issues.

• Secure access to utilities, boiler rooms, and other maintenance/facilities operations locations. Examine and enhance physical security measures related to outside access to heating, ventilation, and air-conditioning systems (HVAC), utility controls (electrical, gas, water, phone), and related facility operations mechanisms. Secure chemical and cleaning product storage areas, and maintain appropriate records of such items according to local, state, and federal guidelines.

• Evaluate food and beverage service stock, storage, and protection procedures. Determine if schools have adequate water, food, and related supplies in the event that students and staff would have to be detained at the school for an extended period of time beyond normal school hours. Examine measures for securing access to food and beverage products and food service areas during normal food service periods and after hours.

• Assess school health and medical preparedness. Evaluate school nurse staffing levels. Make sure that schools maintain an adequate number and level of emergency kits and medical supplies. Maintain a stock of at least three days worth of medications for students required to have medications at school. Consider offering first-aid/first-responder training to faculty members who are interested in volunteering for such training so as to increase the number of trained individuals available to assist in the event of medical emergencies.

• Conduct a status check of emergency communications mechanisms. Be sure two-way radio units and cell phones are functioning and have back-up batteries charged. Make sure that the public address system is fully functioning. Test the fire alarm system. Review procedures for emergency communications with parents, notify parents in advance how school officials will communicate with them in an emergency (media, district website), discuss importance of parents not flocking to the school if directed during an active crisis, review family reunification procedures, and communicate other relevant information to ease parent concerns.

• Review procedures for mobilizing mental health services for students and staff in the event of a crisis. Plan in advance how adults will communicate with children in a time of crisis. Discuss approaches for age and developmentally appropriate communications with students about violence and threatening issues. Be familiar with community mental health resources for families and have plans for securing supplemental mental health services from outside of the school/district in a major crisis.

• Evaluate and enforce employee screening procedures. Review guidelines for subcontractors and identify all individuals working on school property.

• Implement *information security* programs. Evaluate the storage, access, and security of sensitive information. Create guidelines and conduct periodic assessments of school and district websites to avoid posting of security-sensitive information.

• Identify higher risk facilities, organizations, and potential terrorist targets in the community surrounding schools. Such entities might include military facilities, government offices and facilities, nuclear power plants, airports and airport flight paths, railroads, chemical companies, and so on. Develop appropriate security countermeasures and crisis preparedness planning guidelines accordingly.

• Continue local field trips unless specific threat assessments suggest otherwise, using safety plans that include adequate supervision, communications capabilities, and so on. Evaluate national travel decisions based upon ongoing threat assessments and common sense. International travel during wartime and terrorist acts is discouraged.

• Develop, review, refine, and test emergency preparedness guidelines. Be sure to have guidelines for both natural disasters and acts of violence. Particular procedures for handling bombs, bomb threats, hostage situations, kidnappings, chemical and biological terrorism, and related information should be reviewed. Review with staff their specific roles and responsibilities consistent with your crisis guidelines. Identify back-up crisis team leaders in case normally assigned leaders are not at the building or are unable to lead.

• Provide K–12 school-specific security, crime prevention, and emergency preparedness training to all staff, including support personnel such as office, food services, custodial and facilities, and transportation support staff (Trump, 2010e).

A number of these examples such as training staff are best practices at all times, not just in times of heightened security. And many of these steps could be taken not only in heightening security in connection with a terrorist threat, but also in response to other threats and needs to beef up awareness and security measures.

BIOLOGICAL AND CHEMICAL THREATS

Following the 9/11 terror attacks in the United States, a number of anthrax scares took place, including at schools. Discussions were held, and continue to be held, on potential biological and chemical terror threats to America. Some considerations in this area for schools include the following:

• Establish procedures for detecting and reporting unusual absence patterns, in particular sudden mass absences caused by reported illnesses. Schools may be in one of the best positions to recognize early signs of such a terrorist attack via major increases in student illness rates. School and community officials should consider having a protocol for school officials to notify public health and/or other appropriate public safety personnel as soon as they detect an unusual occurrence.

• Do not allow students to open school mail. Limit the opening of mail to one individual staff member. Have this person open school mail in a room separate from open, main office areas. Staff who wish to open mail with protective (latex-type) gloves should be allowed to do so if they desire. Educate school staff, especially the person who opens school mail, so that he or she is familiar with issues related to suspicious packages. See U.S. Postal Service poster on suspicious mail and related updates at its site on anthrax-related mail concerns.

• Work with custodial and maintenance personnel to establish procedures for quickly shutting down HVAC systems if needed.

• Review procedures for handling suspicious items such as envelopes with power substances that may be found in hallways, stairwells, restrooms, and other areas of the school. Anticipate that, unfortunately, some hoax incidents may occur. However, all threats should be treated seriously. Firm, fair, and consistent consequences, both administratively and criminally, should be sought, including for hoax scares, and students should be informed of the seriousness of such offenses.

• Review lockdown and evacuation procedures. Note that you may have to have a simultaneous lockdown of one section of the building while evacuating other parts of the school, so both lockdowns and evacuations may need to occur at the same time.

• Create Shelter-in-Place plans to supplement lockdown and evacuation plans. Identify safe areas, preferably with no windows, in the building where students can be relocated if need be. Confer with local fire, HAZMAT (hazardous materials), emergency management, and police officials for specific advice.

• Create plans for bringing in students outside and where to locate them if contaminated (away from others), including discussing if/how you would have contaminated individuals shower and put on second set of stored clothes. Remember to have a procedure to shut down HVAC system as soon as possible, and discuss backup heating for winter and related other concerns. Custodial and maintenance staff should be a part of the school's emergency planning and response team.

• A significant amount of discussion took place around the nation after 9/11 about having duct tape and plastic to seal windows, vents, doorways, and related areas. A number of officials recommended having duct tape and plastic to cover windows and to seal off Shelter-in-Place areas. Those discussions subsided a great deal, and in fact became somewhat of a point of jokes and humor as time moved on. In the worst possible scenario and under the proper conditions, this is an extra resource which may help schools serve some purpose. But a number of school and safety officials appropriately expressed concern about an overemphasis placed on this strategy. In particular, several school officials stated that reviews of air circulation needs suggested that individuals sheltered in areas designated for Shelter in Place in their schools would have a limited amount of air over a number of hours to survive under conditions where HVAC was shut down, areas sealed off, and so on. Schools should consider this issue, evaluate their own unique environment, and plan accordingly. Schools may wish to prepare Shelter-in-Place kit materials in advance. This might include battery-operated AM/FM radios; flashlights with fresh batteries; bottled water and adequate food supply; towels; candles; matches; first-aid kit; medicines for students who normally have them at school; charged batteries for cell phones for school's crisis team; personal cleaning supplies and hand sanitizers. Again, schools wishing to include duct tape and plastic for extreme situations may wish to do so if it is viewed in context and as a part of a broader preparedness plan.

• Confer with HAZMAT officials, fire, emergency medical, law enforcement, emergency management, and other local, county, or state officials to establish specific response and prevention protocols, and to educate your school faculty, staff, crisis teams, and community on biological and chemical terrorism issues.

Schools should work particularly close with their first-responders to develop relationships and specific emergency guidelines for these and other situations. Fire departments and emergency management agencies are particularly good resources for conversations and planning on issues related to HAZMAT incidents, sheltering, community-wide disasters, and related issues.

GENERAL CONSIDERATIONS IN TIMES OF TERRORISM AND WAR

Today's world is one of uncertainty. Considerations in times of terrorism and war might include the following:

• Determine which schools in a district are designated community shelters. Be sure all principals know this, especially as new principals move into schools as a result of retirements and personnel changes. What exactly would be expected of the school district and individual school in a community disaster where schools are used as shelters? Create, maintain, and update written agreements with community emergency management agencies, the Red Cross, and others that include the expectations of school officials when schools are used as community shelters.

• Identify school and community mental health support services available to students and their families, and communicate the availability of these services to members of the school community.

• Communicate openly and honestly with students. Attempt to maintain a sense of normalcy in school operations as best possible while still providing adequate and appropriate opportunities for students to share their feelings, concerns, thoughts, and so on. When communicating with students, mental health professionals typically suggest that adults: (1) Keep discussions age and developmentally appropriate; (2) let students know when they are having normal reactions to abnormal situations; (3) include facts and be honest; (4) reaffirm existing adult support of students; and (5) reassure students of measures taken to keep them safe.

• Maintain a balanced, commonsense approach to school safety and security. School and safety officials should maintain a heightened awareness for potential spin-off incidents. In light of the nature of the national incidents, particular awareness and preparation for possible spin-off incidents involving bomb threats, suspicious devices, and hate crimes may be worthy of consideration. It would also be prudent for school officials to develop, refine, or review with staff their policies and procedures related to school threat assessment and threat management.

• School officials may wish to review security issues related to access control, perimeter visibility and security, and other crime prevention measures. The importance of adult supervision before, during, and after school, both inside school buildings and on campus, should also be reviewed and reinforced. Involve all school staff, including support personnel such as secretaries, custodians, and bus drivers, in your school safety review.

• Communicate hotline numbers and other methods that students, parents, staff, and members of the school community can use to report safety and related concerns.

• Use school district call-in lines, websites, and other information sources that can be accessed by the school community to provide ongoing information to the school community (Trump 2010e).

As is the case in our broader society, there is no perfect security or preparedness program that can eliminate the threat of terrorism. But we can take steps to reduce the risks, to make our schools less soft of a target, and to improve preparedness measures for responding to incidents that cannot be prevented. The first step is acknowledging the risk, and the next challenging step is making awareness, balanced security measures, and a mindset of preparedness a part of our school and community culture.

8 Managing School Safety on Tight Budgets

Tight budgets are no excuse for failing to be proactive with school safety. In fact, school leaders must be especially attentive to sustaining prevention and security programs during times when economic woes are increasing stressors on kids, their families, and school staff. But there will be times when school administrators face tighter budgets than others, and school safety will still be the top priority of parents who will not consider tight budgets to be a legitimate reason for not taking every possible step to keep kids safe.

PRACTICAL SCHOOL SAFETY CONSIDERATIONS ON LIMITED BUDGETS

School leaders can still do many things school to keep schools safe when the coffers start to get bare. These include the following:

• *Keep your head out of the sand.* A suburban school board member recently said to me, "We don't have a violence problem. We have a budget problem." His message was simple: "We are not worried about school safety. We are worried about the budget." Boards and administrators with this mentality scare me. Although no school district has a blank check for school safety expenses, school leaders do not have the luxury of simply eliminating school safety measures and ignoring the whole issue. Safety goes hand-in-hand with academic achievement, and the smaller dollars saved in cuts to school safety budgets in the short-term can be a lot less than the loss of a life or the litigation costs in the long haul.

• *Focus on what you can do, not what you can't do.* Reframe the focus and conversation on what *can* be done to keep schools safe. Do not go *doom and gloom* and do nothing if budgets do get cut.

• *Engage affected parties in cost-cutting decisions.* Avoid arbitrary cuts to prevention and security programs. Get input from affected staff and stakeholders. Often those staff running the programs can provide valuable input into potential areas for savings that would have a less severe impact on their program, but they are never consulted. Decisions made by bean counters may look good for the budget, but they may not be in the long-term best interest of school safety and the kids.

• *Expect other government and community agencies to be partners, but not to take on the whole load.* Remember that they, too, may likely be under the same financial climate conditions as the schools.

• *Conduct an internal assessment of school safety strengths and needs.*

  o Tap into building and district-level school safety/crisis committees for ideas.
  o Conduct safety surveys of students, parents, and staff.
  o Get input from community partners such as first-responders, mental health professionals, and other stakeholders.
  o Create prioritized lists of what is working well and what is needed to help guide funding decisions.

• *Create and follow a strategic plan developed in cooperation with school safety professionals.*

  o Consider using limited school safety funds to have a comprehensive, independent external professional school safety assessment to build upon your internal needs assessment.
  o An external assessment by independent, non-product-affiliated school safety professionals can produce findings to be used over a 3-year to 5-year period as a strategic plan to prioritize school safety activities.
  o Costs paid up front for a professional assessment by quality experts could save your schools a lot of wasted time and money over time.
  o Avoid knee-jerk reactions to specific security incidents.
  o School boards and superintendents should not cave into pressure to throw up unnecessary metal detectors, more cameras, and other big-cost items in response to parent and media pressure after a high-profile incident.

○ Use your strategic plan for school safety after a high-profile incident, rumored threat, or other school safety issue in their school-community to avoid costly knee-jerk reactions.

- *Proactively communicate about school safety with your school community.* See tips in Chapter 15 on communicating with media and parents.

- *Communicate school safety funding needs to state and federal legislators.* Boards and superintendents should let their state and national education association staff know of the need for greater advocacy specifically for school safety funding. Make sure advocacy messages for school safety stand separate from, not as a footnote to, other lobbying efforts for other education programs and resources. The key time to start lobbying legislators about school safety funding, however, should be when there is *not* a crisis in the news, not after high-profile events or only after school safety budgets have been cut.

BUDGETING FOR SCHOOL SAFETY, SECURITY, AND EMERGENCY PREPAREDNESS

Boards and superintendents can no longer view school safety as a grant-funded luxury. For too many years, school boards, superintendents, and principals have become dependent upon state and federal grants, and other outside sources of funding, to build their prevention, security, and preparedness plans for school safety. School leaders cannot sit idly waiting to get lucky by having a grant application funded while they do little to nothing out of their own school district budgets to address the safety needs they feel warranted applying for a grant in the first place.

Although no school district has an endless checkbook, there are some basic areas for school safety that should be incorporated into local school district budgets. What the exact amount can and will be will vary by district and should be a topic of quality discussion and planning. These areas include the following:

- Prevention and intervention support services (mental health, counseling, school psychologists, social workers, prevention programs, intervention staff).
- Security and police staffing for day-to-day operations and for special events (athletic, dances, large-scale events).
- Physical security measures (security equipment, communications systems, access control).

- Professional development training for all staff, including support personnel such as office support, food services, transportation, and custodial/maintenance staff.
- Consultant services (security assessments, emergency planning evaluations).

Many school districts have dedicated line items in their budgets to fund some of these areas, and a number of districts are funding all of them. But many are not funding them adequately, and some of the areas are not being funded at all on a regular basis. Although grants can, and should, be pursued to augment these and other school safety programs, school boards, superintendents, and principals are ultimately the school leaders looked to by their parents, students, and staff as having final responsibility for school prevention, security, and preparedness efforts. Viewing school safety as a grant-funded luxury is no longer an acceptable option.

LOW-COST AND NO-COST SCHOOL SAFETY STRATEGIES

School budgets may be tight, but educators and safety officials should be able to fill several pages of paper with lists of things they can do that may cost some time but generally will not cost money.

Examples of things we remind school leaders they can do when the economy hits them hard and school budgets are stretched thin, as well as when they are not, include the following:

- *Apply the 5-minute rule.* My business associate and long-time friend, Chuck Hibbert, advocates taking 5 minutes at every faculty meeting to discuss one topic from your school's safety or crisis plan. Be sure to do it at the end of the meeting, Chuck says, or your entire meeting will end up focusing on safety. This approach can be extended to department, grade-level, and other group meetings within schools.

- *Diversify drills.* Conduct lockdown drills during nontraditional times such as lunch periods, between class changes, during student arrival, and just prior to dismissal. Block exits (unannounced) during fire drills to teach students and staff to think on their feet. Pull a couple of students out of line during fire drills to see how much time passes before someone notices they are missing, and do the same with a teacher to see who will step in for the teacher. Lock down one section of your school while evacuating another area during the same drill. Hold your first faculty meeting of each school year at your walking-distance evacuation site. Monitor not only the time it takes to exist a school for a fire drill, but how quickly students can be recalled into the building.

• *Engage students.* Draw students into school safety plans through student leader group discussions, poster contests, and awareness of drills. Train students not to open exterior doors for strangers or others during the school day. Involve students in school climate improvement.

• *Reach out to nontraditional partners.* Work with your county emergency management agency to update crisis plans, participate in drills with first-responders, and collaborate on joint applications for security grants. Engage your broader community in a community-wide school safety planning group, and have the group put together a directory of prevention, intervention, and other youth safety programs and resources available in the school-community.

• *Conduct mini-tabletop exercises.* Build abbreviated tabletop scenarios into building-level faculty meetings and at districtwide principal meetings several times during each school year.

• *Cross-train crisis team members so they are familiar with the duties of other team members.* For example, teach principals how to shut off the gas at their buildings in the event the custodian is unable to do so. Train a core group of district nontransportation staff to drive school buses so they are available on short notice in a crisis situation where regular drivers may not be available.

• *Hold a safety roundtable.* Add an agenda item to districtwide principal meetings for sharing successful safety and crisis preparedness practices in place in district schools. Too often principals share common problems but do not share common solutions.

• *Strengthen school safety communications:* Proactively communicate the many positive things being done in the schools to improve and maintain safety. Let the school community know that although budgets may be tight, the schools are still doing many proactive things to keep schools safe. (See Chapter 15 for tips on communicating with parents and the media.)

Many other things can improve school safety that involve more time than money. Many of these are detailed in this book, and the majority of things herein take more time and leadership than money to get done. Tight budgets are not an excuse for not strengthening school safety and emergency preparedness plans.

9 Parents and School Safety

Parents will forgive school leaders if student test scores go down. Parents are much less forgiving if something happens to their child at school that could have been prevented or better managed when it occurred.

What does a parent need to know? What should a parent look for and ask about related to safety at their child's school? And what questions should school administrators and safety officials be prepared to answer if asked by a parent?

PRACTICAL THINGS PARENTS CAN DO TO ASSESS SCHOOL SECURITY AND EMERGENCY PREPAREDNESS

Parents want to know what to look for and what questions to ask about safety at their child's school, but typically they do not know the specific things to look for or specific questions to ask.

Here are a number of questions and issues parents should consider, and school officials should be prepared to answer and address, if asked by a parent:

- *Ask your child about safety in his or her school.* Students often know where gaps in security exist and what can be done to improve school safety. Where do they feel most safe? Least safe? Why? What can be done to improve safety?

- *Identify comfort levels and methods for reporting safety concerns.* Do students have at least one adult they would feel comfortable in reporting safety concerns to at school? Are there other methods (hotlines, e-mail tip lines) for students to report concerns? Are parents comfortable in addressing safety concerns with school administrators?

- *Examine access to your school.* Are there a reduced number of doors that can be accessed from the outside (while still allowing children to exit from the inside in an emergency)? Do faculty and staff greet visitors, challenge strangers, and know who is in their school? Are there sign-in procedures, visitor identification badges, and so on?

- *Find out if your school has policies and procedures on security and emergency preparedness.* Does your board and administration have written policies and procedures related to security, crisis preparedness planning, and overall school safety planning? If so, are they communicated clearly and regularly to students, school employees, and parents? How? When?

- *Determine if your school has an active school safety team, safety plan, and ongoing process, as well as a school crisis team and school emergency/crisis preparedness guidelines.* Does your school have a school safety committee to develop an overall plan for prevention, intervention, and security issues? Are these plans balanced and not just prevention-only or security-only? Is there a school crisis team to deal with emergency planning? Who are members of the safety committee and crisis team? How often do they meet? When was the last time they met? Is there a written school crisis plan? Are there written emergency/crisis guidelines? Are these plans and guidelines reviewed regularly—at least once a year? (Note: Many schools have one overall team to address both overall safety planning and crisis preparedness. Two separate groups are not necessary as long as they are dealing with all of the various issues and components.)

- *Inquire with school and public safety officials as to whether school officials use internal security specialists and outside public safety resources to develop safety plans and crisis guidelines.* Do school officials actively involve internal school security specialists, School Resource Officers (SROs), and other school safety specialists in developing safety plans and crisis guidelines? Do school officials have meaningful, working relationships with police, fire, and other public safety agencies serving their schools? Are they involved on school safety committees and teams or do they have direct input on school plans? Are parents a part of the district and school crisis planning teams?

- *Ask if school emergency/crisis guidelines are tested and exercised.* Do school officials test and exercise written crisis guidelines? What type of tests do they do? For example, if they have a lockdown procedure, do they conduct periodic drills to practice them? If they cannot have full-scale exercises of emergency plans (which are very time and labor intensive to do), do they at least do tabletop exercises to test written plans?

- *Determine whether school employees, including support personnel, have received training on school security and crisis preparedness issues.* Have school employees received training on security and emergency strategies by local, state, or national specialists? Have employees also received training on their school/district specific crisis guidelines? Are all employees, including support personnel such as secretaries and custodians, included in such training? How often is such training provided? Is the training provided by qualified and experienced instructors with knowledge of K–12 specific safety issues?

• *Find out if school officials use outside resources and sources in their ongoing school safety assessments.* Do school officials subscribe to current publications addressing security issues? Do they attend conferences and programs on school safety? Have they reviewed their security measures, crisis guidelines, and safety plans with recommendations by school safety experts?

• *Honestly evaluate whether you, as a parent, are doing your part in making schools safe.* Do you follow parking, visitor, and other safety procedures at your school? Do you support teachers and administrators with safety initiatives, including by asking the above questions in a supportive, nonblaming manner? Do you talk with your child about personal safety considerations, drug and violence prevention issues, and related topics early and regularly at home? Do you seek professional help for your child in a timely manner, if needed (Trump, 2010c)?

HOW PARENTS CAN REDUCE CHILD SAFETY RISKS AT HOME

Parents can take many steps to address the threats to child safety in schools, at home, and in the community. Examples of such steps include the following:

• Talk with children early and regularly about bullying, cyberbullying, online safety threats, gangs, drugs, weapons, school and community safety, and related concerns.

• When talking with children, be honest. Violence and related trauma issues are serious, but more damage can be done by minimizing or exaggerating points than by simply providing children with facts and telling the truth.

• Do not assume that children know even the basic facts about safety and other risks. Kids absorb a lot of information and, unfortunately, much of it is inaccurate or from questionable sources. Let children get all of the information—the correct information—from their parents. And give it to them in a nonthreatening and nonembarrassing time, place, and manner.

Perhaps, then, children will be more willing to come to parents with other questions and problems later on.

- Eliminate access to weapons by youth.

- Be aware of and do not permit gang identifiers.

- Provide order, structure, and consistent discipline in the home.

- Work cooperatively with police and school officials.

- Seek professional assistance when needed and in a timely manner. Do not wait until a problem gets out of control and then look for professional help.

- Parents must provide order, structure, and consistent discipline. Although they love their child, they must realize that he or she is still a kid and will test the limits. Ask probing questions: Where are you going? Who will be with you? And do some follow-up to verify the answers you get.

- Look into your children's online social media sites. On how many sites do they have a presence? How many pages do they have on the same site? It is not unheard of for teens to have one profile page on a social media site to show to their parents and then a second page with less than desirable content of which parents would not approve. Seek out resources to educate parents about the latest social media and other electronic networking, video games, and other communications methods being used by kids.

- Inspect a child's room from time to time. Parents have found gang graffiti on bedroom walls, drug paraphernalia on dresser tops, sexually explicit notes, weapons in bookbags leaving the home, graffiti and revealing information on school notebooks, and much more once they get up the nerve to start snooping. Unfortunately, some parents falsely believe that they should not—or legally cannot—go into their child's room. It is your house and your child—check them both and check them regularly. It is not only the parents' right, but their responsibility (Trump, 2010c).

STEPS PARENTS CAN TAKE TO ADDRESS SCHOOL SAFETY CONCERNS

It is clear many parents do not know how to address their safety concerns with school officials. Many parents get nervous asking pointed, and sometimes challenging, questions to teachers and school administrators. Often this is out of fear (most of the time unwarranted) of reprisal against their students if they, the parents, challenge their student's teacher or principal.

There is a way to ask questions, and a right to ask questions, as a concerned parent. Following progressive steps, doing so in a reasonable and supportive manner, and working as a partner with educators can help parents get answers to their questions. Hopefully the parents can also become part of their school's safety process and practices.

Still, there are times when parents get dismissed and their concerns get marginalized by some school officials. Other times, school administrators may address the situation and it may reoccur. And in some cases, school politics and image concerns prevail, and legitimate issues can fall to the wayside.

Here are some basic steps to help parents bring their school safety concerns to school officials:

• Start closest to the source. If an incident such as bullying, harassment, or threats occurs in the classroom, first talk with the teacher in charge of that classroom.

• Engage the student's counselor. Many schools have counselors, psychologists, social workers, and related support staff. Counselors are there to help students with climate and relationship issues.

• Follow the chain of command. Every now and then, parents may need to take their concerns to the top school leaders (the superintendent or school board). But jumping the chain of command without making an effort to deal with the administrators at the building level is generally not a wise move. Start by talking with the school's assistant principal and principal on specific safety concerns at their school. Then work up the chain of command to the superintendent and school board, if necessary.

• Document your concerns and requests, especially those related to school safety. Written complaints provide a paper trail of a parent's effort to communicate and resolve his or her concerns.

• Notify police if a potential crime is involved.

• Educate yourself on district policies and appeals processes. Many parent safety concerns I receive are questioning disciplinary action or inaction by school administrators. Parents should familiarize themselves with student and parent handbooks, school board policies, and related documents to help determine if they have a legitimate complaint. Understand due process appeal procedures if you believe your child has been unfairly disciplined. Appeal up the chain of command if your safety complaints are not reasonably resolved.

• Constructively communicate with school officials. Going on the attack, pointing fingers, placing blame, and making threats will not move the conversation closer to resolving a concern or issue. Try to sincerely work with school administrators cooperatively, not in an adversarial manner.

- Consider if there is strength in numbers in addressing the concern. Specific incidents are typically best handled individually on a one-on-one basis. But some issues, such as getting easy access inside a school or chronic safety hazards not addressed over time, may be shared by many parents. If parents collectively communicate these concerns through the school's parent organization or as an informal but collective group, greater attention may be paid to the matter by school administrators or the school board.

- Consult outside support if necessary. If you have taken issues to the teacher, counselors, principal, superintendent, and school board, and they remain unresolved, then you may need to seek outside assistance. Personal legal counsel may be necessary in extreme unresolved matters. Unfortunately, in some cases needed change may not occur until legal inquiries and media inquiries push issues to the front burner for school decision makers. But legal and media intervention should be last resorts and on extreme situations. Try to work within the system and through all steps in the system first. The best scenario is where parents and school officials work cooperatively, sincerely, and collaboratively to resolve issues in a manner focused on the best interests of the child (Trump, 2010g).

This is not an exhaustive list, but it is a good starting point for parents to consider regardless of the specific complaint or concern they want to address at their child's school.

I leave parents with three simple tips for keeping your kids safe, each of them being a challenge busy parents must consciously work at every day:

1. Talk with, not at, your kids.

2. Give them, not your smart phone, your full attention.

3. Work to live, don't live to work.

Build a relationship with your kids today!

Part III

Readiness and Emergency Management for Schools

The U.S. Department of Education (2010b) identifies four phases of emergency management for its Readiness and Emergency Management for Schools program:

1. *Prevention-Mitigation:* Identifying all potential hazards and vulnerabilities and reducing the potential damage they can cause;

2. *Preparedness:* Collaborating with community partners to develop plans and protocols to prepare for the possibility that the identified hazards, vulnerabilities, or emergencies will occur;

3. *Response:* Working closely with first-responders and community partners to effectively contain and resolve an emergency in, or around, a school or campus; and

4. *Recovery:* Teaming with community partners to assist students and staff in the healing process, and restoring a healthy and safe learning environment following an emergency event.

Chapters 10–16 lay out a complex body of lessons learned and best practices to address these four areas. The information is not laid out by category, per se, but prevention-mitigation, preparedness, response, and recovery are represented throughout the seven chapters. In fact, the majority of this book, including areas on proactive security practices, also fit in the model.

It is virtually impossible to put everything known, discussed, debated, and implemented into one book. This book is not meant to be an all-inclusive encyclopedia of school emergency planning. Instead, it serves as a source of discussion of the fundamental issues and basic best practices in the field, while providing most school administrators enough things to work on for the next 5 to 10 years of their career.

The professional discipline of school emergency planning has grown dramatically since the pre-Columbine era and continues to evolve. Although we have many lessons learned and best practices today that did not exist prior to the school shootings of the late 1990s, we continue to learn and build upon the knowledge base that exists to date. Chances are good that there will be plenty of room for future editions of this book and others to communicate even further progress and changes in this field in the years to come.

Parents, the media, and potentially a judge and jury want to know two things:

1. What steps did your school have in place to prevent an incident of crime or violence?

2. How well prepared was your school to manage what could not be prevented?

The following chapters, and this book as a whole, provide educators with best practices to help them answer these questions.

10 Early Warning Signs of Violence

A re there children who are ticking time bombs ready to explode with violent behavior in our schools and in our communities? School violence incidents have lead many people to ask if there are early warning signs indicating the potential for violent behaviors by youths, and many opinions have subsequently been offered on the subject. Although most professionals agree that there are some red flags that should, at a minimum, raise some adult eyebrows as to a child's potential for involvement in violence, agreement upon what those flags actually look like and how they should be identified is much less common. The key is finding a balance between recognizing the red flags of potential violence that should raise educators' eyebrows while still exercising care and caution to avoid inappropriate labeling and misidentification of children.

CONCERNS AND CAVEATS

Following the series of school violence tragedies in the late 1990s, a number of checklists, computer software programs, overnight expert consultants, and other resources were made available to help school officials and others identify potentially violent offenders before an actual incident. One computer program reportedly analyzed student essays for the purpose of identifying violent words that would indicate a potentially violent student. Heaven help the poor child who writes an essay on war.

In one workshop on school crisis preparedness, I spoke with two principals who were looking at a checklist of common characteristics of potentially violent youthful offenders. One administrator commented, "Over 90% of my student population fits this list of characteristics, but I don't believe that 90% of them are very likely to shoot up or blow up our school." The other administrator responded: "And I can't think of one kid in my school who fits this so-called profile, but I can think of about a half-dozen kids who I'm sure are higher risk for bringing in anything they can get their hands on and destroying all of us!"

An understanding of youth and delinquent psychology can unquestionably help parents, school officials, and other youth service providers to better deal with potentially violent youths. However, the explosion of overnight expert consultants, checklists, and other evaluation mechanisms following school violence incidents has, in a sense, created some dilemmas in addressing the entire issue of recognizing early warning signs of potentially violent youths. Particular concerns include the following:

• *Parents, school officials, and other youth service providers placed in the role of pseudo-psychologists.* Psychology and counseling are professions that require extensive training, certification, and other professional preparation. Lists of early warning signs and other products need to be viewed within an appropriate context and in a reasonable manner. Authoring a checklist does not automatically make someone an expert in psychology. When a red flag pops up, educators and others should remember to consult with professionals, such as licensed psychologists or counselors, when concerns arise.

• *Misuse of early warning sign resources.* Caution should be exercised not to allow checklists or computer software programs to be used to stereotype or classify children, or to over- or underreact to the potential for youth violence. Some schools may have a large number of children with characteristics on an early warning sign list, yet none of them will commit a violent, tragic act. Other schools may have children who show none of the characteristics on such a guide, yet one may commit a violent offense. Lists and other products need to be viewed within an appropriate context and in a reasonable manner.

• *Unwarranted fears that only experts can effectively identify and work with high-risk youths.* Media and public attention to school violence incidents may unintentionally communicate to parents, educators, and others that only highly trained experts can have an impact with high-risk youths. Although an understanding of and increased training on youth and delinquent behavior can be quite helpful and is to be encouraged, parents and others who work with children should not resign themselves to inaction because they do not have a degree in abnormal psychology or counseling. Such a paralysis of adults can only contribute to youth violence by driving the average parent or teacher away from the children, not closer where they need to be to help control and prevent it.

CHECKLISTS AND GURUS

Certain behavioral indicators should serve as red flags for adults in terms of recognizing that there is at least the potential that they might be dealing with a youth at a higher level of risk for committing violence. However, the use, and potential for misuse, of various so-called checklists and similar products being produced in response to this issue should cause concern. Some questions that need to be asked when these lists and similar resources are offered include the following:

- Who made the checklists, and what are their qualifications and perspectives in doing so? Have they ever worked on a full-time basis with youths, violent juvenile offenders, and K–12 school safety issues?
- Who will use these checklists and in what context? Will everyone, from the custodian to the superintendent, be checking off lists to identify potentially violent kids? Is the assessment limited to self-reports by the student or to the perspective of the evaluator? What about parent and family input?
- What will be done once these items are used? Assuming that you have a valid reference tool and qualified people to use it, what will be done with a potentially violent offender once he or she is identified? What services are available, and how are they engaged and sustained? What do you do if the parents or the child refuse services? Does the school have, or even want to have, a policy mandating evaluation before a child can attend school?

These and a number of other issues need to be examined closely before using checklists and other products.

WE ARE FEDERAL AGENTS AND WE ARE HERE TO HELP YOU

The emergence of various checklists and software products following the late-1990s school violence shootings stirred up a number of media, conference, and other professional debates around concerns of labeling or misidentifying children as potentially violent offenders. The debates and polarization grew even stronger following the publication of an article in the September issue of *FBI Law Enforcement Bulletin* (Band & Harpold, 1999) that included sections on violence indicators, and in particular an offender profile, in connection with the school shootings of previous years. A number of professionals, especially educators, questioned everything from the validity of the offender profile to the expertise and appropriateness of the Federal Bureau of Investigation (FBI) having involvement in the school violence arena.

According to the article, the FBI's involvement began when it moderated an August 1998 2-day school violence summit held in Arkansas with representatives from six cities that had experienced recent school shootings. The lessons learned from the shooting were summarized in the article and in presentations made by FBI officials to school and law enforcement personnel in various conferences across the country the following year. Although a number of issues in the lessons learned covered logistical and coordination preparation suggestions, public and media attention seemed to focus strongly on the profiling aspect; that is, on suggestions that the FBI was teaching educators how to profile potentially violent offenders.

In the September 1999 article, the agents identified several factors "that may indicate that individuals have the potential to commit violence" (p. 13), including the following:

- Low self-esteem.
- Previous acts of cruelty to animals.
- Fascination with firearms.
- Disrespect from mothers or other family members.
- Seeing violence as the alternative left for them.

Although these indicators were made with several references to the six school shootings, the article did indicate that they were "by no means certain or present in every case of violence" (p. 13).

Probably even more controversial was the title and concept behind the article's offender profile section. Here, the agents indicated that the suspects from the six shootings displayed similar traits, including that they

- were white males under 18 years old with mass- or spree-murder traits;
- sought to defend narcissistic views or favorable views about themselves;
- experienced an event prior to their acts that resulted in depression and suicidal thoughts turned homicidal;
- had or perceived a lack of family support and felt rejected and wronged by others;

- had a history of mental health treatment;
- were influenced by satanic or cult-type beliefs;
- listened to songs that promoted violence;
- appeared isolated and felt powerless;
- openly expressed a desire to kill and an interest in previous killings, and had no remorse after the killings.

The agents again qualified this section by noting that "any one of these characteristics alone may not describe a potential school shooter," although they did add that, "taken together, they provide a profile that may assist law enforcement, schools, and communities to identify at-risk students" (p. 14).

I strongly suspect that the connotation of the word *profile* in itself triggered a number of strong feelings leading to the voicing of concern regarding the FBI's involvement in the school safety issue. General public opinion and a number of news stories claiming that law enforcement authorities were using race to profile highway drivers for traffic stops in order to conduct drug searches received high-profile attention around this same time, making the word *profile* automatically mean *racial profiling* or *suspected drugs* in the eyes of a number of citizens. This, in itself, appeared to be reason enough for some automatically to dismiss the points raised in the FBI article and other public discussions on the topic.

It is also arguable not only that the FBI's involvement stemmed from their interest to take a leadership role by gleaning some commonality from the various incidents, but that their higher profile in doing so could easily have been driven from higher up in the federal government where political pressures existed to initiate some highly visible efforts. Doing so would give the federal government something visible to point to in terms of their efforts to stop school shootings, which many people felt were out of control. What better claim could a politician or political appointee make, when challenged by reporters or their political foes, than saying, "We even have the FBI working on these issues. What more can we do?"

Shortly thereafter, the U.S. Secret Service jumped into the fray, edging out the FBI after the Columbine attack and taking the lead throughout the decade as federal experts in "threat assessment." The Secret Service produced several studies and reports, in cooperation with the U.S. Department of Education, which became repeated references in education and media circles when discussing threat assessment. The federal government frequently pointed to the Secret Service reports when asked by media and others as to what the Feds were doing to address school shootings.

Certainly the federal agents working on these projects have been sincere in their efforts. And lessons learned from their work are interesting resources upon which we can glean insights in approaching violent school offenders. But it is also true that federal agents, while experts in their respective fields, typically work with adults and not juveniles, and have little to no experience working in K–12 school settings.

The *wow* factor sets in, though, when educators sit in on a workshop provided by the Secret Service. Oftentimes these workshops narrowly focus on a handful of case studies, show video of interviews from shooting suspects, and present some common themes from these cases. But the mystique of being taught by the Secret Service and the intrigue of watching interviews of convicted shooters often appears to overshadow the fact that many experienced third-grade teachers can reach the same conclusion on early warning signs of violent children without having been trained as a federal agent.

We certainly should respect the professional expertise of the FBI and Secret Service and consider the contributions they bring to assessing violence. We also have to acknowledge the political climate surrounding the onset of their entry into the school safety field. And as some have privately pointed out, we also have to recognize that their involvement has led some federal agents into retirement jobs as school security directors and school safety consultants.

Whether the FBI and Secret Service contributed any groundbreaking insights that did not exist prior to their involvement, though, remains questionable. As my colleague and school safety consultant Chuck Hibbert often points out, most experienced second-grade teachers can point out the children showing early warning signs of violence. The question is what should be done once the child is identified, making the focus on response more the issue than simply identification.

EARLY WARNING, TIMELY RESPONSE

Following a number of the high-profile school shootings, the U.S. Departments of Education and Justice published a document titled *Early Warning, Timely Response: A Guide to Safe Schools* (Dwyer, Osher, & Warger, 1998) in an effort to "develop an early warning guide to help adults reach out to troubled children quickly and effectively" (Riley & Reno, 1998, p. 1). The guide focuses on a number of safe schools perspectives, including characteristics of safe schools, getting help for children, and developing prevention and crisis response plans. The section on early warning signs, however, appears to have captured the most public attention.

The authors appropriately indicated early on in the document the potential dangers of misinterpreting these identified signs, and they encouraged readers not to use the publication as a checklist for labeling or stereotyping children. They also stressed that violence and aggression must be viewed and understood within environmental and developmental contexts. By placing a number of qualifying statements in the publication to avoid misunderstandings and misuse, the authors professionally and responsibly presented complex information in a clear and useful manner.

Early warning signs were presented in the report with the stipulation that all signs are not equally significant, that the items were not presented in the text in order of seriousness, and that it is inappropriate and potentially harmful to use the signs alone as an index for predicting aggression and violence. The authors also noted that troubled children typically exhibit multiple warning signs and that this often occurs repeatedly and with increasing intensity over a period of time. With these qualifiers, the authors presented a series of early warning signs, which includes the following:

- Social withdrawal.
- Excessive feelings of isolation and being alone.
- Excessive feelings of rejection.
- Being a victim of violence.
- Feelings of being picked on and persecuted.
- Low school interest and poor academic performance.
- Expression of violence in writings and drawings.
- Uncontrolled anger.
- Patterns of impulsive and chronic hitting, intimidation, and bullying behaviors.
- A history of discipline problems.
- A history of violent and aggressive behavior.
- Intolerance for differences and prejudicial attitudes.
- Drug use and alcohol use.
- Affiliation with gangs.
- Inappropriate access to, possession of, and use of firearms.
- Serious threats of violence.

The authors distinguished these early warning signs from what they called "imminent warning signs," which indicate a greater potential for a student to behave in a potentially dangerous manner and that require an immediate response. These signs include the following:

- Serious physical fighting with peers or family members.
- Severe destruction of property.
- Severe rage for seemingly minor reasons.
- Detailed threats of lethal violence.
- Possession and/or use of firearms and other weapons.
- Other self-injurious behaviors or threats of suicides.

The authors stressed that safety must be the first priority and that action must be taken immediately when these signs exist. They also stressed the importance of notifying parents and involving law enforcement if detailed plans to cause harm, a history of aggression or previous attempts to carry out threats, or possession of a weapon and threats to use it have occurred.

FRONTLINE OBSERVATIONS

Based on more than 25 years of work in the school safety and youth violence fields, my wife (a graduate-degreed, licensed social worker and chemical dependency counselor, and former juvenile probation officer) and I pulled together a number of indicators and themes that we have observed from the frontlines in dealing firsthand with some of the most violent young offenders on our streets. These observations are simply that: observations. They are not the result of formal research and, although a number of them appear to be consistent with both research and the positions of a number of other established professionals discussing these issues, they are presented here simply to illustrate that we have observed, at least in our professional experiences, a number of red flags that should alert individuals living and working with potentially violent youths of possible trouble.

The same qualifying factors presented by the authors of *Early Warning, Timely Response* (Dwyer, Osher, & Warger, 1998) most certainly apply to our observations. They should not be used as a checklist or profile by educators or other youth-serving professionals to predict violence or aggression. They also should be viewed within environmental and developmental contexts. We agree that the presence of multiple physical or behavioral indicators and an increase in frequency and intensity of behavioral indicators should be noted—and a great deal of common sense must be applied—by those processing this entire issue to avoid mislabeling or misidentifying youths.

In addition to the various indicators, an equally strong emphasis must be placed on what is done once particular physical or behavioral indicators are identified. As I noted previously, we view these as red flags to alert individuals who are not trained and licensed mental health professionals that there may be a need to seek more in-depth assistance from such professionals. The various potential indicators discussed in this chapter should be red flags to stimulate action for seeking professional help, not tools for making individuals who are non–mental health professionals into something they are not qualified to be.

Stressors and Coping Factors

A variety of social and economic factors can contribute to violent and aggressive behavior by children at home, in school, and in the community.

In cases of workplace violence, we tend to look at the offenders to identify what stressors lead them to commit violent acts. Ironically, we tend not to look at our juvenile population from the same perspective, particularly in terms of thinking about prevention and the early recognition of warning signs.

Children, especially teens, are influenced by numerous stress factors. We believe that youth stressors and coping factors deserve a place in our discussions of youth and school violence. Our observations have found some of the more common stressors to include, but not necessarily be limited to, the following:

- Physical, psychological, or emotional abandonment by parents, adults, and significant others.
- Domestic violence, abuse, neglect, or other severe family stress or dysfunction.
- Lack of order, structure, and discipline.
- Self-concept formation, peer pressure, the need to protect reputation, and related developmental issues.
- Alcohol, drug, and similar influences.
- Gang, cult, or other deviant subculture attraction.
- Pressure to succeed academically or to meet parental expectations (real or perceived). Lack of coping skills and resiliency created by parents who are unwilling to allow their children to fail or to learn from their own mistakes.
- Fear of the unknown, fear of rejection, and fear of failure.

These and other influences leave our children with an enormous amount of stress and internal conflict that might contribute toward triggering aggressive and violent behavior. Nevertheless, such stressors in themselves are very common, so the use of these stress factors as a checklist for profiling potentially violent offenders would be stretching it quite a bit, because many, if not all, youths might experience these stressors at one point or another, especially during their teen years.

Knowing that these pressures exist and that some children, especially teens, may lack adequate and appropriate coping skills for dealing with them is important. Perhaps the focus should be on the presence or absence of coping skills and support mechanisms, along with identifying what triggers the transition from stressor to violent behavior, rather than just the presence or absence of the stress characteristics alone. It is reasonable, then, to say that we are almost automatically dealing with a higher risk population simply because they are teenagers, and in working with them we should have a heightened awareness (but not fear or panic) of the importance of being attuned to stress and related coping issues.

Behavioral and Physical Observations

We looked back over 25 years at the hundreds of violent youthful offenders we have dealt with in urban and suburban settings, which included some of the most hard-core gang members, drug traffickers, and aggressive youths at elementary and secondary school levels, as well as those outside of school settings. The most common behavioral and physical indicators and themes we observed are listed below (these are not ranked in terms of seriousness or frequency of our observations):

- Poor interpersonal skills.
- Lack of trust, bonding, and relationships.
- Impulsiveness, spontaneity, an addiction to excitement, and a high need for instant gratification.
- Strong focus on receiving respect and the need to protect one's reputation.
- Very short-term focus with no vision of a future and a distrust of long-range commitments.
- Early and lengthy history of substance abuse.
- Sexual activity, particularly at younger ages and with multiple consenting partners, or with pressured and unwilling partners.
- Unmet physical and/or mental health needs.
- Poor educational and/or employment performance.
- Functioning well in negative subcultures, often with high self-esteem in that arena, along with effective use of survival skills, a strong drive for goals (typically negative goals), and an intense affiliation to the subculture.
- Skills in negotiation and manipulation.
- Competitive, seeks challenges, and action-oriented.
- Strong need for approval and adult status.

As previously stated, it is important that these characteristics not be viewed as a checklist, *per se*. Readers should also understand that one or more characteristic alone is generally less likely to raise major red flags. However, clusters of the behavioral responses described in this chapter, especially when these responses increase in frequency or intensity to particular triggers or stimuli, understandably justify further attention and probable referral for more professional mental health attention.

Similar to the imminent warning signs mentioned in *Early Warning, Timely Response* (Dwyer, Osher, & Warger, 1998), the following indicators raise our red flags very quickly and heighten the urgency of providing professional mental health services:

- Suicidal thoughts or attempts, and related self-injury and harm.
- Attempting to cause the death of or serious physical harm to another.
- Intentional abuse of animals.
- Setting fires.
- Hallucinations or other delusions.
- Specific plans, especially detailed ones, for committing violence.

Again, red flags should indicate the need to seek help from mental health professionals specifically experienced in working with troubled, violent youths. These signs are not intended to represent a diagnostic checklist or tool for laypersons to use to draw clinical conclusions or as the sole deciding factor for specific administrative, disciplinary, or criminal action in connection with an individual student.

A Continuum of Aggression and Violence

Although the initial public accounts of school shootings or other youth violence may suggest that the violent acts came totally unexpected and without warning, the picture typically changes as the story unravels. Days, weeks, or months later, it is not uncommon for a progressive series of behavioral deterioration in the offender to become more visible. In short, the circumstances behind these high-profile events rarely develop overnight.

References to increases in frequency and intensity of violence have been made in several sections of this chapter. Perhaps the movement from lower levels of aggression to higher profile violence is best characterized using the framework of the spectrum of aggressive behavior (Silver & Yudofsky, 1992). This spectrum or continuum includes the following:

- Verbal aggression, ranging from shouting and insults to clear threats of violence.
- Physical aggression against objects, including property damage, fire setting, and similar harm to inanimate objects.
- Physical aggression against self, including physical self-harm, mutilation, or suicidal behavior.
- Physical aggression against others, such as assaults and serious physical injury or death to others.

Although every situation may not be traceable to a systematic move through these stages, there are often indicators associated with progression through this spectrum that tend to be missed until armchair quarterbacking is performed on higher profile incidents.

Consideration of behavioral and physical indicators alone will only provide a portion of the available insight into a youth's mental health world. An analysis of other environmental and contextual influences provide other important pieces of information for assessing a youth's behavior and related violence concerns.

Youth Supervision and Discipline

It is not uncommon to hear people from all walks of life blaming parents, school officials, and other adults associated with violent youthful offenders for allowing a lack of discipline and supervision to exist, which, in people's opinions, caused a violent behavior. In our years of observations with violent youths, we have found the following related themes:

- Inconsistent presence of parental authority figures.
- Inconsistent discipline or extremes in terms of too little or too much discipline for a particular situation.
- Parent-child role reversals, where the child often seems to be in control rather than the other way around.
- Confidence that there will be no timely and appropriate consequences for negative behavior.
- Minimal supervision of or ineffective limits of control over a youth.
- Unmet minimal basic needs beyond mere physical survival.

Although discipline and supervision alone may not be the only factors playing into violent youthful behavior, the presence of firm, fair, and consistent discipline and supervision certainly reduces the risks.

Family Stress and Dysfunction

Stress, dysfunction, and related dynamics within the family unquestionably play a major role in influencing a youth's behavior. Common themes observed in families of the violent children with whom we have worked have included the following:

- Physical, sexual, or emotional abuse.
- Domestic violence, intimidation, and/or viewing significant others as objects and, therefore, as less human.
- Parental abandonment, either physically or emotionally, due to divorce or separation, parental incarceration, parental mental health problems, parental substance use/abuse, parental physical health problems, or parental work obligations, all of which may draw attention to other

lifestyle or household management issues while detracting from the attention to youth needs and behavior.

- Feelings of rejection because of parental alcohol or drug abuse, mental health issues, criminal history, or incarceration.
- Unstable residences or caretakers.
- Lack of defined family or family boundaries.
- Abused siblings, neglected siblings, or siblings involved in crime and violence.

Again, these factors do not necessarily predict violent youthful behavior in themselves, but they should be recognized as possible contributing factors, especially when they are one of a cluster of conditions.

Youth Worker Characteristics

The tendency to look at youths, their families, and related dynamics often fails to include an examination of the characteristics of the individuals who are working with the youth and how these characteristics are sometimes counterproductive to reducing risks of youth violence and adverse behavior. Some particular observations we have made over the years include the tendency of many youth workers and youth-serving organizations and systems to be as follows:

- Rigid, bureaucratic, and restricted in operations and service delivery.
- Traditional, predictable, and routine in terms of what the youth can expect of the workers and the system.
- Demanding, pushing the youth to adapt to a system that might not be designed or operated in a manner that meets the youth's issues and needs.
- Inconsiderate of how the youth and his or her significant others define and perceive their issues and needs, delivering services from a worker's point of view.
- Unreasonable in expecting immediate trust, bonding, and relationships with the client youth and families.
- Unreasonable in seeking and expecting quick progress and success, often failing to realize that they are attempting to undo years of adverse behavior patterns in a relatively short period of time, which often leads them to terminate or alter services too quickly or inappropriately because they perceive an absence of progress or change.

This is not to suggest that the workers or the systems are solely to blame for youth violence or the failure of youths to change behavioral directions. It is, however, meant to suggest that those adults working with youths need to take their perspective, and the perspective of their own organization and its service delivery, into consideration when evaluating individual cases.

A Holistic Assessment

It should be clear from the preceding sections of this chapter that individuals attempting to look for early warning signs to determine whether a referral for more professional mental health assistance is needed cannot simply rely on a checklist. Instead, they need to consider a variety of areas of youth functioning. These may include paying attention to the following:

- Behavior changes at home, including in relationships with parents and siblings.
- The general mood and attitude of the youth, (e.g., psychological state, depression).
- Physical signs, such as medical needs, physical injuries, illness, and personal hygiene.
- Social changes in terms of peer relationships, how peer conflicts are managed, activities the youth is engaged in, and any significant changes.
- School performance.
- Work performance.
- Family history, including issues of substance use and abuse, domestic violence, sexual abuse, physical abuse, emotional abuse, and mental illness.
- Legal/court involvement.
- Sexuality.
- Family residential stability (e.g., mobility, transitions).
- Changes in family economic status or needs.
- The loss of a loved one through death, separation, or abandonment.
- Other trauma or the concerns of others knowledgeable about the youth.

Although many people, especially educators, enjoy the checklist approach to addressing issues, human behavior and, in particular, youth behavior and violence are simply not that easy. Unlike with many adults, who are often set in their ways, *normal* youth behavior is very experimental, and therefore can change for an ongoing period of time, particularly during adolescence. If we agree that attempts to accurately predict adult behavior is extremely challenging, then it should be clear that such an approach is even more difficult when applied to children and teens.

PREVENTION, INTERVENTION, AND TREATMENT ISSUES

Parents and Educators

Parents, school officials, and other youth service providers can take numerous steps to reduce the stressors on children and, in turn, to help lower the risks of stress-triggered violent behavior. Some of these steps might include the following:

1. Establish ongoing, sincere, and trusting relationships with youths built on regular, quality communications.

2. Be sensitive to the stressors influencing children and provide timely intervention support.

3. Be alert for, and promptly respond to, such issues as:

   o Detachment or a lack of bonding and connectedness to others.
   o Withdrawal or perceptions of hopelessness.
   o Threats—and the efforts to establish the means and opportunity to carry out the threats.
   o Disciplinary problems in school or delinquent, criminal activity in schools or communities.
   o Unusual interest or preoccupation with weapons, bombs, violent entertainment forms (e.g., music, movies).
   o Abuse of animals, suicide threats or attempts, self-mutilation, and so on.

4. Be consistent in expectations and in disciplining youths.

5. Listen to kids with a nonjudgmental attitude, even if you disagree with their perspectives. The emphasis is on listening, not on having to agree with what you hear.

6. Be alert to small, incremental changes in youth behavior instead of waiting for *the* major event. The importance of looking at *changes* in behavior, rather than for a specific list of behaviors, cannot be overstated. And to be able to detect a change in behavior, adults working with youths first need to know what is standard behavior for that child before they can detect a change. You will be less likely to detect a change in Johnny's behavior on Friday if you do not know what Johnny's typical behavior is on Monday, Tuesday, Wednesday, and Thursday. Although this does not easily lend itself to those who prefer a checklist or cookie-cutter approach to dealing

with kids, it does provide an accurate depiction of reality, in that the key to dealing with at-risk youths and preventing youth and school violence rests strongly in knowing and working with children as individuals.

Parents and professionals working with youths should especially remember to talk with children honestly and, when necessary, to seek professional help before a situation reaches a crisis level. Dealing with small concerns is a much more manageable task than dealing with crises.

Professional and Program Considerations

Like any professional who works with violent youths, my wife and I have developed some basic beliefs about how prevention, intervention, and treatment for such youths should be approached. These beliefs include, but are not necessarily limited to, the need

- to focus on individualized approaches to at-risk and violent youths, instead of using cookie-cutter approaches and programs for all;
- to recognize that multiple attempts may very well need to be made with the same kid before progress is seen;
- for individuals working with youths to attempt to understand, even if they do not agree with, the logic and thinking of the youth as he or she views issues, needs, or concerns;
- for a commitment to skilled interviewing and communications with youths in terms of recognizing the need to check multiple sources of information (not simply the child or a particular adult), the tendency of youths to answer questions literally or in a very narrow and specific manner, and the tendency of many youths to exaggerate, minimize, or rationalize behaviors;
- for continuous monitoring, supervision, and support;
- for simple, direct, and concrete communications to be made when setting rules and expectations;
- for firmness, fairness, and consistency, with an emphasis on order and structure, in discipline and supervision;
- to engage constructive, and sometimes new, methods for youths to cope with stress, conflict, and related dynamics;
- to focus on building and maintaining long-term relationships, which are often absent but needed in violence-prone youths;
- for strong drug prevention, education, and employment plan, which are necessary to keep youths in the direction of progress;

- to recognize that even the most violent youths may be clever, creative, skillful, and manipulative—in either a positive or a negative manner depending upon the circumstances;
- to address concretely issues of self-respect, respect of others, and challenges to respect;
- to acknowledge that youths, and especially at-risk or violence-prone youths, often require meaningful challenges, mental and physical stimulation, exposure to new areas, and involvement in the planning and process for prevention, intervention, or treatment;
- to emphasize meaningful and useful short-term tasks, along with immediate and tangible pay-offs and feedback, which may be the most successful approach in dealing with at-risk or violence-prone youths;
- to recognize that youths—and adults—must learn patience with the process, and to acknowledge the importance of long-term goals in addition to the short-term issues;
- for youths to understand and distinguish between the short- and long-term consequences of adverse behavior;
- for youths (and for that matter, many adults, too) to learn to differentiate wants from needs;
- for youths to be able to recognize negative behavior in others (including in their role models), to evaluate the depth of their friendships with and the motivations of others, and to respond appropriately;
- for a balance of rights with responsibilities;
- to include social skills issues in working with at-risk or violence-prone youths, and to focus on teaching youths how to ask for help and assistance, manage embarrassment, deal with disrespect, and handle rumors, change, and related concerns.

ANOTHER CALL FOR COMMON SENSE

Psychology, mental health, crime, violence, and aggression are all very complex issues. Although we cannot bypass or look only at the surface of these issues and expect that we will not miss some major warning signs, we also do not need *paralysis by analysis* to the point where we believe that only individuals with doctoral degrees and dozens of years of experience in a mental health profession can detect potential initial indicators of violence. Parents, teachers, and others who work with kids should not fear that the issues are too complex or that they cannot recognize early warning signs.

The reality is that good observation skills and common sense can alert many adults to impending problems. For example, art and English teachers are in excellent positions to detect early warning signs of potentially violent youths by looking closely at their drawings, essays, and related projects for themes of violence. Common sense should indicate that if the project is on war, then the project may reasonably include such themes, but if projects show in-depth themes of violence, especially on an ongoing basis, then it might be a good idea to refer concerns to a school counselor, psychologist, or administrator.

In the end, common sense and a heightened awareness of early warning signs, combined with timely and appropriate follow-through, can help prevent school and other youth violence tragedies while avoiding inappropriate labeling and misidentification of youths as violent offenders.

11 Assessing and Managing Threats

What do you do when you find a student in possession of a hit list of students and staff to be killed? How do you handle the report that a student threatened to kill a group of other students? What do you do when a teacher reports that a student threatened to kill him or her?

All threats must be treated seriously. There must be an understanding that there is no such thing as joking when it comes to threatening harm to others. Educators need to have a protocol in place to evaluate threats and to manage threats in a balanced yet firm and efficient manner.

Unique factors exist between dealing with school-based, student threats and the kind of threats typically handled by law enforcement officials responsible for protective details for public officials and foreign dignitaries. The most notable difference is that, in handling school-based threats, educators and law enforcement personnel are dealing with youth behavior and not with the typical adult, terrorist, or other more mature threat sources involved in executive protection. Although lessons can be learned from threat assessment outside of the school setting, caution needs to be exercised when considering the various computer software, checklists, and so-called experts attempting to take their expertise from adult settings and apply it directly to school settings without first studying and understanding the differences between adult and juvenile behavior in social settings.

THREAT ASSESSMENT PROTOCOL

School officials should establish a basic protocol to be followed in assessing and managing student threats. Students need to understand that making threats, even when the student thinks they are not serious, is inappropriate behavior in the school setting. Air travelers cannot joke about guns, bombs, hijacking, or similar issues in an airport, and a similar level of seriousness about threats should be applied to the school.

Threat Assessment Questions

No expert can accurately predict the exact circumstances surrounding every potential threat that school personnel might encounter. Therefore, educators who rely upon checklists of particular circumstances or individual characteristics might not get an accurate read or the best direction for handling every case of student threats. However, school and public safety officials can ask a few questions to help them gather as much information as possible to best assess most student threats and to evaluate their best course of action for managing these situations.

Before asking these questions, however, school officials should consider some important lessons learned both from past school violence tragedies and from the experiences of school safety professionals who have prevented violent offenses from occurring elsewhere:

• There is no particular look or appearance that characterizes every individual who might act violently. School officials should therefore exercise caution and should not evaluate an individual's desire or ability to carry out an act of violence based on appearance. Potential offenders do not necessarily look crazy or present an abnormal outward physical appearance. Offenders can look, and indeed have looked, like any other average, ordinary student in a given school.

• Officials evaluating threats should focus on *behavior, behavior, behavior!* Educators and public safety officials need to focus on what the threatmakers have done and are doing, not on who they are or appear to be. The threat assessment should be based on the thinking processes and corresponding behaviors of the threatmakers, their position in a continuum of violence or potential violence, and related considerations.

• A threat alone will not guarantee violence, nor does the absence of a threat guarantee that violence will not occur.

• Although violent offenders may not make a threat directly to school officials or other potential targets of their violence, they have often told someone that they know, typically other students, about their intended actions. Verbal or other indicators need not be loud and flashy, but they do tend to be present and often detectable by those who are paying close attention.

- The actions of high-profile violent offenders in schools do not appear to be spontaneous or the result of their acting on impulse, but instead often appear to be planned, thought out, and more organized than a spur-of-the-moment action. In fact, the violent actions in a number of school violence tragedies appear to occur after a progression of deteriorating events and possibly undiagnosed or untreated depression. They often occur when offenders have reached a point where they feel that they are at the end of the road with no way to turn back, and no adults or significant others are in their life who care about them. When these circumstances exist, or are perceived to exist by the offenders, the resulting violence is often their method for solving such real or perceived problems. Given these conditions, in the end a very thin line may exist between homicide and suicide.

Understanding the mind-set and thinking processes of potentially serious offenders may therefore help educators and public safety officials obtain a more clear and accurate threat assessment.

Keeping the above information in mind, some questions that can guide school officials in assessing any threats coming to their attention include the following:

- What was the motivation of the threat? Are there identifiable reasons why the threat was made?
- What exactly was communicated in the threat? How was it communicated—verbally or in writing? To whom was the threat communicated?
- In what context did the communication threat occur? Was it, for example, in the heat of a fight? In a letter? In a spur-of-the-moment comment?
- What was the intensity of the communication threat? Was it detailed?
- Does the threatmaker show an unusual interest in violence, weapons, self-abuse, suicide, abuse of animals, or other progressions of violent behavior?
- Has the threatmaker shown an unusual interest in acts of violence committed by others that are similar to those he or she is threatening? Has the person sought out details or studied other similar offenses? Has this unusual action been accompanied by related planning or actions?
- Are there signs of emotional detachment by the threatmaker? If so, to what degree? Is there progressively increasing detachment?
- Has the person making the threat previously engaged in threatening, menacing, harassing, or similar behavior?
- Has the person making the threat previously engaged in planning or committing violent acts?

- If there is a history of violent or threatening behavior, is there a change in the frequency or intensity of the incidents?
- Has the person engaged in any specific information-gathering, stalking, or similar activities to learn about the target of his or her threat?
- Does the threatmaker have a plan? If so, how specific is it? Did it include specific steps, maps, or other supportive materials to carry out the threat?
- Does the threatmaker have the ability to carry out the threat?
- Is the threatmaker's overall behavior consistent with his or her threats?
- Does the threatmaker have current or prior undiagnosed or untreated mental illness or emotional disturbances, such as depression, delusion, hallucinations, feelings of desperation, feelings of persecution, or similar conditions?
- Have there been any other major stressors or changes in the threatmaker's environment that might affect his or her desire or ability to carry out the threat?
- What action, if any, has been taken in addressing threats previously made by the individual?
- Does the threatmaker have a social support system in school? Outside of school? What is the threatmaker's desire and willingness to seek and accept help?
- Have as many individuals as possible who are familiar with the threatmaker (e.g., teachers, counselors, psychologists, social workers, school support staff, law enforcement, parents, and others) been consulted to obtain a complete picture of the individual? Have others familiar with the threatmaker expressed concern about threats made by the individual?
- Are there any gaps or pieces of missing information that could influence the assessment of the threat?

These and other questions could assist school and public safety officials in focusing on the thinking process and behavior of threatmakers, their position in a continuum of violence or potential violence, and the amount of planning and preparation related to their threat. These questions are not a panacea for evaluating threats and should not be viewed as a definitive assessment tool. Nor are they a substitute for professional evaluation. They should, however, illustrate to school officials the importance of establishing some type of guiding protocol questions to help school threat assessment teams process threat incidents. Flying by the seat of one's pants, rather than having some predetermined questions to ask, will certainly increase the potential for problems.

Threat Management Procedures

Suggested procedures for managing threats once they come to an administrator's attention include, but are not necessarily limited to, the following:

• Treat all threats seriously, and engage a standard, rational response protocol for investigating and documenting threats and related actions taken in response to the threats by multidisciplinary school threat assessment teams consisting of administrators, counselors, psychologists, teachers, security/law enforcement personnel, and support staff.

• Interview witnesses to the threat and obtain written witness statements immediately upon notification of the threat.

• Interview the alleged threatmaker, and obtain a written statement from him or her.

• Because one of the more reliable predictors of future behavior is often past behavior, review records of the past disciplinary and criminal behavior of the threatmaker to ascertain if there is a history of such actions.

• Within the legal parameters set on confidentiality, review the psychological history of the threatmaker and confer with counselors or psychologists familiar with the individual.

• Assess weapons availability by asking the threatmaker if he or she has access to weapons at home or from other sources.

• Assess weapons availability by asking the threatmaker's parents or guardians if the student has access to weapons and if they are aware of any other threats made by the student.

• Process the various questions and considerations listed in the previous section of this chapter.

• Inspect notebooks, lockers, book-bags, and school computers for items such as weapons, drawings or essays with violent themes, hit lists, or similar indicators as appropriate. (Reasonable suspicion and related standards for searches will likely need to be taken into consideration. Consult with school attorneys for developing guidelines for such actions.)

• Obtain input from other staff members who know the student, law enforcement officials, and others familiar with the individual and his or her background.

• Notify the police, if appropriate, and do so in a timely manner.

- Secure and maintain custody of related evidence.

- Administer the appropriate disciplinary action.

- Take the necessary steps, if consistent with school policies and procedures, to facilitate formal professional mental health evaluations before the threatmaker returns to school.

- Document the incident.

- Assess the need to provide additional security measures or protection to threatened individuals.

- Advise potential victims of administrative, criminal, civil, and other options available to them, such as restraining orders or steps for reporting additional threats or concerns, to prevent or reduce risks of future harm.

- If the threatmaker legally must return to the school following disciplinary or criminal action, provide an appropriate level of monitoring and follow-up to gauge the individual's behavior.

Recording Threats

Written incident reports of threats and the actions taken to address them should be completed and retained by school and other appropriate personnel. These reports should include, but not necessarily be limited to, the following:

- The name and identification information of the threatmaker, victims, and witnesses.
- When and where the threat was made.
- How the incident occurred, including conditions and circumstances preceding, surrounding, and following the threat.
- Specific language and/or actions associated with the threat.
- The names and actions of teachers, support staff, administrators, and other officials involved in assessing and managing the threat.
- The steps taken to prevent the threatmaker from carrying out the current threat or to prevent future threats.
- Steps taken to advise and counsel the victim(s) of the threat.

The reports will provide not only documentation of the steps taken by school and other officials to properly manage the threat, but also a written history available for review in assessing related threats that may occur in the future. Issues regarding the retention of these records, security of the records and information contained therein, and legalities of reciprocal information sharing will, of course, also need to be addressed.

LIMITATIONS

These steps certainly will not guarantee that threatened harm or additional threats will not occur. However, they do provide school officials with some guidance for treating threats seriously and in a balanced, rational way without over- or underreacting to a threatening situation.

12 Lessons Learned From School Crisis Incidents

If we can learn nothing but two things from the experiences of the victims of school crises, remember that *it can happen here* and that there *are* things that can be done to prevent and prepare for such tragedies.

It is important for school officials to practice what is preached in the education community: Learn from the experiences of others. School officials cannot do the job alone, however; emergency service providers, parents, students, and community leaders must also examine how, or perhaps even if, they will be mentally and operationally prepared for a crisis.

School and community leaders can begin their preparations by learning from the experiences of those who have already experienced such tragedies.

BE PREPARED, NOT SCARED

The two most common messages heard over and over in news and other accounts of school crisis incidents have been the following:

1. "We never thought it could happen here."

2. "There was nothing we could do to train or prepare for such a tragedy."

If nothing else is remembered from the school crises that have occurred in our nation, school and community officials must learn from the experiences of others that it *can* happen here, regardless of where *here* is located, and that although every incident cannot be prevented, steps can be taken to reduce the risks for such incidents, and preparations can be made to more effectively manage a crisis, should one occur.

It is human nature for individuals to deny, or at least to avoid thinking about, a possible tragedy in their school or community. And educators should not go to work each day in fear or in a state of paranoia. However, one of the best ways to increase the risk of experiencing a crisis or of being victimized by violence is to let down one's guard and to operate with a mind-set isolated from reality.

Educators should not be scared; they must, however, be prepared.

PRIORITY ONE: EMERGENCY PREPAREDNESS

A debriefing of officials from several cities that experienced school shootings in 1997 and 1998 identified as one of the primary lessons from their experiences the importance of having a well-defined crisis response team, one with the ability to communicate and effectively collaborate on responding to and managing crisis incidents (Reisman, 1998). Because a school crisis quickly becomes a community crisis, it is important for response teams to include coordination not only among the key players within the school district, but also with those in the broader community. Crisis preparedness is also an ongoing process, not a solitary event, and so it requires testing and exercising crisis guidelines, not simply putting together a fancy document and leaving it in the principal's office until a crisis strikes the school.

More than a dozen years following this 1998 debriefing, we are still addressing the same issues with schools: Have a well-defined crisis team, be able to communicate and coordinate with community partners, make planning an ongoing process, and test and exercise guidelines instead of leaving plans on a shelf until a crisis threatens the school. In many schools, the message has been heard. But in too many schools, the lessons have not been learned or have not been put into practice.

Cathy Danyluk, a school safety expert with the Indiana Department of Education, best described the importance of preparedness when she noted, "The offenders in school shooting incidents came to school with a plan. So should educators" (C. Danyluk, personal communication, May 3, 1998). The only difference, she added, is that "educators need to make sure that they have tested and exercised their plans more thoroughly than those who actually have thought out their own plan to commit the offenses."

PREVENTION: AN EQUAL PRIORITY

The first line of effective prevention planning is having comprehensive, effective school security and crisis preparedness measures in place. Unfortunately, these items are often not viewed as prevention. However, most school security personnel and school resource officers report that they have prevented a greater number of potentially violent situations than they have reacted to incidents culminating in an arrest. Effective school security, school-based policing, and school preparedness planning play a role in school violence prevention.

Other specific prevention and intervention issues and strategies were discussed in Chapter 3 on comprehensive school safety leadership, Chapter 5 on hot topics and strategies, Chapter 10 on early warning signs, and Chapter 11 on assessing and managing threats.

DEAL WITH SMALL PROBLEMS

Most veteran school administrators and security personnel tend to agree that dealing with small problems while they are still small will prevent larger problems from arising down the road. The most three most common small problems that trigger more serious school violence incidents are as follows:

1. "He said/she said/they said" rumors.

2. Boyfriend or girlfriend conflicts or rumors.

3. Disrespect, or "dissin'," in the words of the kids, both real and perceived (Trump, 1998).

Although educators realistically cannot spend all day dealing with each of these types of conflicts, they should exercise care not to overlook or dismiss these problems without addressing them in an appropriate and meaningful manner.

Those who fail to deal with these issues should not be surprised at the result of their inaction. The student who accidentally bumps into someone in the hallway at 7:30 a.m. and exchanges derogatory remarks instead of offering a simple "excuse me" may very well be the same person who pulls out a razor blade and slashes the other person in the face after school. Disrespect, along with the rumor mill of "he said/she said" comments, can quickly transform a small conflict into a major incident in very little time.

The issue of disrespect, in particular, warrants much closer attention by adults than it is often given. Disrespect may be real or perceived, and it may come in a variety of forms, including the following:

- Staring, dirty looks, eye rolling, lip smacking, or other nonverbal communications intended to mock, disrespect, or intimidate another student.
- Verbal put downs.
- Rumors and gossip
- Bullying, cyberbullying, and teasing.
- Pushing, shoving, hallway horseplay, or similar physical intimidation, often dismissed by adults as being too minor for their involvement.
- Alienation and isolation (i.e., making someone an outcast).

These are a few examples, but certainly not an exhaustive list.

So many incidents of in-school violence, even some of the higher profile cases and cases involving gang conflicts, often start with these lower profile forms of disrespect and aggressive behavior. Goldstein (1999) best describes this, arguing that

> we as a society have far too often ignored the very manifestations of low-level aggression that, when rewarded, grow (often rapidly) into those several forms of often intractable high-level aggression that are currently receiving a great deal of society's attention. (p. 2)

The small problems described above, and the resulting high-profile problems that result if they go unattended, represent a perfect example of how this applies to school settings.

SCHOOL CLIMATE

The need to deal with disrespect and other lower level forms of aggression illustrates the importance of addressing school climate issues in general. The tendency of educators to focus solely on climate issues and not on security and crisis preparedness historically created a critical imbalance in the approach to school safety. Respect, sensitivity to diversity, appropriate language and behavior, peaceable conflict resolution, a sense of belonging, and related characteristics of a positive and supportive learning environment play significant roles in reducing safety risks.

Schools should address climate along with security and emergency preparedness, not one or the other. Too often climate is pitted against security, instead of focusing on both. Schools can be warm, welcoming, and trusting environments and still have balanced security measures and comprehensive emergency preparedness guidelines.

OVERCOMING STUDENT DENIAL

Denial of school safety concerns and issues became an issue following the spate of high-profile school shootings. However, the focus has primarily been on denial by school officials, parents, politicians, and other adults in the broader school community, when, in fact, there is also a level of denial present in many students. In a number of discussions with youths, I have discovered that the *it can't happen here* mentality is as equally present with students as it is with adults.

It is possible, if not probable, that one reason for student denial of the potential for a high-profile school violence incident is that they believe and are modeling the denial of the many adults with whom they come into contact. It is also reasonable to conclude, however, that youths, and in particular teens, often have a false sense of security generated by their perception that they know other students in the school and that none of these other students would commit a shooting or other major offense. Combined with their natural perception of self-invincibility, the confidence gained from the belief that they know each other and that, from their perspectives, these other youths would not commit such offenses, fosters a tendency not to see the potential for a critical incident to occur.

Overcoming youth denial is as sensitive an issue as overcoming adult denial. A number of educators believe that by discussing these incidents head-on, they will actually create a fear in students that otherwise would not exist. Unfortunately, such an adult mind-set only fosters both more denial and an unrealistic mind-set in students, who often seem to handle crises better than some adults do anyway.

The real focus needs to be placed not on *if* the adults will discuss school safety issues and concerns with students, but *how* they will do so. Discussions of these type need to be honest and need to offer direct explanations of safety concerns, the rationale behind such school safety strategies as lockdowns, and the importance of the procedures and practices put in place to deal with security and crisis situations. Students typically understand and appreciate such communications and will respond as desired in a drill or an actual crisis.

A SWITCH FROM SNITCH

The need for educators to create ways for students, parents, and other individuals to report threats, rumored violence, and other safety concerns is another important lesson learned from recent school crises. Students and others often know about a potential violent act before the incident occurs, yet many times this information does not make its way to those who can prevent the violence until after an incident has happened. Reasons for the withholding of information range from fear of reprisals if the reporting person is identified, to denial of the "We never thought that he would actually do what he said he was going to do" or "Kids will be kids" sort.

The most common way adults find out about a student who is bringing a weapon to school is when other students report it. Kids want to know that two things will occur when they do report: First, that they will remain anonymous, and, second, that someone will follow up on what they report.

School staff members need to realize that this anonymity means not only that will they not tell other students, but also that they will not tell other staff members aside from an administrator or other official authorized to act on the information.

Students also need to know about the follow-up when they report something. For example, one teacher shared her concern about a student who had not attended school since the day that the student reported seeing a gun fall from another student's backpack. The principal had promised that he would meet her in the same stairwell the day following the incident so that the student could identify this otherwise unknown gun-toting student, but the principal did not show up. The student then decided to not attend school again, because she perceived that her report was not taken seriously and that there was not going to be a follow-up as promised.

In addition to assuring anonymity and doing proper follow-up on reports, we also need to reeducate children that providing information related to threats to safety is not *snitching*, but instead may indeed be life-saving. The life saved may be that of the reporting person, his or her friend, or others in the school. This education process needs to take place quickly and thoroughly in all schools, beginning at the elementary level.

A variety of mechanisms have been created to promote an anonymous and more timely reporting of concerns about violence, including the following:

- Telephone hotlines, within schools or school districts, consisting of a dedicated phone line with an answering machine that is checked regularly.

- Government hotlines through city, county, or state police, education, and other agencies.
- Commercial hotline services that offer to operate a fee-based 24-hour, 7 days per week staffed hotline for school districts.
- Hotlines connected to the school system's voice mail service, which alert administrators to pending messages.
- Electronic mail hotlines and text messaging reporting processes, where students can send tips to designated officials, thereby capitalizing on the interest children have in the technological world.

Regardless of how it is done, the mechanism for reporting must be made very widely known to students and must be promoted on an ongoing basis to get the most use of it.

LISTEN TO KIDS AND PARENTS

One group of students had some very serious complaints about the installation of metal detectors in their school. Although most adults expected these complaints to focus on the delays in getting into school because of the inspections, student complaints actually centered on their belief that the adults were not checking their backpacks thoroughly enough when they activated the metal detector. At another school, one student, who was the victim of an extortion but saw no action taken when he reported it to an administrator, asked, "How can we learn to be serious about crime when we don't see crime being dealt with seriously in our own school?"

The awakening of the silent majority of parents to school safety issues following the high-profile national incidents of violence provided a clear indicator to school officials that safety is, indeed, a top priority to parents. Although no administrator wants to experience what occurred during and after the Columbine tragedy in 1999, educators should keep in the back of their minds the extent of parental uproar about school safety that occurred after these and subsequent incidents. In fact, progressive administrators will remember to seek out input and recommendations periodically from both students and parents, in addition to staff and outside public safety officials, at times during the school year when there is not a crisis incident triggering them to do so.

Although facts and data should largely drive decisions, educators and safety officials must also address perceptions about school safety. Actual school conditions may be significantly safer than they are perceived to be by some members of the school community, but these perceptions must be acknowledged and addressed. Perception can often turn into reality when left unchecked, and school administrators should ensure that they communicate about school safety accurately, clearly, and regularly.

RELY ON LOCAL DATA

National data on school crime and violence are extremely flawed and misleading for a variety of reasons, as discussed in Chapter 2, so it is not uncommon to see two reports from the same national source identify conflicting trends within weeks of their publication. In light of the political and logistical constraints prohibiting accurate national school violence data, school officials would be wise to focus on local data to help identify security threat trends and areas for preventative action. Such local data would include school discipline data, school crime data, police crime data for the communities in which students reside, staff surveys, parent surveys, student surveys, and focus groups.

The value of student surveys and input should not be underestimated. Students often see things differently and much more clearly than their adult counterparts. Adult perspectives tend to be clouded with personal biases, political agendas, philosophical twists, and, in general, more theoretical and conceptual thinking than those of students.

For example, in one discussion with adults and students about who or what is responsible for school violence, the majority of adults tended to blame guns and the media, whereas kids identified the individual offenders and their actions as the source primarily responsible for the violence. The students were much more practical and realistic, whereas adults tended to point fingers, place blame, and spout rhetoric. It was not surprising, then, that the kids also had more practical and realistic strategies for preventing and managing school violence, too.

Survey data should be combined with incident data to get a clearer picture of school safety issues. Too often, we hear arguments for use of crime incident data or only for survey data. We should be using both to create a more comprehensive perspective on school safety issues.

WHY SUBURBAN WHITE KIDS KILL

Often I am asked why so many of the higher profile school violence incidents happened in rural or suburban areas. "Is it just the revenge of the nerds?" one principal asked seriously, suggesting that the shooters may have been "getting even" for years of harassment and being made outcasts from the more popular students.

Although harassment and disrespect toward the offenders may have played a role in adding to the stressors of school shooters, it is unlikely that these factors were the sole causes of these incidents. Other likely factors include the following:

• *Suburban and rural communities have generally looked at violence and crisis issues as inner-city problems.* The level of security and crisis preparedness in these cities had therefore been minimal or, more often than not, nonexistent. Unfortunately, the "We never thought it would happen here" mentality was, and in some places still is, alive and well. Security and emergency preparedness measures were, up until the high profile school shootings, seen as unnecessary and alarmist in the eyes of many suburban and rural educators, parents, and public officials because, in their minds, "those things" only happened in the inner city.

• *Race, money, and politics are directly related to the perception that violence is an inner-city issue.* While working in a predominantly minority inner-city school district, for example, I observed that the common adult focus was on arresting and prosecuting students caught with drugs in schools—period. This was certainly a legal and appropriate response. In contrast, when I worked in a suburban school district, the message was to get treatment for the children caught with drugs, but to think twice as to whether school officials should really be so punitive as to pursue arrest and prosecution. In essence, many suburban and rural areas, especially those where residents are predominantly white and affluent or are relatives of politically connected or highly positioned professionals, have sheltered their children from the legal consequences for their criminal acts and, in many cases, have even sheltered them from disciplinary consequences by school administrators for violations of school rules.

• *Parents and children often focus too much on material items.* "I bought everything for this kid, and he still turned out to be violent," one mother said at a parent workshop on school safety. "I could not even go into his bedroom because he told me that it is against state law," she added. Although urban parents may also overindulge their children with material items, it is especially predominant in many suburban and rural communities, where parents often have more resources to buy things for their children and to give them money whenever they request it. This focus on material wealth, when coupled with a lack of discipline, teaches too many children that they have to work for very little, and that money, not time and love, are the most important things parents have to give them. Add together money, mobility, and few, if any, consequences for misbehaviors, and you have a formula for disaster. (And, no, there was no such state law prohibiting a parent from going into their child's bedroom in their own home.)

● *Denial and neglect are factors, too.* Many children from more affluent families have easier access to professional assistance such as counseling, drug treatment, and other mental health services, but this certainly does not mean that they get the services. In fact, because of concerns about family image, parental guilt, and just plain denial, many suburban and rural children do not receive the mental health and professional services that they truly need. Such circumstances foster trouble, and children become like a number of pots just waiting to boil over. Violent outbursts by children from suburban and rural areas should therefore really be no more of a surprise than the outbursts by children from inner-city communities.

● *Parents who are unwilling to allow their children to fail or to learn from their own mistakes.* Too often, especially in suburban and affluent communities, I see families I refer to as *The Perfects.* Parents want their children to be *perfect* and do everything for them instead of allowing the children to do things, make mistakes, and learn from their mistakes. We then end up with children who have minimal to no coping skills and resiliency for bouncing back when they encounter nonroutine circumstances or critical issues. This in turn leads to increased risks for violent reactions against others or self-harm.

● *Raising children as little adults, rather than letting kids be kids, while parents chase the suburban dream.* Children in suburban and affluent communities are often overscheduled with activities, overstressed to behave like mini-adult robots, and passed off on a heartbeat to relatives, babysitters, or nannies while their parents are busy at their work or social lives. The opportunity to simply act like a kid, be a kid, and enjoy childhood has been stolen from many kids. It should not be surprising when we see children with these backgrounds having untreated or undiagnosed mental health issues, particularly in those cases that lead to high-profile acts of violence. Far too often I see suburban and affluent parents so busy chasing what they believe is the suburban dream that they are missing the opportunity to live it.

● *Inner-city schools are typically far ahead in the game when it comes to preventing violence.* Although many large urban school districts may have a larger volume of violent incidents than their suburban and rural counterparts, the reality is that many of these inner-city schools have addressed security procedures, crisis planning, and similar risk reduction and awareness measures far sooner than these other districts. More doors are routinely secured, visitors and strangers are challenged more quickly, teachers and staff are better trained and experienced in dealing with crime and violence issues, crisis preparedness plans have long been established and tested in real life as well as in training, early warning signs are detected by staff more quickly, and so on. Meanwhile, in many suburban and rural schools, every door in a school could be found open at any given time until the spate of high-profile school violence incidents forced such schools to take precautions. Why should we be surprised that a violent incident could occur in suburban and rural schools, especially after considering that there was little done in terms of security and crisis training, planning, and procedure implementation? If anything, we should be surprised that it has not happened sooner and more often.

A number of other potential factors may very well play into the urban/ suburban debate on school violence. Although the point is not to identify them all here, it is important that we stop acting so shocked and surprised when we hear of violence in our suburban and rural areas. In the words of veteran educator and internationally known youth safety consultant Steve Sroka, "The major difference between the inner city and suburban communities is that, in the suburbs, drugs and violence hide behind lawns, lawyers, and fences" (S. Sroka, personal communication, September 4, 1999).

TRAIN EMERGENCY SERVICE PERSONNEL

Columbine had a dramatic impact on law enforcement training. Prior to that time, the standard police response to a Columbine-like situation was to set up a perimeter and dispatch the SWAT team. It was not until the tactical team arrived that police entered the building where the incident was occurring.

This changed after Columbine. "Active shooter" training became a best practice in law enforcement training for addressing school and other locations where an attacker is actively shooting. Active shooter response typically involves the first officers on scene (often the first 3 to 4 officers based upon variations described to me by officers around the nation) entering the school with the sole purpose of neutralizing the shooter.

Historically, many police, fire, and medical units did not train together. While this improved post-Columbine and post-9/11, many of these entities across the nation have had, at best, limited exposure to the schools in their communities. Aside from responding to individual and isolated calls for specific incidents several times a year, many emergency service providers have been inside the schools only if their own children happen to attend. Many schools have opened their doors to police tactical teams post-Columbine, but oftentimes this does not include fire and emergency medical personnel, and in many communities, police tactical teams still have not practiced in their community schools or have done so only once.

School resource officer (SRO) programs provide a bridge between schools and law enforcement agencies. SROs prevent many incidents because of the positive working relationships they form with students and, in fact, have prevented a number of high-profile incidents. School-based officers can also facilitate the exchange of tactical information and training, such as active shooter training, to help both the school and the law enforcement agency better prepare for a tactical emergency response.

THINKING SECURITY WHEN THERE IS NOT A CRISIS

Everyone remembers the motherly advice, "It's what you don't know that might hurt you." Truer words were never spoken when it comes to school security and crisis preparedness. Although high-profile incidents certainly provide a focus for learning important lessons, educators and others in the school community need to think about school security when there is *not* a crisis.

A number of reporters asked me after high-profile school shootings whether or not it was a wake-up call for schools to do a better job at school security. My answer was simply that the question was not whether the shootings were wake-up calls, but whether or not as a society we would keep hitting the snooze button and going back to sleep. Educators need to concentrate on security and crisis preparedness at all times, not just after a particular incident.

In fairness to educators, the tendency to react rather than act is a national trait. Americans focus on terrorism after a terrorist bombing, workplace violence after an office shooting, and airline crashes after an airline accident. Yet when these items are no longer in the headlines, Americans put the issues on the back burners and move on to other hot topics, to return to these types of issues only when the next crisis arises. Oddly enough, we then spend even more time wondering aloud why such incidents continue to happen!

This tendency to run hot and cold is even more entrenched in the education community because of the absence of any type of accurate, strong, coordinated, and ongoing national information source on school crimes, violence, and related prevention, intervention, enforcement, and crisis preparedness strategies. There have been a number of well-funded think tanks, centers, and institutes that studied, collected, and analyzed information on school and youth violence, only to be eliminated or dramatically downsized a few years down the road when budgets got tight; of course, many of these efforts were politically driven or politically funded, and tended to be limited in scope and usefulness to educators on the front lines anyway. Although there are dozens of theories on the causes of school violence and hundreds, if not thousands, of different violence prevention programs claiming to be the answer to school and youth violence, the reality is that we do not know even how many crimes are committed in schools each year because our data collection mechanisms are inadequate and school-based crimes are under-reported on a national level.

To stay current, I follow national news stories about school safety through a variety of traditional and new technology sources, in addition to working in the field with those on the front lines. The average educator and administrator in our workshops turns out to be shocked when we show him or her the cases of violent incidents taking place across the nation on an ongoing basis that do not make their local news. Although I do not believe that school violence should dominate the headlines each day, I do believe that educators need to recognize that, in terms of security and crisis preparedness, they should pay attention not just to the higher profile incidents, but also recognize there are many incidents going on in schools every day that they never hear about.

BUYER BEWARE: OVERNIGHT EXPERTS, GURUS, AND GADGETS

One of the foremost lessons learned from the school violence tragedies has been that educators must be prepared for the attack of the overnight experts, charlatans, and product-pushers who emerge after a crisis or crises to exploit these incidents and the resulting state of fear for personal or business gain. Following the series of school violence incidents in the late 1990s, everyone from academicians to politicians—and even former magicians—began spouting their theories and solutions for improving school safety. Likewise, an extraordinary number of security equipment and other vendors began popping out of the woodwork in an effort to get their products into the school marketplace, regardless of whether it was designed or tailored to fit there.

Overnight Experts and Charlatans Abound

In the months following the first series of school shootings, and particularly in those months following the tragedy at Columbine High School in April of 1999, my office was flooded with calls, letters, faxes, and e-mail messages from individuals looking to change careers, enter the consulting field, or sell products and services to educators to prevent such violent incidents from occurring in their schools. Here is a sample of some of the contacts we received, along with those we reviewed from various other sources.

- A former federal law enforcement agent wanted to buy all of my slides and videos so that he would go out to schools the following month to sell his services as a school security expert.

- Two military security specialists, one whose expertise included "special weapons site security" and the other whose expertise included being, as he put it, a "qualified expert with pistol, shotgun, and rifle," submitted unsolicited resumes because they wanted to be hired as school security expert consultants.

- Numerous educators and former educators, including a retired school personnel director and former principal, a current elementary school principal, a high school athletic coach, a former superintendent of a private school, and several educators advertising themselves as former law enforcement officers (although they had been law enforcement officers for only a few years and then spent several dozen years in education), were promoting themselves as school safety experts.

- A number of potential investors sought to contribute funds to our company, even though we are a private firm and do not offer stock.

- Several academicians and researchers who, although their backgrounds had never included issues related to school security, now wanted to collaborate to seek funds for studying school violence prevention, security measures, and related issues.

- Dozens of current and former local and state law enforcement officers who had never worked in schools or with kids as a primary part of their law enforcement jobs, decided that their expertise in school safety offered more options for better income than did performing security functions off-duty at football games, basketball games, dances, or other security guard part-time jobs, and began consulting as school security specialists almost overnight. One contacted our office five times, pleading for me to teach him how to enter the school security consulting business because, as he said, "There is enough work out there for all of us to make a buck."

- School security experts whose backgrounds prior to the time of the shootings included being bodyguards, private detectives, drug counselors, security guard providers, insurance adjusters, magicians, and numerous other unrelated professions contacted us.

- Computer programmers offered new software designed to analyze student writing assignments to identify violent kids, develop threat assessment profiles by answering a series of questions, conduct risk assessments of schools, track school crime, and develop school crisis plans.

- A corporate conference planner sought to shift to a new career putting on school safety programs across the nation.

- A former federal law enforcement agent whose expertise prior to retirement included scientific laboratory operations, white-collar crimes, and international drug cartels sent us an unsolicited resume. He wanted to discuss "how [his] experience would be of benefit" to our company in providing school security services.

- A group of former law enforcement officials, in addition to providing investigative services, threat assessments, and workplace violence prevention training, now offered school violence training to decrease serious behavioral incidents and increase student attendance and success rates.

- Dozens of security product vendors offered everything from ID cards to locks, fiber optics, surveillance cameras, digital imaging, Web-based information services, safety newsletters and publications, and every other product one could possibly imagine.

- Security consultants with backgrounds in providing services or consultation to utility companies, government agencies, embassies, private corporations, and other institutions unrelated to K–12 schools, became *school* security consultants almost overnight.

And the list goes on. As school shootings occur subsequent to Columbine, the same type of contacts continue to surface.

Although there are a number of experienced, educated, and qualified school security consultants across the nation, it is clear that there is also a significant number of individuals and companies who attempted to capitalize, in one way or another, on the tragedies and losses experienced at numerous schools across our nation. The majority of these individuals have little or no history of ongoing education in or experience with the field of school safety. Nevertheless, a number of schools hired such individuals or purchased such products, failing to realize that the costs of hiring a poorly selected, unqualified consultant, or of purchasing products for the sake of doing something will likely increase the very risks and liability that they were hoping to reduce.

Lessons Learned About Experts

A number of important lessons can be learned from these and other examples of overnight experts:

- *Law enforcement or security experience alone does not automatically equate to school security expertise.* An individual may have an outstanding career in law enforcement, but this does not immediately make him or her a school security expert. Unique differences exist between the law enforcement and security communities, and also unique differences exist between security in K–12 schools and security in other environments, such as military security, utility companies, or private industry. It is difficult to understand why some educators will accept individuals with no experience in working with children, schools, or K–12 school security as school security experts. School officials should not allow impressive titles and careers in other fields alone to command respect as a school security specialist.

- *School administrators must learn to check for borderline backgrounds and misleading qualifications.* They need to examine the backgrounds of so-called school security experts to see whether they actually have experience in school-specific environments, in security-specific capacities, and in working with youths and schools. Unfortunately, there are individuals, ranging from former law enforcement officers to former educators, claiming school security expertise without ever having had responsibilities for school safety issues. Simply because someone is a former or current school administrator does not automatically qualify him or her as a school safety expert. Just because someone has a college degree does not mean that the person is automatically qualified to be a teacher or a school principal. Why then would it be assumed that someone with a degree and some type of position working in a school is automatically qualified to be a security professional?

- *Administrators also need to check credentials.* School officials must be cautious about vague comments intended to mislead them to believe that a person has more qualifications than he or she actually does. For example, the phrases "attended XYZ University" or "has a degree from XYZ University" are vague. Did the person *graduate* from XYZ University? Is the degree a two-year degree or a PhD? School officials should approach these people and organizations with caution: If someone would misrepresent himself or her organization before being hired, what would they do once a contract is signed?

- *We must learn to scrutinize the academic answers to security problems.* Some academicians, unfortunately, have shifted their research or academic interests to fit the hot issues of the times—and to follow the money. Individuals who have had no previous interest or experience in school safety issues are now professing near overnight expertise in this area, including some who have remotely studied youth issues in other arenas and are now attempting to apply their backgrounds to school security.

Some have never worked in K–12 schools, and most have never focused on school security and crisis preparedness as their full-time career. Simply because some claim that they have studied it or written an article about it does not mean that they are immediately qualified to be school security and crisis preparedness experts. Make sure that their experience reflects an understanding of K–12 school-specific security issues and needs.

• *Experience should also have taught us to be skeptical of many product vendors.* Many sincere security vendors exist who want to work with schools to create or adapt technology to the school environment for the purpose of improving school safety. However, many vendors also exist who are more concerned about breaking into the school market—and into the school budgets—with the sole purpose of making more money. School officials should scrutinize trainers and consultants to make sure that they do not misrepresent their qualifications, experience, abilities, and knowledge of school security and crisis preparedness for the purpose of selling products to their schools.

• *Administrators also need to check the credibility, track record, experience, and references of the company and staff, specifically in the K–12 school security field.* Officials should investigate the nature of organizations providing school security and crisis preparedness resources, and should not let fancy names or titles mislead them. Is the nonprofit or research organization simply a cover for a personal consulting business? Are consultants using these titles and organizational classification in a misleading effort to enhance their credibility and convince potential clients that they are something that they are not? Are individuals associated with such legitimate organizations using it as a backdrop for their personal consulting? Are they really experts in a different area who are now adding school security to their list of alleged qualifications? These questions will help school officials make sure that companies offering school security services are truly specialized experts in this field and that slick names are not really an effort to create an appearance of enhanced legitimacy and professional interest for what is, in essence, a consulting business. A truly competent, professional consulting business should be able and willing to identify itself up front. Real school security and crisis preparedness specialists should have school-specific security and crisis preparedness experience as well as school-specific services to offer.

Critical Questions in Hiring a School Security Consultant

Answers to these and related questions should provide school officials with a better awareness of the potential capabilities and motives of consultants seeking to do business with their districts. Of course, references and backgrounds should always be thoroughly checked before hiring any consultant.

- Was the consultant in business to provide school security-specific services on a regular, ongoing basis before high-profile school violence tragedies?
- Is the consultant affiliated with a product?
- Does the consultant have a long-term history of working firsthand with violent and delinquent children? In particular, was this a position of full-time responsibility for school security and crisis issues in K–12 school settings? Is the consultant now twisting work experience in a remotely related area into a proclaimed expertise in school security?
- Is this the consultant's primary, full-time employment, or is this a part-time income, postretirement job or new market expansion by a company whose primary expertise is in other areas?
- Does the consultant's perspective come primarily from an academic or theoretical perspective, or has he or she worked in K–12 schools— and worked specifically with violent youth and school safety issues?
- Is your school district being used as a guinea pig so that the consultant can build a client list of school districts? (Is this perhaps why some experts are offering their school safety expertise and services for free?)
- Does the consultant and his or her company have a well-established, long-term reputation? Do their peers in the school safety field recognize them, and are they recognized as being independent, credible, and on the cutting edge in the field?
- Does the consulting firm have a history primarily in a peripherally related area of service, such as in providing security guards or private detective investigations, military security, or law enforcement, or is it in K–12 school security?
- Is the consultant or his or her firm hiding behind titles like *nonprofit organization* or *research foundation,* or other institutional or organizational names when, in essence, they are primarily for-profit consultants?
- Is the consulting firm a larger, more generalized company seeking to *widgetize* the school security industry by packaging and mass-producing generic, canned programs and services for sale to many schools for the purpose of broadening their income base?

These and other questions can help educators dig a little deeper beyond self-promotional marketing materials and claims by prospective school safety consultants.

13 Emergency Preparedness Planning and Preparation

No person can perfectly script every possible crisis, but having no guidelines at all in today's education world could legitimately be considered as negligence. The key rests somewhere between doing nothing and *paralysis by analysis.*

So where do we start? Where do we stop? These are two common questions about the emergency planning process. Giving recommendations for where to start is not too difficult depending on where the people asking the question actually are in the process. Knowing when enough is enough, however, is the more difficult task.

This chapter offers a starting point to beginners and a refresher to the veteran crisis planner. In both cases, crisis planners will need to ask a number of questions when developing their guidelines. No book or expert can answer all of these questions without being familiar with the individual school or school district.

One note: The words *emergency* and *crisis* are used interchangeably and fairly loosely in the education community. In the broader field of emergency management, we hear the phrase *emergency planning* more than *crisis planning.* My colleague and school safety consultant, Chuck Hibbert, distinguishes the two by referring to *crisis* more as the aftermath, such as mental health recovery, after an *emergency.* Given the interchangeability in the education field, readers should anticipate some interchangeability of the words here in this book, too. It is simply a curse of more than 25 years in the school safety profession.

FOUR PHASES OF EMERGENCY MANAGEMENT

In introducing Part III of this book, I highlighted the U.S. Department of Education's (2010b) four phases of emergency management for its Readiness and Emergency Management for Schools (REMS) program:

1. **Prevention-Mitigation**: Identifying all potential hazards and vulnerabilities and reducing the potential damage they can cause;

2. **Preparedness**: Collaborating with community partners to develop plans and protocols to prepare for the possibility that the identified hazards, vulnerabilities, or emergencies will occur;

3. **Response**: Working closely with first-responders and community partners to effectively contain and resolve an emergency in, or around, a school or campus; and

4. **Recovery**: Teaming with community partners to assist students and staff in the healing process, and restore a healthy and safe learning environment following an emergency event.

The 2010 REMS grants also had several "absolute priorities" the federal government views as important in school emergency planning:

- Projects designed to develop and enhance local emergency management capacity. Projects must include training for school personnel in emergency management, procedures, plans for communicating school emergency management policies and reunification procedures for parents and guardians, and coordination with community partners.
- Coordination of plans with state or local homeland security plan.
- Develop an infectious disease plan.
- Develop a food defense plan.
- Agree to develop plans that take into consideration the communication, medical, and evacuation needs of individuals with disabilities within the schools.
- Implement the grant consistent with National Incident Management System (NIMS).

Many schools are developing Continuity of Operations Plans (COOP) to lay out how the school system would operate in the event of an emergency situation prohibiting or significantly disrupting normal use of facilities. These are certainly best practices and should be considerations in local school emergency planning processes.

In working with school districts across the nation on implementing REMS grants, I periodically find individuals who get so bogged down with the four-phase model and lingo that they miss the bigger point of focusing on the tasks that fall within the model.

But a model is just that: One model. This is a framework put forth by the Education Department for its REMS grantees, not a federal mandated law which all schools must follow. Most schools are already doing things that fall into these categories. School leaders should understand the concept of the framework but focus on the tasks that define what these concepts really mean in practice.

NORMALIZATION NONSENSE

A number of academicians, educators, and others have claimed that the presence of security and related emergency preparedness measures normalize violence, imply that violence is expected, or actually increase the level of fear by sending the message that kids are vulnerable to violence because of their presence. Although this might sound logical in theory, it lacks practicality and common sense when used to justify not having reasonable security and emergency preparedness measures in and around our schools.

Using this same line of thought, it could then be considered logical and acceptable to do the following:

- Stop conducting fire drills because they increase the fear that a fire may occur.
- Eliminate law enforcement personnel from our society because their presence might send a message that violence is to be expected.
- Remove security personnel, metal detectors, and X-ray machines from airports so that we do not communicate our fear and distrust to terrorists and bombers.
- Leave the doors and windows to our homes open when we are not present so that we do not communicate to burglars that we expect someone might break into our homes, steal our valuables, or harm us upon our return.

These thoughts are, of course, as ludicrous as the suggestion that school security and emergency preparedness measures, police presence and collaboration with schools, and related measures contribute to school violence.

Unfortunately, this type of Ivory Tower theory received an excessive amount of coverage in the media in the months after Columbine, and from time to time resurfaces in debates on school safety issues. This problem is further exacerbated by the absence of substantial research on school security and emergency preparedness measures. One can only assume that individuals who subscribe to this type of thinking, and who in turn advocate not having professional security and emergency preparedness programs, must have experienced unprofessional security programs, must never been victims of crime, or are so far removed from reality that their ability to influence school or public policy should be closely scrutinized.

A reasonable number of security and emergency preparedness measures are necessary to reduce the risks posed by security threats and to minimize losses that may occur in managing crises. Testing emergency guidelines is necessary to ensure that the guidelines do not just look good on paper, but that they also work. Security guidelines and measures also reflect reality, making everyone aware of what needs to be done in the event of a crisis situation.

School officials should, however, consciously balance the need to reduce risks and prepare for crises with the need to avoid creating fear or panic. The most effective way to do so is for school officials to communicate clearly the rationale for conducting such exercises to students, staff, and parents, and to plan actual exercises that are carefully thought out from both an operational and legal perspective. When properly informed, these individuals typically understand why the activities are taking place and, more important, appreciate that school and safety officials are taking steps to reduce risks and to prepare for successfully managing a crisis incident, should one occur.

Lockdown drills, for example, have falsely been equated to prison lockdowns by some individuals. Although lockdown procedures have grown tremendously as a result of the attention to high-profile school shootings, a number of reasons exist as to why a school official may want to have students and staff quickly cleared from the hallways and relocated to more secure areas of the school, including a number of reasons that have nothing to do with crimes. For example, a loose hostile animal biting children in the school's hallway might be a very good reason for calling a lockdown throughout the school.

The bottom line on both sides of this issue is common sense. Schools should not resemble prisons, nor should students be treated like prisoners. The adults running schools, however, also have a responsibility to take reasonable steps to protect students and staff and to prepare to manage effectively those security violations and crisis incidents that may not be preventable.

THE PROCESS

The emergency preparedness planning process should include at least 10 basic steps:

1. Appoint a district-level crisis team and building-level crisis team.

2. Determine realistic goals and objectives for the crisis teams.

3. Research guidelines and resources for developing crisis guidelines that are in place in other schools.

4. Review and, if necessary, modify existing school policies, and recommend new policies, if appropriate.

5. Identify resources within the individual school, at the district level, and within the community, and consider the following questions:

    o   What is the source and level of response to be anticipated from local emergency service personnel, such as police, fire, and medical? What type of equipment and resources will these agencies have available? Will a serious incident, such as a bomb threat or suspicious device, hazardous material exposure, or other crisis, require emergency service expertise from outside of the regular departments, and, if so, how long do we wait and what should we do (or not do) while waiting?

    o   If counselors, psychologists, and other mental health professionals are needed, can they be drawn from other schools within the district, and, if so, how? Will they need to come from other districts or community agencies? If yes, what is the mobilization process, and is it documented? If school buses are needed from other districts, are mutual aid agreements in place?

    o   What communications capabilities exist or do not exist? In addition to telephones, are there adequate numbers of two-way radio units, and who has them? Do they function in all, or just some, areas of the school and surrounding campus? Are multiagency communications systems compatible with one another? What are the limitations of the phone communications system in the general school area or elsewhere? What, if any, alternative communications plan exists? How can technology be effectively utilized to manage communications concerns?

6. Conduct, or have a qualified professional conduct, a school security assessment, and review and reevaluate plans at least annually.

7. Develop crisis guidelines in a two-directional manner to ensure that guidelines are not simply issued in a top-down fashion without the input and ownership of the building staff and that individual building teams are not putting together different sets of guidelines.

8. Have the final draft versions of the crisis guidelines reviewed by key stakeholders in the process within and outside of the district, including emergency service providers and school attorneys.

9. Test and revise the guidelines, and train all staff on them.

10. Understand the role of the emergency preparedness guidelines in relation to the broader, more comprehensive school safety plan, and make planning for both an ongoing process within the school community.

Staying focused and keeping the steps in the process to a manageable number will help school officials develop worthwhile guidelines without falling into paralysis by analysis.

Crisis Team Levels and Composition

District-level crisis teams should coordinate central office support with the building crisis team staff, and crisis teams at the building level should focus on directly managing students, staff, parents, and others with whom they are the most familiar. Certainly the work of the two teams will overlap, but building-level school staff are typically more familiar with the individuals directly affected by the crisis incident as well as with the physical school plant itself; they will, therefore, be better positioned to interact effectively with those directly involved in the crisis. District-level staff typically are in a better position quickly to mobilize additional resources, such as transportation, counselors and personnel from other district schools, community-based resources, media liaison officials, and other support services to assist building-level crisis officials in restoring order and crisis recovery efforts.

Crisis team members at the building level should include the following:

- The principal, assistant principals, or deans.
- School resource officers and security personnel or campus supervisors.
- Counselors, social workers, and psychologists.
- Custodians.
- Secretaries.
- School nurses.
- The food services manager.
- Key teachers.
- A parent representative.
- A student representative.
- Others identified by crisis team members as playing key roles in crisis management.

District-level crisis team members should include the following:

- A representative of the school board.
- The superintendent and assistant superintendent(s).

- The district safety and security director.
- The business manager.
- The transportation director.
- The food services director.
- The communications director or media spokesperson.
- Maintenance or physical plant supervisors.
- Counseling and psychological support service supervisors.
- The supervisor of discipline and related support services.
- The school attorney and other key district-level support personnel who would provide critical support to schools during a crisis.

Although both teams should interact with emergency service personnel and other key agencies and individuals in the broader community, the district-level crisis team should take a lead in formulating formal and informal relationships with those community members outside of the school district who would play an important role in crisis prevention and management. Such organizations might include the following:

- The police.
- The fire department.
- Emergency medical services.
- Hazardous materials crews.
- City, county, or state emergency management agencies.
- Public health agencies.
- Mental health and social service agencies.
- Criminal justice professionals (e.g., court, probation, and parole officers).
- The clergy.
- The media.
- Elected officials.
- Members of the business community.
- Other community leaders.

The key is for district crisis team members to take the lead in formalizing relationships with individuals and agencies in the larger community who will interact with school officials in a crisis situation.

Team Member Characteristics

Community and school district size, available resources, and individual personalities will all play a role in determining the characteristics of your crisis team membership. Desired characteristics of crisis team members include the following:

- Strong verbal and written communication abilities.
- The ability to remain calm, confident, deliberate, and focused.
- The ability and authority to make logical decisions under stress.
- A willingness and ability to take directions, to work as a team, and also to work independently when necessary.
- Flexibility, adaptability, and the ability to go with the flow.
- Being task oriented, but with ability to empathize and be people oriented as well.
- Firmness, fairness, and consistency in dealing with others.

Crisis team leaders should be familiar with the team members, their strengths and weaknesses, and the best possible match between members and team roles whenever possible.

EMERGENCY GUIDELINE DOCUMENTS

Once the parameters of the emergency preparedness process have been identified and the crisis team members have been selected, the next questions tend to be, "What should the final product of the process include?" and "How should it look when it is completed?"

Begin With a Board Policy

School board leaders should establish a policy requiring that their districts establish emergency guidelines for themselves and their individual buildings. The policy should include the following:

- A position statement demonstrating that the need to be proactive on safety and emergency preparedness issues is recognized by school leaders.
- A direction to district administrators to implement a comprehensive school safety plan that includes security and emergency preparedness, prevention and intervention, mental health, firm and fair discipline, school climate, and other related school safety components.

School board members may wish to research the policies of neighboring districts and those on file with their state and national professional associations when developing the parameters of their own policy. Exploring what other districts in the area are doing can be helpful for any unique issues being addressed in the region. Furthermore, all policies should be reviewed by school district legal counsel before implementation.

Plagiarism Versus Modified Borrowing

Educators are notorious for *borrowing* materials and ideas from other school districts on a variety of matters. Providing that appropriate credit is given and that plagiarism does not occur, there is nothing wrong with one school adapting the lessons learned from other schools to their particular school or district. The key, however, is to have the borrowed information or materials *modified and adapted* to the school or district doing the borrowing.

Pressures and time constraints for having emergency guidelines in school districts has, unfortunately, led some school officials simply to take documents from one district, change the names on the document, and then disseminate it as their own emergency guidelines document. This effort to have a product simply for the sake of having a product is exceptionally dangerous because it has not been adapted to fit the borrowing school or district and because it lacks ownership by that group's members. It also represents a potentially increased liability to borrowing school officials should they be legally challenged as to the source of their plan, how it was developed, and related issues.

Plans or Guidelines? A Lesson Plan for Crises

Many educators struggle to understand exactly what an emergency plan or guideline actually is meant to be. The best way for educators to conceptualize emergency guidelines is to view them as they do their classroom lesson plans.

The purpose of a lesson plan is to provide some guidance and direction for the teacher to follow in managing the instructional session. Lesson plans typically identify goals and objectives, and then build a guiding framework for the teacher to follow in getting to the desired end result of the lesson. Most experienced teachers use lesson plans as guides rather than as rigid scripts to be followed without flexibility or adaptation. In short, although they are called *plans,* they are really guidelines used to move progressively through a process to reach a desired outcome. (Perhaps the name should be changed to lesson *guidelines?*)

My colleague and school safety consultant, Chuck Hibbert, has long pointed out that while possibly a minor, trivial difference in the eyes of some, a closer look at the term *guidelines* suggests something different from plans. Although the term *plan* suggests a very concrete, rigid, and sequential step-by-step process, guidelines are as follows:

- Structured, yet flexible.
- Guiding, but less scripted.
- Adaptable to allow effective management of the changing and unpredictable flow of a crisis.

Real-life crisis situations cannot be scripted down to the last detail, and, for emergency guidelines to be effective, they must allow crisis responders to exercise some level of adaptability, flexibility, and movement as the crisis unfolds, just as a teacher does with lesson plans.

This distinction of conceptualization and verbiage is not only important in emergency preparedness process and final product, but it could also very well play a role in litigation if a district is challenged on its emergency preparedness and response. It would seem much more reasonable to indicate that the end product produced by crisis teams should be viewed as guidelines, with room for adaptability and flexibility, rather than as rigid procedural plans that must be followed to the letter regardless of the circumstances.

The Document Format

The last thing most people will do in the middle of a crisis is read a 300-page manual to tell them what to do in a crisis! Yet, ironically, we have seen a number of emergency guideline documents that are inches (if not more than a foot) thick.

Although a more detailed manual might be appropriate for top central office administrators and perhaps the building principal's reference, documents for building administrators, teachers, and support staff should be simple, accessible, clear, and direct. A multilayered flip chart with bulleted steps or checklists seems to be the most practical format for use by those on the front lines of the crisis. The importance of keeping it simple, direct, and accessible to those who need it cannot be overstated.

Defining a School Crisis

As I have been advised by a number of superintendents and board members, what may be a crisis for one person might not necessarily be a crisis to another in day-to-day operations. In a crisis, however, it is important for everyone to be on the same page in terms of defining what is and is not a crisis. A common definition should therefore be established by the crisis team.

A school crisis may be defined as

an incident occurring at a location under school control or in the community that negatively affects a large number of students, staff, and/or other members of the school community.

This is only one example, however, and whether a definition is appropriate ultimately depends on whether or not it is agreed upon and recognized as such by crisis team members and those who are being served by the crisis guidelines (i.e., students, staff).

206 ● Readiness and Emergency Management for Schools

Establishing Crisis Criteria

To help make any crisis definition operational, school officials may wish to elaborate on the definition by establishing criteria that must be present for an incident to be considered a crisis. These might include incidents that

- are life threatening;
- pose a threat to the health, safety, and welfare of students, staff, and community;
- create, or have the potential to create, a severe disruption to or interruption of the education process or normal school operations;
- might not appear to be a crisis, but that are judged, based on past experiences or circumstances unique to the school or community, to have a potential to create crisis conditions.

A general understanding of the crisis definition and its criteria is critical to ensuring a timely response. It is also very wise to work with public safety officials on the definition as well so that all players within the community are on the same page from the onset of emergency preparedness planning.

Crisis Levels

Different types of crisis situations warrant different levels of response. Crisis team members may wish to distinguish the differences among types of crisis situations by their potential severity and corresponding responses. For example, school officials could create a three-tiered system:

1. *Level One.* Crisis situations that pose a minor disruption to school operations or pose a lower-level threat to student and staff safety but are outside of daily disciplinary issues and require prompt attention. Level One situations typically would be handled by officials within the school.

2. *Level Two.* Crisis situations that pose a moderate disruption to school operations or pose a moderate threat to student and staff safety. Level Two situations would require limited assistance from outside of the school.

3. *Level Three.* Crisis situations that pose a serious disruption to school operations or pose a serious threat to student and staff safety. Level Three situations would require a large amount of support from elsewhere within the school district and from the outside community.

These three levels are very generic examples. Crisis team members interested in applying a multilevel system for classifying crisis situations should spend some time discussing the various types of "What if?" situations and the types of responses to these situations when defining the various crisis levels for their guidelines.

Minimum Emergency Guideline Components

How far is far enough in terms of what to include in emergency documents? How do you avoid a 300-page emergency document when there are so many possibilities that could be included in the guidelines? These are typically the first questions on the minds of most school administrators and crisis team members who take on the task of developing an emergency guideline document.

A number of crisis guidelines that I have reviewed over the years have focused either on the mental health crisis perspective (e.g., on providing counselors and psychologists dealing with deaths, suicide threats) or on the criminal perspective (e.g., on dealing with shootings, hostage situations). Others have focused largely on dealing with the media or have listed more background information on policies, procedures, or preventative programs as their crisis guidelines. Fewer schools have had a comprehensive, yet clear and concise, guideline document that covers emergency response procedures clearly without adding up to an extremely large end product.

First, school officials should distinguish their emergency guidelines from documents listing their policies, procedures, and prevention and intervention programs. These areas are all important components of the overall school safety plan, but they are not something that will need to be read by people on the front lines in the middle of the crisis incident.

Emergency guideline documents should include the following four basic sections and the various subcategories that may develop under each:

1. A bullet-style list of guidelines for "What if?" situations (see later sections in this chapter), along with evacuation and lockdown guidelines, staging area information, and associated response-related materials.

2. Relevant information on the expected roles and responsibilities for specific staff positions or individuals on the crisis team.

Two areas that are important but should stand separately from the immediate-response oriented documents but still be readily accessible include the following:

3. Counseling, healing, and related mental health support guidelines.

4. Crisis communications guidelines (internal and external) and related resource listings, such as individual names, agencies, phone numbers, and other contact information used in follow-up (not direct response) activities.

It is difficult to keep the amount of information under each of these sections as focused and concise as possible, but these categories should provide crisis team members with some reasonable parameters for feeling comfortable that they have covered the critical areas needed in the emergency guidelines without overkill.

"What If?" Situations

Addressing "What if?" situations simply means playing out a particular scenario or type of crisis incident: What if there is a bus accident and we have a large number of students injured? What if there is a shooting in the cafeteria? What if we have a hostage situation?

By walking through a tabletop or other discussion-like types of "What if?" situations and creating bullet-style lists of things that would need to be done, crisis team members can develop some practical, realistic steps to be included in their emergency guidelines. This need not be an extremely long process; in fact, I demonstrate how easily and effectively this can be done in our crisis workshops by tossing out a pre-established "What if?" scenario to crisis team members and having them report their steps back to the larger group in less than 10 minutes. Participants are often amazed at how much they were able to list in such a short time, illustrating the point that although the emergency preparedness process requires more time and effort than it does money and equipment, a rather comprehensive list of things to do can be developed in a relatively short period of time.

There are two keys to success in this process, however:

1. Have the right players at the table so that all of the different perspectives are represented and have input. The teacher's perspective on what will need to be done is typically different from that of the principal, which is also different from the secretary's perspective or the superintendent's, and so on.

2. Use common sense to know when to draw the line in the "What if?" process. I have watched people play out "What if?" scenarios to the extreme. For example, in one scenario involving a bomb threat evacuation, team

members appropriately played out the scenario to ensure that they moved children not only out of the building where a suspicious device had been found, but also away from cars in the parking lot to an adjacent open school field in case additional bomb devices had been planted in the cars. This demonstrated a good level of thinking things out, but then the group got carried away with other "What if?" possibilities: What if there are snipers on the hills around the schools? What if somebody does a drive-by shooting?

Crisis team members need to be flexible, creative, and insightful enough to carry their thinking out beyond the surface of a situation. But they also need to apply common sense and, most important, to recognize the importance of limiting how far they carry out the process, because the realm of possible scenarios is endless. Those who fail to draw the line are, unfortunately, the people who tend to be pulling out their hair in this process.

Some general suggestions apply to almost all crisis situations. These should be common to most "What if?" situations and, to avoid unnecessary duplication, could be provided in crisis guideline documents under one general heading instead of being repeated in the bulleted list for every type of incident. They include the following:

- Remain as calm and composed as possible.
- Focus on protecting lives and assisting the injured as opposed to protecting school property or personal belongings.
- Give clear, short, specific, and direct verbal commands, and, if appropriate, reinforce them with simple and understandable hand commands when directing students and others in a crisis.
- Know how to report situations: that is, to provide information on *where, what, who, when,* and *how* when reporting concerns to or seeking assistance from outside agencies or internally to other school officials.
- Once an incident is over and your immediate recovery needs have been met, document your observations and actions in a timely and thorough manner.

Noncriminal "What If?" Situations

School officials have generally done a good job in preparing for noncriminal "What if?" situations, such as fires, weather and natural disasters, or unanticipated deaths of students or staff. In developing school emergency guidelines, the noncriminal "What if?" situations covered could include the following:

- Accidents with a large number of injuries, such as a school bus accident, airplane crash, or other mass catastrophe.
- Death, serious illness, or other medical situations involving students or staff.
- Environmental issues, such as hazardous materials release, chemical spills, or toxic waste.
- Fire or explosions (such as a boiler explosion).
- Utility-related situations, such as a gas leak or a power or water outage.
- Student or adult demonstrations or protests (note, however, that these could translate into criminal situations).
- Weather-related situations, such as a tornado, a severe storm, floods, hurricanes, earthquakes, or other area-specific possibilities.

Criminal "What If?" Situations

Schools historically did not included a substantial number of situations in their emergency guidelines related to violence or criminal activity, although many more have since the spate of school shootings in the late 1990s to mid-2000s. Situations that could be included in this section include the following:

- Abductions, such as kidnapping and abductions of children by a noncustodial parent.
- Altercations or riots, including large-scale fights, racially motivated conflicts, and gang-related disruptions.
- Bomb threats and suspicious devices.
- Larger scale drug-related incidents.
- Gunfire in the school or on school grounds.
- Hostage situations.
- Terroristic threats, including anthrax scares.
- Trespassers, suspicious persons, or other "intruders."
- Weapons possession, threats, and use.
- Violations of other laws and ordinances.

Unique conditions in individual schools and communities may very well warrant the expansion of both the noncriminal and criminal "What if?" categories. These lists are included here as a starting point, not as a panacea.

The key part of this type of planning is to identify common issues and responses needed across various types of emergencies. These might include lockdowns, evacuations, communications logistics, a need for staging areas for parents and media, parent-student reunification, and so on. The type of emergency may vary, but often these and other underlying responses will be engaged in a number of specific types of emergency situations.

Going through "What if?" situations as a part of emergency preparedness planning, coupled with adequate in-service training, can help educators reduce their fear of the unknown and prepare to better manage incidents of crime and violence for which they otherwise would not received training. For example, in a hostage situation, it is generally advisable to remain calm and avoid being agitated; to be patient and allow time to pass without losing confidence in the police negotiators; to keep distance from the hostage-taker and avoid aggressive or threatening body movements; and consciously to remember that, as a hostage, educators are no longer authority figures. Knowing a few basic tips and what to expect from law enforcement response units in a hostage situation can prevent educators from unintentionally escalating, instead of a deescalating, of a life-threatening situation.

Evacuations and Lockdown Procedures

Depending on the nature of the crisis, school officials may have to evacuate the building, lock down the building, or do both simultaneously. For example, evacuations may be necessary in a fire situation, bomb threat, or location of a suspicious device, whereas a lockdown may be needed during situations with intruders, hostages, gunfire, or similar circumstances. Evacuations and lockdowns may need to occur at the same time if a crisis situation requires students and staff in one area of the school to remain there while others, located elsewhere, are ordered to exit the building.

Evacuations and Alternative Sites

Schools have generally done good jobs with evacuations for fire drills, and, depending on the situation, the same general procedure may be appropriate for other situations. In some cases, however, it may not be adequate. For example, evacuation to a parking lot area may work fine in a fire drill, but in a bomb scare school officials may prefer to locate students in an adjacent open field so that they are away from vehicles in the event that someone placed a bomb in one or more of the cars.

An alternative evacuation site should be established for every school district building. In ideal situations, these sites would be places near the school, such as a church, community center, business facility, or other adequately sized location to which students and staff could simply walk from the school. In many cases, however, this is not possible, so school officials will also have to include plans for quickly mobilizing school district transportation in crisis situations to get students and staff to the alternative site if it is impractical or impossible to release kids directly from the school. (If students can logistically be released, accounting for all of these students, whose custody they are released to, and how this is verified and approved all remain as major planning issues.)

In some areas, it may be most practical for school transportation buses to be the initial holding site for students upon evacuation. This may especially be true in areas experiencing adverse weather conditions (e.g., freezing temperatures, snowstorms, or heavy rain) during the time of the crisis incident. Advance planning with school transportation directors is critical so that building administrators have reasonable expectation of response times for buses during school hours when bus drivers are typically not working en mass, such as midday.

School officials may also wish to establish a secondary alternative site in the event that the first alternative site is unavailable or if the first alternative site is also the scene of a crisis situation. If at all possible, both primary and secondary alternative evacuation sites should *not* be other schools, because the evacuation of children and staff from one school to another could cause increased risks for disruptions, along with a possible transfer of psychological trauma, to the students and staff of the alternative site. Unfortunately, school officials may be unable to locate nonschool alternative sites; if required to use other schools, officials should have steps in their emergency guidelines for providing an adequate level of supervision and mental health support to everyone involved, including those students and staff at the receiving site.

School administrators should hold the first faculty meeting of each school year at their walking distance evacuation site and have faculty walk to that location for the meeting. This helps to identify who on staff can and cannot physically walk to this site—something administrators would want to know before a crisis. It also helps familiarize school staff with the design, layout, and other aspects of the evacuation site facility.

If the evacuation site is a nonschool site, school administrators should have a written letter of agreement updated annually with each hosting site. School officials may wish to request a set of keys to community facilities such as churches, where there may not be staff present at all times during the school day when school leaders may need emergency access. Student management and supervision, parent-student reunification procedures, and related logistics should be formally planned out by each school's crisis team well in advance of their needing to engage the plan.

Emergency planners should also prepare for the worst-case scenario of not being able to return immediately to their home school. This could occur as a result of damage to physical facilities, extended declaration of the school as a crime scene, or other unforeseen reasons. Plans for long-term continuity of educational services should therefore be included in school emergency planning.

Lockdown Procedures

The school shootings of the late 1990s brought new meaning to the word *lockdown* in schools. Lockdown drills were established in a number of schools in response to concerns about the need to clear students and staff quickly from the hallways and to move them to safer areas away from a potential security threat. Unfortunately, as a result of media attention and many misunderstandings, the term was perceived by many to be punitive, associated with the concept of prison lockdowns, or reminiscent of the nuclear and bomb drills practiced by many of the adults who now are working in schools or are parents of school children.

In reality, a lockdown is, in essence, a reverse fire drill. The purpose of a fire drill is to get students and staff safely out of harm's way by relocating them outside of the school. Typically, this means inside locked classrooms or other secure areas. Students and staff become proficient and efficient in doing so through practice.

Basic procedures for a typical lockdown generally include the following:

1. Turn off all lights.

2. Move as far away from the doors and windows as soon as possible.

3. Minimize physical exposure and, if appropriate, seek protective cover.

4. Remain calm and absolutely quiet.

5. Wait for an all clear from an established or credible source.

I am often asked whether windows be covered and blinds be pulled down. Typically we find law enforcement agencies prefer they be left open so police tactical response officers can see what is occurring inside. From time to time, we find some local law enforcement agencies prefer to have them covered, so we encourage all school crisis teams to consult with their local law enforcement agency that would be responding to determine their preference.

I also frequently get asked about schools using red and green cards to slide under their doorways or post in their windows to indicate to first-responders whether or not they have a secure room. Again, I suggest school leaders talk this through with their first-responders. My general feeling is that this adds an extra step in securing the classroom, could present a number of possibilities for the intended outcome not to occur, and in the long run may be less productive than helpful.

One of the most important steps is to remain calm and absolutely quiet. In one lockdown drill that I observed, the majority of classrooms followed the established procedures perfectly. In one classroom, however, the students were not taking the process seriously, and that noise—and, in turn, their physical presence—was quickly and easily detected by those of us who could have been the bad guys out in the hall. Unfortunately, the students did not take the process seriously because their teacher did not treat the drill seriously, allowing the students to carry on conversations during the drill.

Educators have a number of questions about lockdowns that are difficult, if not impossible, for another person to answer. Some questions that school officials must ask of themselves, and that only they can answer, include the following:

- Can the doors to my classroom be locked? If yes, how? Do I leave them locked all of the time? If no, then what do I do?
- What other levels of protection are available if my doors will not lock?
- What other safe places are in my immediate area in the event that I cannot get to my room?
- If I need to communicate information, can I safely get to a phone? What other options exist if no phone is available?
- If kids or someone else I know knocks on my door demanding entry for their safety after I have shut it for the lockdown, do I open the door or do I let them stay outside? What if the person knocking is really the person who poses a danger?

These and other questions will ultimately have to be answered by the individuals asking them. No consultant or expert, and especially no individual who is unfamiliar with the school, can answer these questions for someone else.

These lockdown suggestions are just that: suggestions. School officials and crisis team members should confer with their local public safety officials in developing specific lockdown guidelines, as well as evacuation and other guidelines, to ensure that the procedures they establish are consistent with local public safety expectations and recommendations, and with circumstances or conditions unique to their school and/or to their community.

Sheltering, Weather, Natural Disasters, and Other Types of Drills

Schools have numerous other drills in addition to evacuations and lockdowns. Shelter-in-Place, tornado, fire, earthquake, nuclear plant evacuations (for schools within a certain radius of such plants), and other unique drills may be required in certain schools. Some drills are relatively routine, while other school sites may face more difficulty because of building design and conditions.

We have run into a number of schools during our emergency planning consultations that, because of the design of the school, are challenged for appropriate locations to place students during tornado drills. These districts have been referred to their local emergency management agencies, Red Cross, and fire departments as local experts best versed in making sheltering recommendations. Schools in such situations should reach out to these and other community partners for their expertise and knowledge of local/regional threats and best options on a site-by-site basis for sheltering, exercising, and so on.

Drills to Teach Students to Attack Armed Intruders

At several points over the past decade, individuals have proposed teaching students to attack armed intruders. The rationale behind this argument is that lockdowns teach students to be *sitting ducks* for a mass massacre by a gunman. On the surface, this sounds logical, but the devil is in the details of implementation.

Teaching students to throw books, notebooks, pens, chairs, and other items raises many questions when considering the age-appropriateness and realistic expectations of response for students in K–12 schools. Although such an approach may have some application in a college or university setting, it is very questionable as to its applicability and practicality in K–12 settings. Many questions and concerns arise in considering such an approach, including the following:

- It is unrealistic to expect 25 students and a teacher to react simultaneously, with split-second accuracy and timing, when a person with a gun unexpectedly walks into a room. Coaches spend hours, weeks, and years working with youth to perfect athletic skills, and team dynamics often do not generate such skilled snap judgment capabilities and physical precision in non-life-and-death circumstances. We do not have a student show up to one football or basketball game practice for an hour or two, never come back to practice, and then expect them to play effectively 6 months later if we toss them into a game at a critical point. Military units work for weeks, months, and years to develop such skills. Police departments train patrol officers extensively, and SWAT officers practice intensely throughout their assignment in a SWAT unit to develop such skills and abilities. How could anyone who understands training, and especially anyone who understands child learning and behavior, believe that an hour or two presentation or video would adequately prepare students to fight armed intruders?

- It is particularly unrealistic to believe that one, two, or even several hours of instruction can adequately prepare any group of children to have the precise physical responses and split-second judgment to make the life-and-death decisions required when confronting an active shooter. Truly effective physical self-defense training requires both extensive instruction and countless hours of practice. It is highly questionable whether a lecture, with or without videos, or a one-time practical exercise would accomplish the stated goals.

- Would throwing objects incite a suspect to fire his or her gun when he or she might not otherwise do so? Would we want everyone to start throwing items and attacking an armed person, with questionable probability of success, only to trigger more anger and shootings by these typically mentally unstable persons who may not have otherwise planned on shooting everyone?

- It is simply not realistic to recommend such confrontational training for young children because of their developmental levels and related factors. If current practices are considered so inadequate for the middle and high school grades that children must be taught to throw items at and directly attack armed gunmen, what is their plan to protect children in grades Pre–K to 6? Or are the young children simply written off as sitting ducks?

- What consideration does such proposed training take into account for students with special needs (physically challenged, emotionally disturbed, autistic students, medically fragile students, students with learning disabilities, preschool and daycare center children housed in schools), and how would this factor into the proposed theory behind teaching children to throw books and attack armed gunmen?

- Has such proposed training been thoroughly reviewed and endorsed by experts in child developmental issues, child psychology, child learning theory, and related areas? (Note: To date, we have seen no endorsements nor have we heard of any from child development experts.)

- Will the school district mandate every student participate in the training? What about parents who do not approve of the training or who do not wish their child/children to participate? Will parental approval be received for each and every child to participate in the training? And what then is expected of those children who do not wish to participate in the training, whose parents do not want them to participate in the training, or who do not feel safe, comfortable, or capable of reacting in the manner taught in such programs?

- Who will instruct such programs? What is the basis for their qualifications? If they claim certifications to instruct such programs, what is the basis of the certification? Who is the authorizing/certifying agency? Is the certification merely a certificate of attendance for attending a training workshop? Are the trainers representing themselves or acting as agents for a company or a law enforcement agency? What liability insurance do they carry to protect themselves and indemnify school districts if and when lawsuits are filed in connection with such training? Are the instructors (and their agencies, such as police departments in the case of School Resource Officers or other police department training officers), prepared to absorb the potential liability for the outcome of the training they provide to school students and staff? In addition to the outside trainers, is the school board and administration prepared to accept the potential liability for approving such training?

Responses to unfolding incidents by police and adults in schools will vary based upon the facts and nature of unfolding incidents. Responsibility for taking the lead with these judgment calls should be the primary responsibility of well-trained adult professionals, not emotional, frightened children. Some cases may very well warrant fighting back, but the proposition of schools formally attempting to train students to be effective and proficient in doing is unrealistic in today's K–12 setting (Trump, 2010h).

Diversify Drills

In Chapter 8, I highlighted a number of things school leaders could do that cost more time than money as a part of their effort to manage school safety during tight budget times. Diversifying drills is one of those areas. Tweaking drills to reflect different types of scenarios, and requiring different responses, is a better use of drill time than doing the same thing over and over again.

In conducting drills, who are we *really* training? Most people agree we are training the adults even more than the students. In general, students will follow the lead of the adults who are (supposed to be) giving directions to them.

Problems arise when we have educators who have done the same drills, at the same times, and from the same locations in the buildings for their entire career working at the school. One veteran teacher, who was now in her first years as an assistant principal, recently said to me, "I spent most of my career as a teacher believing fires could only happen in my school during second period because that is the only time we ever practice fire drills." Why? Because it was convenient for the administrators and staff to do it that period.

But crises don't follow a script. They don't play by the rules of the written emergency plan that has been sitting for years on the principal's shelf. Often they occur at the worst possible time, in the worst possible location, and under the worst possible conditions (staff shortages, principal out of the building, and so on).

To be truly prepared, we have to practice for reality, not for convenience. One of the best ways to practice for reality is to diversify drills. It gives administrators and safety officials the chance to learn which adults will step up and think well on their feet, and which ones may not do so well. Oftentimes those who handle a situation well, and conversely those who do not, are not necessarily the people administrators would have expected to respond in the manner they do—something good to know ahead of time, not to find out in the middle of a real emergency.

Administrators and crisis teams can shake up the routine of fire, lockdown, and other drills in numerous ways, including the following:

- Conduct lockdown drills during nontraditional times such as lunch periods, between class changes, during student arrival, and just prior to dismissal.
- Block exits (unannounced) during fire drills to teach students and staff to think on their feet.
- Pull a couple of students out of line during fire drills to see how much time passes before someone notices they are missing, and do the same with a teacher to see who will step in for the teacher.
- Lockdown one section of your school while evacuating another area during the same drill.
- Hold your first faculty meeting of each school year at your walking distance evacuation site.
- Monitor not only the time it takes to exist a school for a fire drill, but how quickly students can be recalled into the building.
- Evacuate students onto school buses during the middle of the morning to simulate a mid-morning evacuation to a distant evacuation site.

School officials should not go over the top in diversifying drills to the point of being ridiculous or dangerous in doing so. They should, however, avoid doing the same thing over and over as real-life crises will not follow one particular script. The goal is to teach people, especially the adults responsible for managing the crisis, to be flexible and to think on their feet.

Sharing Emergency Guideline Information

School and emergency service officials should certainly have copies of school emergency guidelines. But should they also be provided to students? To parents? To the media?

School and safety officials should communicate appropriate information on safety and emergency guidelines to students, parents, and the community. However, this does not automatically equate to disseminating printed copies of the full plan. Although students, parents, and the community should know that emergency guidelines exist and should know the reason why they exist, the specific portions and details of the emergency guidelines should be issued on a need-to-know basis as they relate to the roles and expectations of the particular individuals.

For example, students should know what is expected of them in a lockdown. Parents should know what is expected of them if a crisis takes place at their school. However, it would typically be inappropriate to provide the detailed logistics and implementation of the full set of overall emergency guidelines to everyone.

Amazingly, we still see some schools post their emergency guidelines on the Internet and accessible to anyone who visits their school district website. Although a number of school districts have online emergency guidelines, these are typically in reasonably secured and protected sites with restricted access. No school emergency plan should be available online to anyone who should not have authorization for access to such information.

THE PREPARATION

Getting the crisis teams together and developing emergency guideline documents are only part of the preparation to be done for crisis situations. Emergency preparedness planning is a process, and knowledgeable planners realize that the only time that preparing for a crisis really ends is when they retire from their job! A number of preparatory tasks are listed in the following sections.

Establish Command Posts and Staging Areas

School officials, in cooperation with public safety agencies, should identify multiple sites that can serve as a command post from which crisis management could be coordinated in the event of an incident. The reason for having multiple designated sites is so that backup locations are identified in the event that the primary site is the actual scene of the crisis or otherwise inappropriate for use based on crisis circumstances. Potential sites may include the principal's conference room, a library, or, if the site needs to be outside, an athletic field office or other accessible, but safe, location.

Depending on the size and resources of the school district, it might very well be appropriate to have a mobile crisis command center. Perhaps an old school bus, mobile classroom, or delivery vehicle could be equipped with the necessary resources and equipment to serve as a mobile location site for managing a school crisis. In addition, it is wise to have a dedicated command center at the school district's headquarters, adequately equipped with such items as phones, two-way radios, and maps so that school leaders can be centrally located in one room to coordinate decisions and communications in a timely and efficient manner.

Staging areas should also be identified in advance for use by SWAT teams and other emergency service providers (including for multijurisdiction coordination); for use in medical triage, media and press conferences, mental health and related psychological services, and other functions as needed; and for use, if necessary, as command posts.

Establish a District-Level Emergency Operations Center

District-level crisis teams should create a designated emergency operations center (EOC) at which district crisis team members can assemble to coordinate their response to an emergency situation at one or more of their schools. Too often we see well-intended central office administrators and crisis team members either rush out to schools where the emergency is unfolding or given direction to building administrators by phone from their individual offices or cell phones with little to no communication with other district crisis team members. In one instance, a principal told me she had her assistant superintendent on one phone and the transportation director on another phone at the same time, and they gave conflicting information and exact opposite instructions on what steps she should take in response to the incident.

A district-level EOC allows directors and other crisis team members from critical departments to pull together in one location, share information, make joint decisions, and send consistent information to their building administrators during a crisis. Some district crisis team members, such as transportation directors, may be at an off-site location but still could be patched into the district EOC by speaker phone or webcam. Although district crisis team members may, and likely will, respond to the site at some point, there are a number of circumstances in which they may need to make communication decisions from district headquarters, and this should be done in a coordinated manner from a designated EOC when possible.

School district leaders also should have a seat at city, county, or other emergency management agency EOCs. In the event of an emergency impacting the broader community, schools need to have a representative at emergency management EOCs so they are active participants, when appropriate, in community-wide emergencies.

Create Parent-Student Reunification Sites and Procedures

Parents are one of the few groups of people who are likely to arrive on scene at a school crisis faster than the media. Parents often understandably want to remove their child from the school as quickly as possible, at least until control has been regained. Although it is important for students and staff to return to normalcy as quickly as possible, school officials may find it necessary or prudent to reunite students and parents—and, for that matter, staff and their families—as the crisis unfolds.

School and safety officials may be poised most effectively to manage a school crisis if they have a designated location away from the crisis location itself, which depending upon the situation could mean off-site at a walking distance evacuation location or other site. If a crisis is small-scale in nature, a designated location in another wing or adjacent building of the school may suffice. However, in the event of a larger scale incident or an ongoing active scenario, a location totally off-site may be much more appropriate and necessary, even though traffic flow typically becomes overwhelmingly congested and phone systems tend to overload and shut down in a major incident.

Parent-student reunification plans are one of the most undeveloped or underdeveloped aspects of school emergency planning. School officials often grossly underestimate the overwhelming aspect of parents flocking to the school and the overwhelming impact of releasing students to parents in an efficient, effective, and safe manner. A host of issues must be built into such planning including having remote access to student emergency contact and release authorization information, sign-out procedures for students, and the ability to trace back specific information on who students were released to.

School officials should include mechanisms in their crisis communications plans for directing parents to reunification sites at the first appropriate opportunity rather than delaying notifications and having parents reporting to the incident site. Emergency guidelines should include steps for sending crisis team members to the reunification sites, along with student emergency information data, student release cards, communications equipment, and other necessary items described in the emergency kits below.

Parents should be encouraged during the crisis to avoid visiting the regular school site and to avoid calling the regular school or using cell phones so that they do not tie up lines or overload communications systems.

Emergency guidelines for the parent center should involve adequate staffing, including counselors and mental health personnel, at least one school official from the crisis team with decision-making authority, and adequate staff to handle student and parent intake, phone calls, media liaison, and related functions. Because a presumably large number of individuals will be relocating from the crisis scene to this center, it will, in essence, operate much like the command site where the actual crisis is taking place. It is therefore important to have advance arrangements for use of this site and a thorough knowledge of communications capabilities (e.g., phone, fax, and e-mail) and other logistical needs.

Prepare for Medical Emergencies

Most schools are fortunate if they have one school nurse. They are especially lucky if that nurse is on-site at the same school each day of the week on a full-time basis. Relying on the school nurse to handle all medical emergencies in a crisis, particularly if there are mass injuries, is totally unrealistic.

Some steps that can be taken to prepare better for medical needs in an emergency include the following:

- Identifying school staff members interested in being trained as first-responders in a crisis situation, and providing them with at least a basic training session and necessary updates on first-aid, cardiopulmonary resuscitation, automated external defibrillators, and related medical safety techniques.
- Maintaining a list of individuals who have received first-responder training, and including a copy in the emergency guidelines.
- Ensuring that school nurses (if the school is fortunate enough to have such persons) have had training comparable to emergency-room level trauma preparation so that they are best prepared for managing a school crisis.
- Designating a location or locations on the school premises where a medical helicopter could land in the event it's needed to fly injured individuals to hospitals (although this need may exist anywhere, school officials in rural or remote areas in particular should prepare for such support because they are often far from a hospital).
- Placing first-aid kits in various locations inside and outside of the school building, as well as on each school bus, so that they are easily accessible in a crisis; ensuring that crisis team members and others on staff know where these kits are located; and perhaps including a list of these locations in the crisis guideline document.

- Creating a method for identifying individuals sent to the hospital when there are mass injuries: for example, using wristbands on which individual names can be written in indelible ink.
- Determining which hospital or hospitals would be used in the event of mass injuries, and which school representatives will go to these hospitals to identify injured students or staff in a crisis situation.
- Identifying a way for student emergency records to be accessed by authorized school officials during a crisis, and determining how these will be made available if they are needed to authorize medical treatment for a student whose parent cannot be contacted.

Assemble Critical Facility and Tactical Information

The more information that police and public safety agencies have available on the school physical plant and its operations, the better tactical advantage they will have in carrying out search, rescue, and related crisis functions. School officials and their fellow crisis team members, including public safety representatives, should consider the following suggestions:

- Provide police, fire, and other appropriate emergency service agencies with a copy of the blueprints for all schools. An important reminder: before turning over blueprints, school officials should ensure that they are up-to-date and accurate. A number of school officials have been rushing to turn over building blueprints, but have forgotten to check that the blueprints being given to public safety officials accurately reflect building layouts after years of new construction, remodeling, and other changes. Although a number of high-tech mapping products and services have been created post-Columbine, redundancy is an important consideration and having hard copies of blueprints and floor plans even when they are computerized is a wise planning step. In addition, if mapping services are contracted from vendors, and the district's mapping or emergency plans are on a vendor's server and not the district's, logistics regarding access, such as from a walking or distant evacuation site, need to be considered in the emergency planning process. School leaders using contracted mapping services need to explore ongoing costs associated with such services, the ability to regularly update facility changes, and numerous other issues.

- Invite police, fire, and other public safety agencies to the school to discuss safety concerns, and allow them to take a walk-through of the facility so that they may become familiar with it.

- Make the school building and grounds accessible at night and on weekends for police SWAT teams (and other public safety agencies) to train there and even on a school bus so that they become familiar with these environments.

• Consider requiring contractors, especially those hired for new construction where you can build this into their contracts, to produce school blueprints and other facility schematic plans on CD-ROM so that they can easily be accessed on a laptop computer.

• Number both the inside and outside of entranceways to help public service agencies easily identify and reference entry and exit points in a crisis. Make sure the numbering order (counterclockwise or clockwise starting at the main entrance as doorway #1) is consistent across the school district. Use numbers made of reflective material of at least 18 inches in size, with numbers positioned on both the inside and outside of each entranceway. Such numbering can facilitate emergency response to specific areas.

• Create a tactical resource listing of the following locations and information, and provide this information (updated yearly) to public safety agencies serving the school:

  o Power main panels and electrical closets, controls, and the like.
  o Water, gas, electric, and related utility controls and main leads, along with the names and phone numbers for the companies supplying such services.
  o Telephone control boxes.
  o Information on alarms, bells, sprinklers, and related systems.
  o Location of high-risk or critical areas within the school, such as day care centers and areas dedicated to special needs children (i.e., physically challenged, special education, and other students with special needs).
  o Information on heating, ventilation, and air-conditioning system and controls.
  o Location of security cameras and other devices.
  o Main computer circuits and operational controls.
  o Remote shut-off locations for utilities and alarms.
  o Locations of hazardous materials, flammable materials, chemistry labs and supply rooms, or similar sites.
  o Locations of elevators, false ceilings, electrical and other ducts, crawl spaces, and utility access points.
  o Location of all fire extinguishers, first-aid equipment, and other necessary supplies.
  o Emergency telephone, pager, cell phone, or other numbers for crisis team members, maintenance and other facility plant supervisors, and outside utility companies, security or other systems officials, and related contractors.

• Take still photographs of key areas within the school, such as the office area, common areas, and chemistry labs, and, if possible, do a videotaped tour of the school, including office areas, common areas, hallways and stairwells, labs, boiler rooms and custodial areas, media centers, cafeterias, gyms, and other critical areas.

• Take aerial photographs of the school, its campus, and surrounding neighborhoods, and have these blown up in size and made available for use in identifying access and evacuation routes.

• Consider establishing secured boxes immediately outside of school buildings containing access keys to the building for emergency service personnel. Also consider providing a set of school master keys (to buildings, classrooms, and lockers) to the local police department to be kept in the car of each shift's patrol commander, along with other tactical information listed in this section. A similar set of keys should be made available to the school crisis incident manager.

Identify the Locations and Needs of Special Student Populations

Crisis guidelines should include steps for making sure that the needs of special student populations are met during a crisis. These populations may include students with physical disabilities, special education students, or other unique groups, such as children in a high school day care center or preschool children at an elementary school. These students are likely to require additional support, especially during evacuations and other drills. Also keep records of staff with special needs.

Develop Systems for Accounting for Students, Staff, and Others

School officials need to develop plans for checking attendance and accounting for students, staff, substitutes, and volunteers, during a time of crisis, evacuation, or lockdown. Schools should also have the ability to generate absence lists for the day quickly. The last thing needed during a crisis is to have people attempting to track down a missing student who had never showed up at the school in the first place.

Prepare and Maintain Emergency Kits

School officials should assemble emergency kits for use in crisis situations, especially when an evacuation is required. Each crisis team member should have a kit, and additional kits could be placed in multiple strategic locations within the school and in designated areas outside of the school, such as in the trunk of the police shift commander's patrol car, at the school district's central office, and at local police and fire departments.

One school district's crisis kits had the following items: a first-aid kit, including latex gloves; a small tool kit; a box of index cards for student release; a book of floor plans to give to the incident commander; a list of staff members, including substitutes, and their emergency contacts; a large water bottle; a space blanket; crackers and juice (in case of sugar imbalance); the crisis plan; a cell phone/two-way radio, backup batteries, and a list of cell phone numbers for crisis team members; a photo ID; a vest and cap with the logo to identity them as crisis team members; and other necessary materials. Building administrators and district crisis team members have crisis kits available at all times.

All school officials should create emergency crisis kits. These kits should be located at strategic sites, such as in administrative offices, in the departments or vehicle trunks of emergency service responders, at reunification sites, and other key locations. Items to consider including are as follows:

- A list of the trained medical first-responders on staff.
- Communications equipment, including extra cell phones and backup batteries.
- A bullhorn.
- School district and emergency response telephone directories for the school and community.
- A student directory with address, telephone, and parent contract information.
- A staff directory with home and emergency contacts
- Student health and emergency records.
- Telephone numbers, including cell phone numbers, fax numbers, and e-mail information, for crisis team members, staff, and other support services.
- A list of phone trees.
- Floor plans and tactical information.
- Bus routes, numbers, and contact information.
- Yearbooks, student IDs, or other photos.
- Attendance rosters.
- Pens, markers, paper, name tags, and related materials.
- Prefabricated signs, with such messages as PARENTS, COUNSELORS, VOLUNTEERS, POLICE, MEDICAL, MEDIA, KEEP OUT, NEED HELP, and other appropriate messages.
- Flashlights, tape, tools, and related equipment.
- A laptop computer and printer, if possible (a small copy machine might also be located at reunification, alternate sites, and other locations outside of the crisis scene).

School officials can certainly add items within reason as they deem it appropriate, and it is understandable that not everyone will be able to have or to carry all of these items. Technology should be utilized, if at all possible, so that the records, photos, and other items are available on CD-ROM and can be accessed via laptop computers. (Of course, this means that backup batteries and computer supplies would be needed.)

Enhancing Communications Mechanics, Technology, and Language Barrier Planning and Preparedness

School officials should thoroughly evaluate their communications capability and, if necessary, invest in timely improvements. Questions for evaluation should include the following:

- Are there phones in classrooms or, if not, at least in each wing of the building so that teachers and staff can easily call the office or 911?
- Can school officials communicate to and from portable classroom trailers?
- Do all staff members know how to call 911 from school phones? For example, do you have to dial 9 to first get an outside line before dialing 911, or can you dial 911 direct and get an outside direct call to 911? If the phones currently require a 9 or other number to get an outside line, can the telephony system be reprogrammed to allow direct calls to 911.
- Do all school staff know the physical address of the building at which they work? (Hint: Many do not, even having taught and/or worked at the same place for a couple of decades.)
- Are there an adequate number of functional two-way radio units to allow communication among the school administrators, school security or school resource officer, secretary, custodian, and staff who take students outside for physical education class or elementary recess? Are those units and their backup batteries kept charged and accessible? Is there a districtwide two-way radio system?
- Does the school have a mass parent notification system? How does that system operate? Who is authorized to use it? How is it accessed and who has the passwords/codes? What is the reasonable expectation of the accuracy of parent contact information input into the system?
- Can a mechanism be created to allow faster and more direct communications between school and law enforcement personnel, such as through a shared two-way radio frequency?
- Are there charged bullhorns available in the event that a crisis requires crisis team members to communicate clearly and effectively with large groups of students in hallways or outside of the school?

- Are there dedicated, private phone lines available at the school that are separate from the main phone system?
- Does the phone system have caller ID or automatic return calling services to help identify incoming calls? Is there a mechanism for tracking internal calls within the district?
- What support can the telephone service provider offer in tracing bomb threats and other threatening calls?
- Are there cellular phones available at each school for use in a crisis? Are backup batteries kept charged and accessible?
- If school officials have access to computers and e-mail from school offices and classrooms, does the 911 dispatch center (or local police department) have e-mail also so that e-mail messages can be sent from individual classrooms or offices where phone communications may not be possible?
- Do crisis team members have timely and adequate access to bilingual communicators remotely and on-site?
- Does the school have internal TV broadcast abilities? Can this be remotely controlled?
- Are computer hubs within the school and/or district accessible? Are they adequately secured?
- Can the school's website be used to disseminate information to parents, community members, the media, and other interested parties?
- Do schools have broadcast fax, voice mail, and e-mail capabilities for sending mass communications in a crisis?
- Is there a voice-mail line that can be used to call in for updated information?
- Does the school system have a master record of telephone companies and account representatives for local, long distance, cellular, Internet, and other communications? If these services are not all provided by the same company, then are school officials aware of the difference in vendors?
- Is there a specific individual within the school district responsible for coordinating communications systems? Does this individual coordinate information with school safety and technology officials?
- Have school safety and public safety officials shared information on these and other communications capabilities?

A mechanism should also be established to create and maintain open phone lines from school district headquarters to school crisis sites and command posts. In other words, once a connection is made between two points, these lines should be left open, even when they are not being actively used, so that callers do not have to redial and risk encountering busy or overloaded communications lines. Charged backup batteries that provide for the extended use of cell phones, vehicle adapters, and such other items can help extend the life of cell phone batteries.

Fortunately, new technology presents us with hope for only continuing improvements in preparing for crisis situations. Digital imaging, for example, could be used to store student photos on CD-ROMs, which could then, if necessary, be used in a laptop computer to identify students at hospitals or elsewhere outside of the school environment in a crisis.

The technology and mechanics are not the only school emergency planning and preparedness aspects of communications. Language barriers can pose huge complications for effective school emergency management. I have been in school districts over the years that have had up to 100 different languages spoken by children and their families.

Some language considerations include the following:

- How many languages are spoken in your school-community? Conduct a formal assessment and maintain a list.
- Do you have staff at the building and district levels who can serve as translators? Maintain a current list at both levels.
- Incorporate language translation in your emergency response guidelines. Who will go out on scene to the site of a crisis? How will it be determined which translators may be needed? How do you get in touch with these translators, both during and after regular school hours, to dispatch them to the emergency site?
- Are your parent, student, and staff emergency planning informational brochures, website pages, and other communications translated into the appropriate languages? Do parents of non-English-speaking students not deserve the same information as English-speaking parents before, during, and after a crisis? How will your district deliver in this area?
- What type of training is needed for school crisis teams, first-responders, volunteers, and others on language issues?

These and other language and cultural concerns can have a significant impact, either positively or negatively depending upon the district's planning in this area.

Evaluate Public Safety Capabilities in Advance

Police, fire, and emergency medical personnel historically had little training related to school safety and little exposure to school settings. Trends in school violence in the late 1990s and early 2000s shifted the way tactical teams approach their need to secure areas, moving away from only setting up and securing a perimeter to actually conducting a search and rescue because of the presence of active shooters. "Active shooter drills" became a common phrase in law enforcement tactical training as the first arriving officers quickly moved in to track down and neutralize an active shooter versus setting up the perimeter and waiting for tactical units as unfolded internationally with the Columbine attack in 1999.

The ability to control alarms so that emergency service personnel can hear voices and noises, the familiarity tactical officers have with school stairs and hallways, knowledge of how entrances and locks work, and similar information can all aid in an effective tactical response to a school crisis. Law enforcement needs this information and exposure prior to an actual incident. Making schools available to law enforcement for tactical training, such as during nights or weekends when students are not present, is a best practice.

Law enforcement officials face some particular challenges in managing a large-scale critical incident in a school, including

- Difficulties in processing large crime scenes can easily occur when there is a serious incident at a school, especially if a significant portion of the school is designated as a crime scene.
- Hundreds of victim, witness, and suspect interviews may have to be conducted.
- Coordinating the transfer of command and/or the smooth interaction between incident commanders from different agencies involved in a school crisis can, at times, be difficult.
- They need to deal with media information, rumor control, and related issues.
- They need to reduce dangers created by media helicopters broadcasting live from around the crisis area; in fact, law enforcement officials may want to investigate the feasibility of contacting the Federal Aviation Administration to request clearance of airspace around the crisis site, especially if it is a prolonged situation.
- Greater confusion can occur if the lead agency is a small department with few officers; mutual aid pacts and logistical agreements can help reduce, but not necessarily eliminate, some of the confusion.

Another difficulty centers around the common inability of police, fire, and emergency medical personnel to communicate on the same two-way radio frequency in a crisis. Although a number of agencies have been working to improve these interoperability communications issues since Columbine and particularly since the 9/11 terrorist attacks, the problem remains widespread in many communities across the nation. Public safety officials, along with school personnel, need to assess their communications capabilities during a crisis and to move toward closing gaps in communications. Nobody can afford to have public safety and school professionals running messages back and forth on scrap sheets of paper while chaos is growing all around them.

Assess Traffic Flow and Evacuation Routes

School and public safety officials should examine traffic routes in and out of schools to determine how they can contain overflow in a crisis, maintain clear access for emergency service vehicles, and still facilitate an anticipated rush from parents, media, and others to the scene. Unfortunately, if they are not careful, emergency service vehicles themselves can contribute greatly to the problem. Use of aerial photographs and maps can help in the assessment, as well as in an actual incident response.

Officials may wish to install gates at the driveway entrances to schools so that that they can at least attempt to block off an onslaught of vehicles in an emergency situation. Parking lot design, routine traffic routes that split parent drivers from school buses, and other traffic flow considerations should also be taken into consideration. These should be recognized as tools, but not a guarantee, as parents will drive on sidewalks, lawns, and anywhere else to get to their child during a crisis.

Develop Strategies to Address Transportation Needs

School transportation services can play a major role in school crisis situations. A number of steps can be taken to better prepare for transportation-related crisis services and needs:

• Develop an action plan for quickly mobilizing school bus drivers during off-peak driving times, such as during the middle of the school day, so that a mechanism is in place for obtaining an adequate fleet response to such crisis situations as evacuations or transports to alternative sites.

• Equip all buses with two-way communications systems that adequately cover districtwide use. Consider multiple channels, one of which can be designated an emergency-only channel, and discuss communications procedures in a crisis situation.

• Equip drivers who go on field trips or special events with cell phones.

• Ensure that drivers have student rosters, student emergency data, and first-aid kits.

232 Readiness and Emergency Management for Schools

- Trainer drivers to increase awareness of student behavior management strategies, security threat trends and procedures, and crisis preparedness guidelines, including procedures for school evacuations, relocation to alternative sites, and so forth.

- Provide law enforcement agencies an opportunity to use school buses for tactical training exercises.

- Consider putting the bus number in large numbers on the top of the bus unit so that it could be identified from a police helicopter.

- Make sure that all bus units have the name of the school district clearly displayed.

- Place signs on all sides of the bus unit requesting that, in an emergency, passersby first notify 911, and then a designated number at the school district.

- Have drivers conduct periodic bus evacuations.

- Consider having backup drivers for emergencies, and create a list of school employees who do not normally drive, but who have a license to drive, a school bus. (School officials may consider having some additional individuals, such as crisis team members, trained as bus drivers for emergency situations.)

Remember that school bus drivers are typically the first and last school employees to see children each day. Their training and involvement in school security and emergency preparedness planning is critical to having a successful safe schools strategy.

Portable Classrooms, Open Classrooms, and Other Sites

Growing school populations and limited space are plaguing a number of schools, particularly in certain regions, across the country in terms of safety issues. Portable classrooms (i.e., trailers) typically have no public address systems, no phones, no fire or other alarms, and other communications gaps. Evacuation procedures, lockdowns, and other crisis guideline implementation could easily be hampered in these areas, and special consideration should be given to portable classrooms when enhancing physical security measures and developing emergency guidelines.

Open classroom areas, shared space rooms, and similar arrangements also present unique conditions for safety planning. Oftentimes, there are few places to seek shelter in these areas, and securing a room or rooms is frequently almost impossible. When these types of design exist in schools, options for relocation in the general area of such rooms, methods for obtaining protective cover and minimizing physical exposure, and other risk-reduction measures should be examined closely as emergency plans are developed.

Risk-reduction options should be closely examined when these designs exist.

Afterschool Programs, Special Events, and More

Crisis team members must also recognize that crises are not confined to certain times or places. Afterschool programs, special events such as athletic events and dances, adult education sites, and field trips are all subject to experiencing a crisis situation. Security staffing and other adult supervision, access control, communications capabilities and procedures, coordination with public safety agencies, and a number of other logistical considerations for handling crises at these locations and in such nontraditional school settings as alternative schools should also be included in the emergency preparedness planning process.

Training, Exercising, and Debriefing

Emergency preparedness guidelines should be tested and revised as appropriate. In addition, all staff should be trained on the guidelines. Furthermore, the importance of following adult directions and the overall importance of safety-related drills should be communicated to students.

School support staff must be an integral part of emergency preparedness training. School secretaries will take bomb threat calls. Custodians will encounter strangers on campus. Food service workers will be in cafeterias during student riots or incidents sending the school into lockdown. Bus drivers are the first and last school employees to see many students each school day. And all of these key support staff are too often not provided training or a seat at the crisis planning team tables.

Testing crisis guidelines does not automatically equate to a full-dress simulation. Tabletop scenarios alone can help school and other safety officials identify a number of gaps in their guidelines. Furthermore, full simulations, as long as they are conducted with volunteers and the fact that it is a simulation has been made clearly known to all in advance, should also not be objectionable, because both school and law enforcement officials typically learn a great deal as a result of these exercises.

Tabletop exercises provide a simulation of emergency situations in informal, stress-free environments. Tabletop exercise facilitators, school safety professionals experienced in managing school emergencies and crisis situations, provide a scenario and series of events to stimulate discussions by participants who assess and resolve unfolding problems based on their existing plans. The school tabletop exercise allows school participants to examine the roles, responsibilities, tasks, and overall logistics associated with managing a similar real-life emergency situation and make subsequent adjustments in their school emergency/ crisis plans.

Although full-scale drills are very educational, they typically are labor and time intensive. Tabletop exercises can provide a less stressful, more time effective method of taking a school's emergency/crisis planning to the next level. Full- and half-day sessions, often done during school professional development days, allow school leaders to avoid having school emergency/crisis plans collect dust on a shelf.

If a tabletop exercise is properly structured, the critical elements that would be experienced in many, if not most, school emergencies can be weaved into the activity. Tabletop designers and facilitators have to be less of an expert in tabletop design by emergency management standards, and more of an expert in understanding K–12 school climate, culture, community-relations, and operational uniqueness. Properly done, I have seen school crisis teams leave half-day tabletops with enough eye-opening information to rewrite more than half of their entire emergency guidelines thanks to good discussion and analysis during the exercise.

Some common themes we have learned from tabletop exercises include the following:

• Many school crisis teams have unrealistic expectations of their public safety partners in a crisis. For example, school teams often mistakenly believe the number of police officers who would respond to their school in an emergency is much greater than the police department staffing levels can actually immediately provide.

• A number of school crisis teams have a tendency to jump into lockdown modes faster than what may be necessary based upon the threat at hand.

• Managing parents and the media will typically be the two biggest *crisis after the crisis* matters school teams must deal with following an emergency incident. Yet crisis plan evaluations and tabletop exercises consistently find these components of school emergency guidelines to be the weakest parts of school plans.

- School crisis plans too often lack adequate backup levels of leadership and planning.

- Parent communication and parent-student reunification plans are typically not well developed.

- Crisis media protocols, especially joint agency protocols, and crisis media training are often lacking.

Do these describe your schools and school crisis teams? You will never know if you do not exercise your guidelines, and tabletop exercises are a good place to start.

School crisis teams and administrators should also have a process to routinely debrief drills conducted during the school year. This includes fire drills, lockdowns, and evacuations. What went right? Where are the gaps and weak points? Are there individuals who consistently do not take the exercises seriously and, in turn, who pose a risk to successful school emergency response? Do you hold by-name accountability of individuals on staff who repeatedly do not take drills seriously and fail to follow safety guidelines? These can all be learned through drills and remedied through appropriate debriefings.

PULLING IT ALL TOGETHER

It should be clear that preparing for crisis situations is an ongoing process, not a one-time event. Effective planning takes time and is extremely detail oriented. The degree of success school and public safety officials can have in managing a crisis, however, is directly related to their degree of planning and preparation.

14 Emergency Response and Crisis Management

N o matter how much you do to prevent a crisis incident, one can still occur. When the chaos is over and the dust has settled, the first question asked is going to be whether the situation could have been prevented. The majority of the questions thereafter are going to focus on how well prepared you were to manage those situations you could not prevent.

Chapter 13 focused on emergency planning and preparedness. If the majority of preparedness steps listed in Chapter 13 have been taken before an incident occurs, school crisis team members are likely to find that the management of the incident will flow much more smoothly than the traditional approach of flying by the seat of your pants. This chapter focuses on emergency response and crisis management. Chapters 15 and 16 provide guidance on managing the crisis after the crisis once the dust settles from the incident.

EMERGENCY RESPONSE: THE FIRST HALF HOUR

You hear multiple loud popping noises. You answer the call for help. You have heard the most dreaded message a school official will ever hear: *"Shots have been fired in the cafeteria."*

Now what? Where do you go, and what do you do first?

There are four priorities in the initial response to a school crisis. A half hour is used here as a reference to help people put tasks in a time frame and to grasp what should be done and when it should be done. The reality, however, is that a response to these four priority areas may run from the first minutes up to hours into the crisis, depending on the nature of the situation.

These four areas are not ranked, nor are they necessarily chronological in order of occurrence. In fact, under ideal circumstances, they would all be occurring simultaneously. Top priorities should include the following:

1. *Securing all students, staff, and legitimate visitors.* Depending on the crisis, this may involve an evacuation, a lockdown, or a partial lockdown and partial evacuation simultaneously. The focus should be on making sure that all students, staff, and others are legitimately out of harm's way.

2. *Assisting the injured.* Time is of the essence in a medical emergency. In some cases, minutes or even seconds can make a difference between life and death. The steps recommended in Chapter 13 for preparing for medical emergencies might help school officials reduce potential losses by strengthening their capacity to provide a timely and effective response to medical emergencies.

3. *Requesting assistance.* The first call for assistance should be to police, fire, and/or emergency medical services, all typically done by calling 911 in many areas. Amazingly, we have seen delays by school officials in obtaining assistance because they chose to call the superintendent or other central office officials before requesting outside emergency assistance. Although the importance of having top school leaders informed of what is going on cannot be overlooked, it is unlikely that the superintendent is also a police officer, firefighter, or medical technician able to provide direct services to students and staff. Get the call out for outside emergency assistance first, then notify designated central office officials who can help mobilize resources within the district and other outside support in addition to the emergency service providers already contacted.

4. *Engaging crisis team members and emergency guidelines.* This is where the emergency guideline development, training, and related preparation will be put to the real test. Although you will want to make sure that all of the elements of the emergency guidelines are followed, some of the most important subcategories in this area should include the following actions:

   o Secure the crime scene once immediate threats are neutralized. This is a phrase well understood by law enforcement but commonly unknown to or misunderstood by most educators. It is a very important step in the criminal investigation process, however. It means protecting the area where the crisis occurred from tampering, movement, or other disruption until the police arrive. It is so important that it is discussed in more detail below.

o Verify facts and begin documentation. Once control is regained, crisis team members should focus on verifying facts as quickly as possible and documenting these facts as they are obtained. It is suggested that each crisis team have at least one individual who serves as the recorder and focuses exclusively on documenting the crisis and the responses to it.

o Determine the status of the remaining school day. If the crisis occurs before school dismissals, educators will quickly have to determine whether or not school will remain open for the remainder of the school day. Factors to consider in this decision are discussed in more detail below. The decision may not occur within the first 30 minutes, but recognizing in advance that this is a call that will have to be made in a timely manner is an important point to remember, as shutting down school early in itself requires advance thought and planning on logistical considerations involved (transportation, student lunches, parent notifications).

o Activate the communications plan. School officials typically equate a communications plan with dealing with the media. Although the media is one area that should be addressed by a crisis communications plan, it is certainly not the only one. Components of a crisis communication plan are discussed in more detail in Chapter 15.

Although there are only four categories suggested for the first response phase, many subcategories and considerations exist under each of these areas. To be able to complete everything that needs to be done under each of these in one half hour is highly unlikely, especially in a major crisis. By focusing on these areas first, however, crisis responders will be better able to prioritize the many things that they will need to do over the length of the crisis.

Securing Crime Scenes and Preserving Evidence

In lay terms, securing the crime scene basically means protecting the area where the crisis took place and preventing the movement, contamination, destruction, or alteration of evidence. This typically means restricting access to the area and prohibiting items from being moved, removed, or touched. Such items might include, for example, shell casings from discharged weapons, firearms, knives, or the personal property of a shooter or victim.

Securing the area also means *not* cleaning up crisis outcomes, such as blood on the floor (something that educators by nature rush to do, typically to prevent someone from stepping in it, slipping, or simply having to see it) or bullet holes in the wall. Again, this is done by setting up some type of perimeter around the scene of the incident until police arrive; for example, you might block off access all the way around the crime scene with tape or rope (make sure, however, that the person securing the crime scene is also not contaminating it by doing so). Assigning an individual or several individuals on the crisis team responsibility for securing the crime scene would be a wise thing to do.

Only police officials should be allowed access, and once they take over the crime scene, they will typically assume responsibility for it unless they indicate otherwise. Until that time—and, for that matter, usually after that time as well—school officials, parents, media, and all others, including superintendents, board members, crisis team members, and other ranking officials, must be required to remain outside the crime scene perimeter regardless of their title or authority. The only exception, however, would likely be those rendering medical assistance to victims who cannot be removed from the crime scene area.

Although a school cafeteria or classroom may be the crime scene in smaller crisis situations, the entire school could very well be designated a crime scene in others depending on the circumstances. Designating the entire school a crime scene has not only been an effective way to preserve evidence and avoid crime scene contamination, but has also served as a way to help keep media, parents, and others away from the area until the situation is brought under control and the investigators have had an opportunity to make an initial assessment of the scene. It is also easier to designate a larger area than necessary as the crime scene and eventually scale it down than it is to start small and try to expand it at a later time.

It would be prudent for crisis team members, if not the entire school staff, to receive an in-service presentation by their local law enforcement agency on how to secure a crime scene and how to preserve evidence.

Deciding Whether to Close School

School leaders will need to decide on whether or not school will remain open shortly after the incident has unfolded. Poland and McCormick (1999) identify several factors to consider when deciding this issue.

• Emotional support will be needed for the individuals involved in the crisis, and, in general, staff and students who experienced the crisis should be kept together. Exceptions include very young students, such as kindergartners, who should be reunited with the parents or guardians.

• Sending students home would allow staff to dedicate their full attention to managing the crisis and its aftermath.

- The police investigation time, damage to the school, complications with transportation issues, and unsupervised children may require an early closure.

- Parents may wish for their children to go home with them, and this could affect attendance and the processing of the crisis incident.

- The majority of staff members will need to have control of their own emotions in order to assist the students, and if the majority of them are unable to do so, closing school may be a necessity.

- If school remains open, staff will need to know what type of bell schedule to follow. It would typically be appropriate under these circumstances to allow students to stay in one class, such as the one they were in at the time of the incident or their homeroom, until they have had adequate time to deal with the crisis.

Poland and McCormick note that the general recommendation, providing that circumstances allow it, is to keep children in school so that they can receive care and support in coping with the crisis. Even in situations where school is closed the day of the incident, they stress that "your goal should be to return your students to school at some location as quickly as possible—preferably the next day—so that they can receive the assistance of trained school personnel and to decrease the occurrence of 'school phobia' among students" (p. 72).

ROLES AND RESPONSIBILITIES

Responding to serious incidents on a regular basis is the job of police, fire, medical, and other emergency service personnel—not school officials. School personnel must, however, know what their roles and responsibilities will be during a crisis even though it is not a part of their daily job routine.

School staff are not the first-responders to a crisis. They are the *very* first responders. Knowing and understanding their roles in a crisis situation, as well as knowing the systems used by many emergency service providers in responding to serious incidents, will help school crisis team members and their fellow staff members better respond in an actual incident.

Incident Command System

The Incident Command System (ICS) originated as the result of organizational problems, including ineffective communications, lack of accountability, and undefined command structure, identified from multi-agency responses to major wildland fires in Southern California in the 1970s.

ICS was adopted by the National Fire Academy (NFA) to standardize the responses of individual agencies working on the common goal of protecting life, property, and the environment through command, control, and coordination. ICS eventually evolved into an all-risk incident management system for all types of fire and nonfire emergencies (Federal Emergency Management Agency [FEMA], 1995).

ICS is based on the business management practices of planning, directing, organizing, coordinating, communicating, delegating, and evaluating and relies on having functional areas for managing serious incidents. Command is responsible for the overall incident management and may be a single command, where one commander is responsible for incident management, or a unified command, where several individuals appointed by their respective departments jointly determine the incident management strategy. According to FEMA (1995), an effective ICS will include an all-risk system and suitability for use with any type of jurisdiction or agency and will be adaptable to all incidents regardless of size, all users, and new technology.

FEMA (1995) identifies the eight components of an ICS as the following:

1. *Common terminology* to prevent confusion through the use of an incident name and common terms for personnel, equipment, facilities, and procedures.

2. *Modular organization* through the use of an expandable top-down structure, with size depending on the incident's management needs.

3. *Integrated communications* using a communications system with common terminology, standard operating procedures, common frequencies, and so forth.

4. *Unified command structure,* whether single or unified, as described previously.

5. *Consolidated action plans,* including verbal or written (especially if multiple agencies are involved) plans of strategic goals, objectives, and activities.

6. *A manageable span of control* of subordinates being supervised, generally from three to seven.

7. *Designated incident facilities,* such as command posts and staging areas.

8. *Comprehensive resource management,* including use of staging areas, consolidation resources, reduction of communication loads, and ongoing monitoring of resource status.

The ICS functional areas include the following:

1. *Command* function, responsible for overall on-scene management, includes an incident commander (IC) and, depending on the size or complexity of the incident, may include a safety officer to address hazardous or unsafe conditions, a liaison officer to coordinate with other agencies, and an information officer to deal with media and public information.

2. *Operations* function, which is responsible for the actual tactical operations at the incident.

3. *Planning* function in larger incidents, which includes the collection, evaluation, dissemination, and use of information on the incident development and status of resources.

4. *Logistics* function, which is responsible for locating and organizing facilities, services, and materials needed to manage the incident, such as communications, medical support, and food.

5. *Finance* function, which tracks costs and financial considerations associated with the incident management.

It is important that school officials, especially crisis team members, understand that this structure may be in place and that the response of emergency service personnel from public safety agencies may operate following an ICS model. Conversely, local emergency service officials may very well not be familiar with ICS. It would behoove school officials to confer with police, fire, and other emergency service providers during their crisis preparation stages to ascertain whether or not such a response model is used by the agencies and, if so, how the school system will respond in conjunction with such a protocol.

School districts receiving federal school emergency planning grants are required to be compliant with the National Incident Management System (NIMS), which includes the ICS issues. FEMA has free online courses for school officials that can provide an orientation and advanced training on NIMS and ICS. FEMA also has a training program at its headquarters on all-hazards planning where school teams and their community partners can spend about a week to learn emergency management best practices.

School System Interface With ICS

School officials may very likely find out that the roles and responsibilities of their crisis team members fall along the lines of ICS functional areas.

It is unlikely, however, that school officials have conceptualized and formally structured their crisis guidelines to include roles and responsibilities in as detailed of a structure as the ICS. Nevertheless, because school officials are the lead responders until public safety agencies arrive and because that they will have to transfer information on their initial response to the responding personnel, they will need to know the form in which these agencies may be setting up and with whom school crisis team members might need to confer.

For example, ICS-like functions performed by school officials might include the following:

• *Command.* The IC for the school district would likely be the superintendent, and his or her assistant commander would likely be a deputy or assistant superintendent. The school IC would likely have a risk management official fulfilling the safety officer functions and a public/community relations official performing the information officer function with media and other audiences. Depending on the size of the school district, the district's security director, school resource officer, or similar representative responsible for school safety might serve as liaison officer, coordinating with other public safety agencies.

• *Operations.* The school district's representative leading the actual response to the crisis typically would be the building principal, possibly in conjunction with the school security coordinator or school resource officer, or members of the school crisis teams Their focus is on the health, safety, well-being, and accountability of students and staff. Activities might include providing additional support for populations with special needs, student supervision, parent-student reunification, first aid and medical support, overseeing emergency kits and supplies, keeping two-way communications equipment operating, and accounting for all students and staff.

• *Planning.* The school administrator in charge of student services (overseeing such personnel as social workers, counselors, psychologists, nurses, and support programs staff) might be the school official to fulfill the ICS planning role. This function might also be split among the superintendent, building principal, security official, and business manager, depending on the size of the district or nature of the crisis incident. This team plans the roles and responsibilities for specific team members, develops plans for caring for populations with special needs, plans exercises, conducts incident debriefings, completes after-action reports, updates plans, and documents specific events and actions taken during a real emergency. The school's secretary may often be selected to serve as the recorder for the planning team.

- *Logistics.* Facilities, services, grounds, materials, food services, transportation, and perhaps even personnel would typically fall under the direction of the school business manager. Titles for this position may run from *assistant superintendent* to *coordinator,* depending on size of the district, but the functions are typically the same. This team is responsible for securing resources such as buses, backup generators, food, shelter, and so on.

- *Finance.* Financial issues are generally under the direction of a school treasurer, finance director, or business manager. Activities might include ongoing documentation of expenses related to the incident management and recovery, handling insurance and reimbursement claims, and associated tasks.

Based on this type of comparison, the superintendent, the principal of the school in crisis, the safety/security director, the student services director, the business manager, and the treasurer or financial director should play key roles in the overall incident command structure for the school district. These people, in turn, would also be central to the liaison with public safety incident commanders upon their arrival on the scene of the incident. In smaller districts, however, all of these positions may not exist, and individuals may wear multiple (or many) hats.

Superintendents and other top administrators often find it difficult to not jump into the fray at a school with an unfolding crisis, but their presence and decision-making authority is often first needed in a command center where they should interface with decision makers from other agencies. Unfortunately, superintendents and other cabinet members often do not directly participate in school emergency preparedness workshops, drills, exercises, and planning sessions, so they frequently do not understand the nature and importance of incident command. In tabletop exercises we have facilitated for school districts, when superintendents are present we also often see other administrators withdraw from discussions and hesitate to challenge inaccurate decisions and comments from the superintendent, even though the superintendent's actions are inconsistent with district emergency plans and best practices.

More than once we have seen real-life emergencies where superintendents have jumped into the emergency response and made decisions contrary to their own district emergency plans. Although their intentions are good, the outcome can be less than desirable for both safety and school-community relations. Superintendents, cabinet members, and board members need to be a part of school emergency planning, training, drills, exercises, and debriefings so at a minimum they have a basic understanding of incident command, their district's own emergency plan, and best practices in school emergency preparedness.

Specific Roles to Consider

School officials will have to evaluate their own organizational structure, their district and building positions and specialty areas, and related factors to determine which specific person or persons will perform which specific tasks (including those listed previously and following, as well as the many others referenced in Chapters 13). It would be prudent for school officials to assign alternate or backup persons (perhaps at least two or three individuals deep for those mission-critical areas) to complete the emergency functions, as Murphy's Law tends to strike along with an actual crisis (e.g., the primary individual responsible for fulfilling a particular role could be off ill, out-of-town, at a conference, or elsewhere at the time of the incident). The following list highlights specific tasks undertaken by various personnel typically involved in school district crisis responses:

- *Administrator-in-charge.* The school superintendent, principal, or other administrator-in-charge may be responsible for

    o assessing the situation, engaging appropriate crisis guidelines, and monitoring their implementation;
    o serving as the liaison with public safety agency ICs once they arrive, being present and participating in command centers, and coordinating with key individuals and organizations in the broader school community;
    o making or assigning appropriately trained administrator's designee to make timely notifications of deaths and injuries, as applicable to the incident;
    o assigning duties as needed;
    o reviewing and approving public information releases, if possible;
    o providing leadership and direction for the recovery process;
    o approving appropriate requests for additional resources.

- *School safety/security official.* School security or school police officials' roles may include the following:

    o Assigning, supervising, and coordinating school security or police staff to supervise and control the incident site, perimeter, crowds, and access, and to direct traffic and escort visitors.
    o Maintaining liaison with public safety agencies on operational issues.
    o Collecting, organizing, and documenting facts, statements, and information.
    o Briefing incident commanders and other key officials on investigations and security issues.

  o Forecasting ongoing school security and policing needs.
  o Other duties associated with the protection of life, property, and information.

• *Public information officers.* Communications, community, or media relations personnel may do the following:

  o Engage and monitor implementation of the crisis communications plan.
  o Oversee mass parent notification system and other parent crisis communication message development and delivery.
  o Oversee the update of crisis response and recovery information on district and individual school websites.
  o Coordinate appropriate media briefings and other incident-related communications and dissemination of information.
  o Participate in Joint Information Center (JIC) activities with public information officers from other involved agencies.
  o Provide updated fact sheets for secretaries and other persons communicating with parents and the public.
  o Ensure effective and consistent communications, in cooperation with school administrators, with the victims and their families.
  o Maintain as detailed records as possible of the information requested and released.

• *Secretaries/office support staff.* These individuals play a key role in the day-to-day operations of schools and will also play a key role in managing a crisis incident. Their roles may include the following:

  o Having one designated secretary, if possible, on the crisis team to document the actions taken by school officials in managing the crisis.
  o Coordinating requests for additional copying, supplies, and other such items needed to manage the incident.
  o Maintaining a log of phone calls whenever possible.
  o Utilizing fact sheets prepared for communications with parents, community members, and other callers.
  o Referring media inquiries to the designated staff.
  o *Not* speculating or giving opinions.
  o *Not* releasing confidential student, staff, or other information.
  o Limiting the use of office phones during an emergency, especially by students, strangers, and visitors.
  o Knowing how to report emergencies (e.g., knowing what information 911 dispatchers will need to know and how it should be provided).

- o Having and making available updated quick resource reference lists, contact information, and so forth.
- o Knowing how to use, and coordinate the use of, broadcast fax, e-mail, voice mail, and other message systems, including public address systems and bell systems.

- *Teachers and support staff.* Their roles may include the following:

  - o Implementing evacuations, lockdowns, or other directives as issued by crisis management leaders.
  - o Not assuming that everything is secure and back to normal until given an all-clear indication of such.
  - o Meeting the needs of special needs populations.
  - o Staying with and supervising students, with an emphasis on ensuring that they remain as calm and quiet as possible, and that they follow adult directions.
  - o Being prepared to take student roll and to report missing students.
  - o Knowing how to report concerns and needs related to the crisis, and knowing whom to report them to.
  - o Being familiar with, and prepared to deal with, student emotions and psychological reactions to the crisis.
  - o Being flexible and prepared to adapt curriculum and classroom activities in response to the crisis and, in particular, to help students process and manage their reactions to the crisis.
  - o Communicating clearly, concisely, and honestly to students before, during, and after the crisis.

- *School nurse or health aide, counselors, psychologists, social workers, and other mental health professionals.* These personnel may do the following:

  - o Mobilize first aid, assist with triage of victims, coordinate emergency medical service response, identify students transported to hospitals and associated parent notifications, address needs of medicated students, and so on.
  - o Mobilize all available mental health resource personnel and materials from within, and if necessary from outside of, the school district.
  - o Establish and coordinate group and individual counseling opportunities for students, teachers, staff, and others, including self-referral systems.
  - o Identify resources for teachers, parents, and others to help identify the natural progression and management of the grief and healing process.
  - o Coordinate debriefings and make services available to those providing care and management of the crisis.

    o Identify resources for parents and the broader community to deal with grief and healing.

    o Prepare for memorial services, and for the long-term support needed for anniversary dates of the crisis incidents.

    o Implement a comprehensive communication plan for making available services known.

    o Maintain adequate records of services provided.

- *Custodians and maintenance personnel.* Their role may include the following:

    o Assisting in physically securing buildings and grounds, or, when appropriate, providing access to normally secured areas for crisis management officials.

    o Being available to brief public safety responders on building design and operations.

    o Having information available on emergency shutoff controls for utilities, alarms, bells, and so forth.

    o Being prepared for requests to assist in providing additional special needs, such as additional electrical, mechanical, and other resources.

    o Preparing for quick mobilization of staff for major cleanup, repair, and other activities at the appropriate time as directed by incident commanders.

- *Transportation staff.* Such staff, including bus drivers, can play critical roles, including the following:

    o Being available and flexible for short-notice emergency transportation needs.

    o Becoming familiar with alternate site plans, evacuation routes and procedures, and so forth.

    o Knowing how properly to use and maintain two-way radio communications equipment.

    o Having first-aid kits and related supplies on buses at all times.

    o Maintaining rosters and emergency contact information for regular riders.

    o Reporting weather or other emergency conditions, obstacles, or concerns as appropriate.

- *Parents.* Parents can play critical roles in crisis management by doing the following:

    o Following procedures established by school officials for responding in crisis situations, use of alternative sites, and other logistical requests.

o Learning to recognize children's psychological responses of to crisis situations and being familiar with available school and community resources for dealing with these reactions.
o Supporting children and encouraging them to communicate their thoughts and concerns.
o Avoiding finger-pointing and blame, focusing instead on healing and recovery as a first priority.
o Being realistic as to what steps should be taken regarding security changes after a crisis incident.

- *Students.* Student roles in a crisis may include the following:

  o Participating seriously in lockdowns, evacuations, or other steps ordered to secure themselves and the school.
  o Remaining as calm and quiet as possible.
  o Following the directions of adults.
  o Reporting any concerns or needs.
  o Avoiding the use of cell phones and texting messages to forward information about an unfolding incident for which they have no direct knowledge of details.
  o Providing input on steps for recovery and future security and emergency preparedness needs.

These roles, along with additional roles for these and other positions, should be reviewed in the emergency planning and guideline development process.

Transfer of Command

The school district crisis team offers support to building administrators, building crisis team members, and school staff. Although members of the building crisis team are truly the very first crisis responders, some of the functions under their control are taken over by district-level crisis team members upon activation of that team and its guidelines. When first-responders arrive, both building and district crisis teams yield most aspects of command to them, although command over general school issues remains with school administrators.

Public safety officials will, however, likely continue to look to school officials for ongoing input, because school officials are so familiar with students, staff, and some members of the broader community. School officials should, at a minimum, have the principal, custodian, and security official quickly available to brief public safety officials upon their arrival. Key players in the district incident response should also be available to public safety officials to ensure a smooth transfer of incident command management from the school to the public safety commanders.

SPECIFIC CONSIDERATIONS FOR BEFORE, DURING, AND AFTER THE EMERGENCY SERVICE PERSONNEL RESPONSE

The exact steps school officials take in a crisis situation will depend largely on the exact circumstances of the particular crisis. Responses to the "What if?" situations referenced in Chapter 13 should provide district- and building-level crisis team members direction for processing specific types of incidents, providing that they have thoroughly processed these situations before a crisis. The roles and responsibilities identified in the preparatory stages will help guide school officials as to who should do what in various situations. Some important steps, however, are generally applicable to a number of different types of crises.

Before the Arrival of Emergency Services

Once an incident occurs and school officials contact police and other emergency service providers, they will need to continue their role as initial crisis response leaders until emergency personnel arrive. Evacuation, lockdown, or a combination of both is likely to occur during this time. Some suggested actions at this time period, when the circumstances warrant them, include the following:

- Isolating the offender, weapon, and site of the incident.
- Engaging lockdown and/or evacuation procedures.
- Mobilizing school nurses and trained first-responders to assist with medical needs until emergency medical services arrive
- Establishing necessary perimeters and preparing to direct traffic.
- Having assigned crisis team members respond to the designated location to greet and escort first-responders.
- Securing the crime scene and overall building.
- Remembering to secure, control, and communicate to all other students and staff not directly involved in the crisis, in addition to dealing with those directly involved.
- Beginning to prepare for the *immediate* arrival of parents and the media, by engaging family reunification center operations and media liaison coordination.
- Engaging other components of the "What if?" plan, including the role of the crisis team member responsible for documentation.

Assisting Emergency Service Personnel

Once police, fire, medical, and other emergency service personnel arrive, it is important for schools leaders to do the following:

• Make sure that school crisis team members and appropriate school leaders are clearly identifiable as decision makers in the school crisis, such as through the wearing of vests, hats, armbands, or other identifying clothing.

• Ensure access for emergency service personnel to school grounds.

• Assist emergency personnel in gaining direct access to those needing assistance.

• Direct leaders from the school, school district, and emergency service agencies to an area designated as a command post or site for managing the incident, and ensure that the principal and/or assistant principal, custodian, and security representative are immediately available to emergency service personnel.

• Designate a crisis team member or members to control access to the school and crime scene and to escort legitimate officials to the appropriate areas.

• Have the most recent student rosters, attendance or absence lists, teacher absence list, and teacher and substitute lists with emergency contacts and related information quickly available.

• Be prepared for student and staff identification, especially when they are transported to the hospital.

• Identify hospitals where the injured will be taken and identify who will be taken to which hospital; mobilize crisis team members to proceed to these same locations.

• Engage accounting procedures for students and staff, if this has not already been done.

• Engage parent notifications, if this has not already been done, beginning with the parents of those injured.

After the Initial Emergency Service Responses

Once emergency personnel have responded to the site and the crisis response is beginning to stabilize, the work of the crisis team members is just beginning. Crisis officials will need to continue working, particularly in the following areas:

- School representatives at the hospital should be clearly identifiable and should assist with victim identification and with coordination of parents and family, hospital security and staff, public information officials, and others. If possible, separate rooms should be set up for school officials, police officials, immediate family members, nonfamily visitors and guests, media, and others.

- Procedures for handling blood-borne pathogens should be followed within the parameters of not destroying crime scenes or interfering with police investigations.

- Crisis communications plans should be in full swing, including notifying parents, internal communications, and press briefings.

- Student debriefings should take place, as appropriate.

- A faculty meeting should be held to debrief and plan the next steps.

- Arrangements for counseling and mental health support should begin, including critical incident stress debriefing for crisis caregivers and others directly involved in crisis.

- Documentation efforts should be evaluated and continued.

- Provide care to the caretakers. See Chapter 16 on mental health support for the adults.

- School legal counsel should be consulted and engaged as described in Chapter 16.

- Crisis team members should debrief at appropriate times to identify crisis response methods that worked and did not work during their management of the incident and to modify their emergency preparedness guidelines accordingly.

- Schedule in a timely manner a community meeting for parents and the school-community to discuss school safety, security, and emergency preparedness issues.

As in other sections of this book, these are not exhaustive lists. Additional points will likely be raised in individual district and building crisis planning. And although these activities will be very consuming during and immediately after a crisis, the postcrisis crisis that follows can last months or years.

15 The Postcrisis Crisis

*Managing Media and
Parent Communications*

S ome of the most painful and stressful aspects of crisis management
will continue after the initial incident itself has passed. In fact, this
postcrisis crisis often seems just short of, if not sometimes worse than, the
crisis incident itself in terms of length, intensity, and strain.

Aside from managing the mental health recovery (see Chapter 16),
nothing can be more overwhelming and more challenging than managing
media and parent communications during and after a crisis incident.
Communications technology, social media, and the 24-hour news cycle
driven by competitive cable, network, print, radio, and electronic news
outlets have changed the communications dynamics dramatically over the
past decade. Although more than 750 news outlets reportedly responded to
the Columbine incident in 1999, and many lessons were learned as shared
below, crisis communications presents school leaders with one of their most
daunting challenges.

MANAGING CELL PHONES, TEXT MESSAGING, AND SOCIAL MEDIA

The influence of cell phones, and in particular text messaging, has made
a dramatic impact on school emergency preparedness response and postcrisis management. Rumors and messages that used to take hours and
days to spread now move within seconds and minutes. School attendance
can decrease dramatically at the drop of one rumor of a generic threat of
school violence.

School administrators feel overwhelmed and frequently ask if there is anything they can do to counter the swift impact of today's digital communications world. The truth is we will never be able to eliminate the problems caused by text messaging and other rapid communications tools used by kids, their parents, the community, and the media. The strategy for school administrators must be focused on how they can narrow the gap between wildfire rumors spread by digital communications and getting out their messages of more accurate information from the school's perspective.

The key is to be prepared is to fight fire with fire. Today's high-tech world and rapid communications must be countered by school officials who have a solid crisis communications plan for managing rapidly escalating rumors around school safety issues. I now regularly recommend that school officials not only have emergency guidelines for handling incidents and crisis guidelines for the mental health recovery component, but also separate and distinct crisis communications guidelines outlining their plans for communicating about crisis school safety issues.

There are three critical communications components to school officials' effectively countering fast moving rumors and school violence threats. Communications must be as follows:

1. *Accurate*—Although there is growing pressure on school officials to release information quickly in a crisis or in periods of high rumors, accuracy is the most important factor. Whatever information school officials release must be accurate to the best of their knowledge at the time is it released.

2. *Timely*—Released in a timely manner at the onset of the rumors with periodic updates as necessary and appropriate.

3. *Redundant* in dissemination—Educators and safety officials must have redundancy in communication channels and mechanisms used to get out their accurate information. Not all parents and community members get their information from the same sole source.

Remember that when people are anxious and anxiety is high, they have a decreased ability to process what you are saying. In an unfolding crisis, keep your messages short, clear, concise, and focused on what parents want to know about the safety of their kids.

Recommendations to help school and safety officials manage vague threats, text message rumors of school violence, and related rapid spread of fear include the following:

• Anticipate you will have an issue that accelerates like wildfire at some time in your school. Identify ahead of time what mechanisms you will use to counter it.

- Have redundancy in communications: Website, direct communications to students and staff, mass parent notifications, letters to go home, and so on. Messages from school officials must be put out in a timely and accurate manner with appropriate updates as incidents unfold.

- Discuss potential scenarios among district and building administrators and crisis teams to evaluate what the threshold will be for going full speed on your response communications. If you go full speed on every single rumor, you might need two full-time employees just to counter rumors in one average secondary school. Try to get a feel for at what point a situation might rise to the level of being so disruptive or distractive that it warrants a full-fledged communications counterassault by school and police officials.

- School and police officials should have unified communications so as to send consistent messages. We train in our emergency preparedness programs for the use of joint information centers (JICs) in a major critical incident response. But even on lower scale incidents, it is important for school leaders to be sending a message consistent with that of public safety officials to their school-communities.

- Have a formal crisis communications plan and professionally train your administrators and crisis team members on communicating effectively with media and parents. Professional outside communications consultants, district communications staff (for those with such in-house resources), and related specialists can help develop and audit crisis communications plans, and to train staff.

- School leaders should review their board policies, student handbooks, and related discipline policies to make sure they have solid legal and administrative provisions for disciplinary action related to students who make threats, to address text messaging and cell phone use that is disruptive to the educational process, and related measures. School administrators and boards should have proactive discussions about the firm, fair, and consistent enforcement of these rules if and when incidents arise.

- Educate students about their roles and behavioral expectations related to preventing and reporting rumors and threats of violence as well as cell phone and text messaging use, especially during an emergency. Students need to know that responsible behavior is expected of them, that consequences will occur for inappropriate behavior, and that starting, spreading, and fueling rumors are serious offenses that jeopardize school safety. This education needs to occur prior to actual incidences and, of course, must be reinforced early on if and when incidents do occur.

- Discuss with teachers the importance of their heightened awareness and supervision to monitor against student use of cell phones and text messaging in classrooms and school common areas. Heightened attention to this is particularly important during times of threats, rumors, and related security incidents. Procedures should be in place for teachers to notify school administrators and security personnel of such misuse and abuse, and administrators should be prepared to fulfill firm, fair, and consistent enforcement of related disciplinary rules.

• Communicate with your parents proactively and in advance about how your district will address rumors, threats, and other school violence concerns. Parents and others in the school-community must be prepared ahead of time to know that school officials have plans in place to respond to rumors, processes to investigate them, procedures to administer disciplinary consequences, and when necessary, steps to engage the support of their public safety partners such as police and other support services in criminal investigations and heightened security efforts.

• Consider how your security and preparedness technology can be used in times of rumors and threats. Can your surveillance cameras be used to monitor hallways to help identify persons going in and out of restrooms where threats have been written on bathroom walls? One school reportedly used their cameras to identify students in the hallways who were using a cell phone to video-record fights in the hallways. The administrators, after dealing with the actual fight incident, went back to the cameras and followed up with disciplinary action against those recording the fight against school rules of using cell phones in school. Other applications of existing technology may also be helpful based upon the particular circumstances of the issue at hand.

In an ideal world, we could ban cell phones from schools—period. Although I support those schools that ban cell phones and/or prohibit their use, the reality in many secondary schools today is that the horse is out of the barn, and the cell phones will be there with or without a formal ban. The most important thing for school emergency planning is to assume every student has, and will use, a cell phone during a crisis and develop your emergency guidelines—and your crisis communication guidelines—accordingly.

School leaders are also facing increased security issues arising from social media. Facebook, MySpace, blogs, and other social media outlets are increasingly the sources of rumors, threatening comments, and other safety concerns being brought into school from outside in the community and way outside in cyberspace. The reality is that educators cannot police the Internet 24 hours, 7 days a week. Although they should periodically search social networking sites to run the names of their schools through a search just to see what comes up, or to check in more detail on specific student concerns reported by parents, educators, and other students, it is impossible to filter out these sites from our lives.

As I advise school educators regularly: You should embrace social media on the front-end or it will embrace you on the tail-end. Educators must learn that it is not going to go away and yes, it is indeed something they cannot control. School leaders can either embrace the technology and try to run with doing something to get their messages out using modern technology, or plan on being buried with rumors, misinformation, and communications gaps with their school community.

We are slowly seeing administrators come out of their shells and jump into the school media fray. Superintendents and principals in many school districts are now blogging to get their information out to the school-community. School districts' communications departments are using Facebook, Twitter, blogs, podcasting, and video on their websites to communicate in more modern ways with their school community. One school district created a blog dedicated to dispelling rumors and providing accurate information on issues which have generated buzz within the school community. And mass parent communications systems have increasingly become a tool in the school district's arsenal of crisis communications vehicles for getting the district's messages out in a timely manner.

The tools are available to bridge the gap between the rumor mill generated by cell phones, text messaging, and social media. School leaders need to embrace the new media. Once they have the vehicles in place, they can concentrate on their messages.

DEVELOPING YOUR MESSAGE: PARENT EXPECTATIONS AFTER A SAFETY INCIDENT

School administrators have repeatedly used some terrible sound bites over the years in response to media and parent questions about school safety. For example:

1. "This is an isolated incident." *Translated:* This really does not concern us. It does not happen every day, so why are you alarmed? That is what parents hear when school administrators hide behind the *isolated incident* comment, which is meant to downplay the seriousness of the incident. As my colleague, Chuck Hibbert, so often says: "Following their logic, Columbine and 9/11 were 'isolated incidents' too. They don't happen every day, do they?"

2. "The incident was handled administratively." *Translated:* We failed to call the police, even though it is a crime and we should have called. We hoped no one would catch us in not reporting but darn, you did.

3. "We have implemented a new zero-tolerance policy for. . . ." *Translated:* What did you have last year—a 50% tolerance for violence?

4. "Schools are the safest place in the community." *Translated:* Safer than what? If 25 kids are shot in the community and five are shot in the school, technically by the numbers, the school is safer. But this is not what is important to parents, nor what they want or need to hear after a school shooting. And if my daughter is being sexually harassed in the halls and my son is being extorted for his lunch money every time he goes to the restroom, your safety statistics are irrelevant to my concerns as a parent—and more so, to the concerns of my children.

So my advice to school officials is simple: Ditch the denying and defensive sound bites. Your community and the media can see through the attempted spin. They are not what parents want to hear.

Parents have some pretty simple and consistent expectations in what they want to hear and know when a school safety incident occurs at their child's school. These issues include the following:

- Acknowledge the incident and/or issues.
- Explain how and why it happened.
- Demonstrate an understanding of the concerns of those impacted.
- Identify steps taken to help those who are injured or aggrieved.
- Communicate mechanisms for obtaining the input and involvement of key stakeholders to prevent reoccurrences.
- Identify official steps taken to correct the problem and prevent future incidents.

In general, parents want to know two things after a high-profile school safety incident:

1. What steps did you take to prevent an incident of crime and violence in your school?

2. How well prepared were you to manage the incident(s) that cannot be prevented?

As noted earlier in the book, school administrators often like to hide behind the Family Educational Rights and Privacy Act (FERPA) federal privacy law as a justification for not communicating with parents and the media. And there are legitimately some issues that cannot be discussed because of FERPA. But a number of talking points for parents can be developed from the questions and concerns listed above, allowing school administrators to focus more on the issue of concern to parents—the overall safety of their child—and less on the minutia of the particular incident at hand.

Following high-profile safety or crisis incidents, I encourage school leaders to hold a timely and effectively facilitated public meeting for parents and others in the community. The meeting allows for school community members to voice their questions and concerns. It is not only a way for them to communicate their fears and uncertainties, but it also provides an important transition point in the overall process of community healing from a critical incident.

AN INSIDE LOOK AT THE BUSINESS SIDE OF TODAY'S MEDIA

There are three things you never want to see being made: Legislation, sausage, and the news. All three are ugly processes that make one wonder how the end product stands a chance of being any good.

The more traditional media (cable and network news, newspapers, radio) are businesses. They have corporate structures, are driven by ratings and advertising (translated: money), continue to downsize staff, are often consultant and trend influenced, and are extremely competitive. In many ways, they are like any other business in America.

News reporters are increasingly relatively young in age, often generalists in the topics they cover but specialists in gathering and packaging the information to tell a story. Like people in education, they are increasingly spread thin in numbers while facing individual increases in demands. Many of today's reporters not only have to tell their story, but to do so in multiple media formats (such as in a TV newscast, but also online with one version when the story breaks and a more detailed version, complete with video, online after the story is on the air at its regular newscast time).

News stories are often packaged in an environment intensely pressured by the need for speed. As one reporter jokingly said to me, "It is not an issue of who gets it right. It is just an issue of who gets it first." Many educators believe that is the truth.

Reporters are challenged to communicate complex ideas and issues into quick, simple stories. The evening TV news story length might be 2 minutes and 40 seconds on the air from beginning to end. Not only does the reporter have to tell a complex story in an incredibly short period of time, but your comment as a school official may get a total of 10 seconds in which it can be told.

Because of the competitive nature of the media business, we tend to see more and more drama in the news. What makes a news story today? Stories that are different, provoking, and emotional. As the old media saying goes, "If it bleeds, it leads. If it cries, it flies."

As so is the nature of the beast. Educators can complain about it, whine about it, and be angry about it, but as we often remind them: It is what it is! The story will be told with or without the school's cooperation. Complaining will not change the big picture of the media business, so the best thing educators can do is to try to understand it and be prepared to work with the media as best they can.

TRADITIONAL SCHOOL DISTRICT PARENT AND MEDIA MANAGEMENT: IT DOESN'T WORK TODAY

The caption under a picture of a lone wolf trying to blend in the middle of a pack of hounds reads: "When you are in deep trouble, say nothing and try to look inconspicuous."

This may be good advice for the wolf, but it is not a good practice for school boards and administrators to follow in communicating school safety and crisis issues to parents and the media.

Schools have traditionally taken what I call a 3-D approach to communicating with parents and the media: Deny, defend, and deflect. If denial does not work, they try (sometimes embarrassingly) to defend themselves. If that does not work, then they try to deflect the real issues and spin their way onto other angles or topics.

The problem is that this approach not only was never good to start with, but that it is particularly suicidal in today's world of instant communications and transparency. We are at a rare point in time when how a public official handles an incident may be more important than the actual incident itself. School officials may believe that parents want to be under the belief that everything is perfect in their school, but in reality parents know things happen, and often, because of the inadequacy of communications by school officials who are in hiding, rumors and perceptions become worse than reality.

Effective school and media relations can be defined as: Good behavior, well communicated. First, people have to be doing the right things—or at least doing their best at trying to do the right things. Secondly, this good behavior has to be well communicated.

In the *New School* model of communicating on school safety and crisis issues, school leaders have to keep in mind that people are not trusting the government and public agencies any more. The day of the single spokesperson is gone. Everyone in a school is a spokesperson: students, employees, and parents. *Transparency* is the key word in today's communications.

Smart school leaders therefore recognize that school safety is not only the right thing to do, but is also a public relations tool, not a public relations disaster. Progressive administrators talk about school safety when there is *not* a crisis in the headlines. They realize that getting out in front on the issue helps them add credits to the public relations bank so when a crisis incident does hit their school-community, they have some advance credibility with the people hearing their message that school safety really is a priority to their school leaders.

GETTING OUT FRONT ON SCHOOL SAFETY COMMUNICATIONS

School administrators can proactively communicate about their school safety efforts in a number of ways:

• Include communications on safety issues, programs, and resources in parent newsletters periodically throughout the school year. Make sure parents get school safety information numerous times a year in these publications.

• Create school district Web pages with school safety information, and make sure individual school Web pages within the district point parents to the district Web page in addition to anything specific about safety on each individual school's website.

• Use student school newspapers to promote safety stories and to talk about challenges to school safety such as student use of cell phones in a crisis and forwarding text message rumors.

• Dedicate time at each faculty meeting to discuss one aspect of the school's safety plan, security procedures, or emergency guidelines.

• Create a school safety committee within the district- and building-level parent organizations.

• Host parent awareness training on school and youth safety topics.

• Encourage student-led activities to promote school safety.

• Promote methods for students and parents to report safety concerns such as anonymous hotlines, methods for notifying school administrators of threats and rumors, and so on.

• Use school district cable television shows, local public affairs programs, and other media resources to participate in stories about school safety, emergency preparedness, and topics in youth safety such as bullying, cyber-safety, and so on.

- Dedicate time at school board meetings to highlight prevention, security, and preparedness strategies, programs, and staff.

Students, staff, and parents should be hearing from their school leaders on school safety far before a crisis occurs. Doing so enhances the credibility of school administrators on safety issues far before a crisis occurs—a credit in the bank that administrators will need if a major incident occurs on their watch.

MEDIA CRISIS COMMUNICATIONS GUIDELINES

Communicating with the media is one of the most challenging and frustrating aspects of emergency management for school leaders. Many educators have an inherent distrust of, and dislike for, the media. This predisposition, along with some individual bad experiences along the way, can set school administrators off on a bad foot with the media. Fortunately, an understanding of the media, solid planning for media crisis communications, and some media training by professional communications staff or consultants can better prepare administrators for sharpening their skills and increasing their confidence in managing media crisis communications.

Comprehensive Crisis Communications Guidelines

School officials often falsely believe that a crisis communications plan is something that only lists who will speak with the media—or tells how to avoid speaking with the media. Although media relations is one element of a crisis communications plan, it is certainly not the only component. School officials must look at their internal communications with staff and students, as well as with significant others within the school community, such as parents, when developing comprehensive crisis communications guidelines.

Key Communications Functions

In a special publication to its members that shares the lessons learned from the Columbine tragedy, the National School Public Relations Association (NSPRA) presented a number of areas for structuring communications in a school crisis (Kaufman, Saltzman, Anderson, Carr, Pfeil, Armistead, & Kleinz, 1999). Their discussion included the following:

- Leadership advisement to provide timely and accurate information and advice to the superintendent, board members, and administrative cabinet on issues, such as updates on criminal investigations, status of the injured, news briefing schedules and key messages, media coverage analysis, and special events.

- Internal communication to all staff, employee groups, parents, and students on a daily basis through varied forms of message delivery. (NSPRA emphasized that the internal communications function should be stressed over media responsiveness.)
- External communication to key community leaders and communicators within the broader school community.
- Media communications, including controlling the overwhelming amount of inquiries, researching inquiries, responding to inquiries, and monitoring media coverage.
- Counseling communications coordination among psychologists, counselors, outside support agencies, and others.
- Special events liaison to memorial services, political visitors, and other special activities.
- Donations and volunteers communications to screen, organize, and respond to offers of donations and volunteer services.
- Telephone bank coordination for hotlines, volunteer workers, updated fact sheets, and so forth.
- Communications command center coordinator to assign tasks, disseminate messages, prepare parent letters, develop daily fact sheets for dissemination to staff and district communicators, update district websites, send voice and e-mail messages to staff, and keep records of all communications.

The article points out that a number of steps, such as structuring the communications plan, identifying roles and responsibilities, and related tasks, can and should be done before an actual crisis. For example, school officials may wish to seek donations or purchase communications command center equipment, such as fax machines, networked computers and phones, television sets, cell phones and batteries, and supplies, before it is needed. It would also be wise for local school officials to establish relationships with national associations, such as NSPRA and their respective state chapters.

Media Relations Preparedness

The idea of the media knocking on a school administrator's door sends chills down the back of most school officials. The idea of multiple media representatives on scene at one time turns the chills into a deep freeze. In a crisis situation, however, school officials can count on the media flocking to their doorsteps not only after the crisis, but perhaps even in the middle of the crisis itself.

Understanding Crisis Media Coverage Stages

As a school security supervisor and director, I learned a great deal about working with the media through trial and error. As a national consultant, I carried on my beliefs about the importance of understanding how the media works, what they need, and how to give it to them without hanging yourself and your organization in the process. This experience of now more than two decades of working with the media, along with having fielded hundreds of media interviews after school crisis incidents including well more than 300 media interviews the month following the Columbine tragedy alone, has offered some helpful insights into the media handling of school crises.

Educators can anticipate a number of stages of possible media coverage of a school crisis:

1. *Breaking News Stage.* This stage involves the first level of coverage as a crisis breaks and will focus on getting information out to the public about the crisis as quickly as possible. Generally few facts are known at this stage, but the competition by the various media outlets to get the first facts is fierce. If the crisis is a larger scale incident, educators can expect team coverage by multiple reporters from the same news outlet. Angles they may explore include stories on the victims (those with physical injuries and the overall psychological trauma of the event), heroes, suspect(s) background and connection to the school, law enforcement/tactical preparedness and response, school's security and preparedness measures, parent perspectives and concerns, student viewpoints, perspectives of teachers and staff, impact of cell phones and texting or school media, and other angles unique to the incident.

2. *Investigation Stage.* Media representatives will shift from the breaking news stage quickly as soon as the investigation by police, school, and other officials is underway. Again, the focus at this stage is on securing as many details as possible about what exactly happened. Media representatives may also begin seeking information on how the crisis is affecting people and school operations, and may request access to buildings and students.

3. *Analysis Stage.* As the facts of the crisis begin to emerge, the media will attempt to provide an analysis, typically through expert opinions, of exactly what occurred, why it occurred as it did, and what its impact on students, staff, school operations will *really* mean. Because of media helicopters, the availability of 24-hours news programs, and other new technology, this stage may occur at the same time as Stages 1 and 2. In fact, it

is not uncommon to see live news coverage of an unfolding school crisis at the same time that reporters make phone calls and attempt interviews to get details; and during all of this, there is an expert in the field being interviewed live from hundreds, if not thousands, of miles away from the crisis. It is also likely that part of the media analysis stage will focus on the impact of the school crisis on other schools in the community, other school districts, and so on, by asking, for example, how other school officials and students are reacting or what measures are in place at other schools to prevent such an incident.

4. *Grief Stage.* Here the media focus shifts to the impact of the crisis on the injured, their families, or the families and friends of deceased individuals. This stage of coverage may last a while, depending on the size and severity of the crisis, and will likely include coverage of funerals and memorials.

5. *Recovery and Return-to-Normal Stage.* Once funerals and memorials are over, the attention typically shifts to the recovery stage. The focus is then on how school officials, students, and the community are returning to normalcy.

6. *Future Predictions and Positive Angle Stage.* As schools and communities return to normal and the media exhaust their coverage of the grief and recovery stages, media outlets may seek to close their loop of coverage by focusing on what people can expect to occur in the future at the school crisis site or at other schools. The media may also take the approach of temporarily closing out coverage with a positive story about some aspect of the school or its operation.

7. *Anniversary Stage.* Depending on the nature of the crisis, the media may return to the crisis issue anywhere from 1 month to 6 months—or even 1 year—after the incident to acknowledge the anniversary of the crisis incident. The appearance of the media after wounds are starting to heal could simply reopen them. School officials need to note such dates on their calendar and should anticipate return media coverage at that time.

These stages are not set in stone, and some that occur may overlap at any given point in time. The purpose is for educators to understand the various levels and stages of coverage. Most of all, school officials need to realize that no matter how much they may want the story to disappear, it is not going to happen. Preparing with the idea that schools will need to respond, in some form and fashion, to media needs is a necessary part of their crisis communications planning.

Why School Officials Should Talk

School officials must recognize that by saying, "No comment," they are placing their reputation, and that of the school and district itself, in tremendous jeopardy. Reasons for talking to the media, especially at a time of crisis, include the following:

- If the media does not talk *with* you, they will talk *about* you.

- Talking with the media affords schools an opportunity to position themselves as being in charge and in control of the situation.

- The reputations and integrity of the school, the school district, and its leaders are at stake.

- The media provide the vehicle for school officials to reach their key audiences with timely and important messages.

No matter how much they dislike the media, educators must remember that if someone representing their school system does not communicate with the media, then the media will move on to other, and potentially less credible, sources who may be less familiar with the incident and the rationale behind the school response. School officials must be articulate, credible, decisive, confident, compassionate, empathetic, and clear not only in their actions while managing the crisis, but also in the messages they deliver during and after the crisis.

Managing the Media Madness

The NSPRA publication mentioned above best describes the impact of the media at a school crisis incident in its description of the Columbine High School crisis:

> Soon after the shooting began at Columbine High, more than 750 media outlets converged on Jeffco's [Jefferson County's] doorstep, creating a makeshift city that filled a nearby park. As Jeffco soon learned, the immediacy of today's media, with its global deadlines, around-the-clock coverage, and multiple communication channels creates nearly impossible demands. (Kaufman et al., 1999, p. 5)

Some tips provided by the NSPRA as a result of this experience include the following:

- Stick to your media policy once it is created.

- Identify spokespersons in advance, give them media training, and make sure that all staff know to refer media inquiries to the designated communications staff.

- Stress internal communications over media communications.

- Triage media inquiries, with priority going to local media over national and international media.

- Be prepared for the new media, such as 24-hour news shows, online magazines, chat rooms, and other new technology media.

- Control media access, as appropriate, and include regularly scheduled news briefings and use of media pools when necessary.

- Develop key messages, stick to them, and ensure that the communications team works with the legal team.

Other Media Preparedness Tips and Lessons Learned

Some additional preparation tips include the following:

- Establish joint information-sharing protocols among the school public information officer(s) (PIOs), PIOs for first-responders, and PIOs for elected officials in your school-community. It is especially important for school and first-responder PIOs to act collaboratively.

- Create plans for a Joint Information Center (JIC) where, in a major incident, the PIOs from schools, first-responder agencies, and other impacted organizations can formulate and disseminate information in a unified and coordinated manner with consistent messages.

- Remember that one school PIO is just that: One person. Too often, in tabletop exercises we see building-level administrators overemphasize the expectations of what the district's communications director or PIO will be capable of handling by herself/himself in a major crisis incident. Building principals are more than willing to say "no comment—see the communications director" as hypothetical incidents unfold in a tabletop exercise, only later to realize the communications director/PIO would be overwhelmed with local and national media, parent inquiries, information tasks for board members and cabinet level administrators, calls from principals from multiple district buildings at once, and so on. Given the 24/7 news cycle involving media outlets of all types (cable and network news, print media, radio stations, online publications, international media, and so on), the best school communications cannot meet all of the demands while working alone for multiple days with limited or no rest. Backup plans should made for providing support for communications staff in the event of a major incident. Plans should be created for obtaining *mutual aid* from neighboring school district PIOs if needed in a major event, and tapping into state affiliates and the NSPRA should also be a part of school crisis communications planning.

- Create and maintain an updated emergency contact list of key communicators with names and phone numbers. I recommend that a database with names, phone numbers, fax numbers, and e-mail addresses be established and, if at all possible, that a broadcast group be created on fax machines, e-mail, and at least internally on voice mail so that messages can be sent quickly and easily if a crisis creates a need for mass messaging.

- Create a fact sheet for the district and for each school with the school name, address, and phone number; administrators' names; the number of students and staff, along with related demographics; grade levels; building details, including the age of school and number of classrooms; and information on any special programs or achievements.

- Determine who will be spokesperson ahead of time, use that person consistently, and, if at all possible, avoid having board members, the superintendent, or the principal as the lead spokesperson, because they will be needed more to manage the crisis and the recovery than to stay in front of the media all day, for weeks on end. In addition, make sure that the school spokesperson works closely with the public information officers from police and other emergency service agencies.

- Respond quickly and early with available facts, and provide even just a few facts as soon as you know them.

- Hold press conferences away from the scene of the tragedy whenever possible.

- Answer those questions that you can, but do not speculate and do not hesitate to explain why you cannot answer a question.

- View your comments from the eyes of the public, and remember to include compassion and depth in your answers.

- Remind reporters of the need for privacy and healing, and take steps to return the school to normalcy.

- Be able to articulate steps taken to make schools safe, to reduce security risks, and to prepare for effectively managing crisis situations, and discuss how school staff followed the guidelines in place to best handle the situation.

- Have key communications staff and administrators professionally trained on skills for bridging, message discipline, and other techniques for effectively communicating key messages in parent meetings and in media interviews.

- Know your audience, prepare for interviews and press conferences, develop and communicate your key messages, make sure that everyone being interviewed is on the same page, and remember that good public and media relations is not *spin*, but involves effectively communicating good practices and behavior, which must be in place before—and during—the crisis.

• Recognize the trajectory of media stories, that is, the ability of a local incident to become a national news stories in a very short period of time. Understand the next phone you pick up in the middle of a school crisis incident could easily be a national news producer thousands of miles away.

CRISIS CREDIBILITY AND REPUTATION MANAGEMENT

School communicators find themselves in trouble when there are mixed messages, late information releases, paternalistic attitudes, and failure to counter rumors in a timely manner.

The Centers for Disease Control (CDC, n.d.) recommends three core principles for crisis and emergency risk communications:

1. Be First.

2. Be Right.

3. Be Credible.

They identify three pillars of successful communications response in a crisis:

1. Empathy—Express empathy early.

2. Action—Give people something constructive and meaningful to do.

3. Respect—Be respectful of others' emotions and coping mechanisms.

Showing competence and expertise, and remaining honest and open, are guiding principles for successful communications through a crisis.

The basic rule for communicating if you make a mistake is simple:

If you mess up, fess up and fix it up!

If mistakes are made, acknowledge it, explain how it happened, and try to work with those negatively impacted. Focus on solving the problem at hand and preventing it from reoccurring. Keeping your school-community informed is critical to maintaining community confidence and the credibility of school leaders.

LESSONS FOR THE MEDIA ON COVERING ONGOING CRISES

Schools, public safety agencies, and other community members are not the only ones to learn lessons from school violence tragedies. The media from time to time come under fire for their coverage of school violence, and closer examinations of their coverage have drawn out some important lessons for them, too. For example, in its examination of the coverage of the school shooting in Jonesboro, Arkansas, in 1998, The Freedom Forum (1998) issued these recommendations for the media on covering school tragedies:

• Editors and news directors should establish guidelines and expectations, set standards for the behavior of journalists, avoid demonizing or glorifying suspects or victims, substantiate information, and know when to get the story off of the front page.

• Reporters and photographers should focus on the impact of the event on the entire community, avoid hyping an already big story, avoid jumping to conclusions and misrepresentation, and report on what worked properly and went well in the response to the incident.

• All media representatives should work on a foundation of trust. They should also consider creating media pools to avoid creating a *media mob* situation.

The Poynter Institute for Media Studies (Steele, 1999) offers the following guidelines for media representatives covering an ongoing crisis situation:

• Assume that the offender(s) has access to the reporting.

• Avoid reporting and showing information that could jeopardize the safety of law enforcement and other public safety officials, including keeping news helicopters away from the area and not reporting information heard over police scanners.

• Notify authorities if the suspect contacts the newsroom, and do not attempt to contact or interview the suspect during the incident.

• Avoid giving comments or analysis of the demands being made by the suspect during the incident.

• Be cautious when interviewing family members and friends so that the interview does not serve as a vehicle for the suspect and his or her family to communicate with each other.

In another publication, the Poynter Institute recommends a number of ethical questions for reporters to ask themselves prior to their coverage of school-related bomb threats (Tompkins, 1999). These questions focus on journalistic duties, story impact, potential consequences of coverage, tone and words used in the coverage, and covering the overall process more than the actual events.

Media management and reporters should discuss and plan for dealing with school and other crisis incidents ahead of time, just as school officials should plan for the prevention and management of an actual crisis.

16 Preparing for the Postcrisis Crisis

Managing Mental Health, Security, Financial, Operational Continuity, Liability, and School-Community Political Issues

School leaders will have to deal with many postcrisis issues long past the point when the incident has ended. Parent and media issues are two of the most significant challenges (thus the reason Chapter 15 is a stand-alone chapter on dealing with parent and media communications issues). This chapter highlights some additional challenges to postcrisis management:

- Mental Health Support—not only for students, but also school faculty, staff, and other caregivers.
- Security and Emergency Preparedness Postcrisis Demands—parent expectations no longer stop at schools dispatching counselors and psychologists after a crisis; parents now demand reviews of security and emergency preparedness plans as well.
- Financial and Continuity of Operations Planning—the costs of providing unbudgeted mental health support, additional security measures, facility repairs, and long-term changes as a result of the

crisis incident, as well as potential sources for recovering some costs; and the need for defined plans for continuing school operations after a catastrophic incident.

- Liability—it is very likely lawsuits challenging security, preparedness, or school response will follow a higher profile school safety incident.
- School-Community Politics—political enemies and agendas can come out of the woodwork using a crisis incident to further broader vendettas and agendas.

MENTAL HEALTH SUPPORT FOR GRIEF AND HEALING

The preparedness perspectives in this book are largely from professional school security and emergency preparedness perspectives, not from that of a school psychologist or other mental health professional. Clearly, the security, tactical, and related public safety perspectives must be balanced with caring, compassion, and an intense amount of mental health support for students, staff, parents, and the overall community affected by a school crisis.

Experts from *School Crisis Response: A CISM Perspective* (Johnson, Casey, Ertl, Everly, & Mitchell, 1999) note that the entire mission of educational organizations is compromised by posttraumatic stress in a variety of ways:

- Children re-experience traumatic events to integrate them into their understanding of the world and, in doing so, create adverse reactions that affect learning.

- Heightened physiological arousal results from the traumatic images and reduces the ability of children to concentrate.

- Any distractions cause a startle reflect, which disrupts attention.

- Children react to trauma by regressing to earlier levels of coping. Children also integrate reenactments of the trauma into play with others, which in turn interferes with socialization.

- Difficulties occur in memory retention and retrieval.

- Children become disassociated.

- Disassociation, attention and concentration difficulties, and associated behaviors can be misread by staff as discipline issues.

- Preoccupation with the traumatic experience detracts from a child's ability to benefit fully from school experiences.

Furthermore, Steele (1998) identifies four possible avenues of exposure to both acute stress reactions and posttraumatic stress disorder (PTSD) reactions:

1. As a surviving victim.

2. As a witness to a potential trauma-inducing incident.

3. Being related to the victim or victims.

4. Verbal exposure to the details of traumatic experiences.

Considering the potential for children to be exposed to traumatic incidents, and knowing the impact such exposure has on educational settings, mental health issues stemming from school crises clearly must be addressed in a timely and effective manner if educators expect children to gain the most from the classroom.

Johnson (1993) notes,

> Reactions to loss can be a part of other crises or they can be the primary focus of the crisis experience. Most people, including children, react to loss in a stereotypical pattern. Most theories hold a core pattern similar to that presented by Elizabeth Kübler-Ross, who, in her book *On Death and Dying*, puts forth a five-step process of denial, anger, bargaining, depression, and acceptance. Other theories include stages of guilt, fear of the future, sadness, and renewal. (p. 102)

Children and adults must therefore understand that when grieving, they are experiencing normal reactions to abnormal situations. The ability of and length of time needed by both students and adults to negotiate through these or similar stages will depend on the severity of the crisis, the individual's understanding of the incident, the support system of the grieving person, and other factors unique to the individual and to the incident. It is important that officials experiencing a school crisis work with mental health specialists to provide services to help both students and staff through the normal grieving process and, if necessary, to facilitate further support for those who experience more adverse reactions.

Poland and McCormick (1999) offer detailed suggestions for what schools can do in the aftermath of a school crisis to help students and staff effectively undergo the grief and healing processes. These include the following:

- Reopening school as soon as possible, especially to reduce the chance of school phobia occurring.
- Avoiding significant alterations of the school environment before students return.

- Adequately preparing teachers and staff for the return of students, and ensuring that they carefully plan for their students' return.
- Continuing to provide emotional assistance to students and staying in contact with parents.
- Providing structure in the days after the crisis, but being flexible enough to modify the curriculum to address the crisis, such as by incorporating artwork, drama skits, music, poems and other writing exercises, and memorial efforts into classroom and school activities.

In Chapter 2 of their book, Poland and McCormick provide detailed guidance for managing the mental health response on the first day of the crisis. Their task list, and subsequent chapters, go into detail on steps mental health crisis response leaders need to consider, including the following:

- Organizing and activating the crisis response team.
- Deciding on the school schedule for the rest of the day.
- Setting, planning, and publicizing family/community meetings that night.
- Sending home letters to parents.
- Finishing and updating crisis fact sheets.
- Evaluating the need for outside assistance and managing volunteers.
- Beginning to attend to the needs of students.
- Eating something and taking care of yourself as the crisis responder.
- Supervising student dismissals
- Processing the crisis with faculty and support staff.
- Scheduling a mandatory faculty meeting for the next morning and preparing materials for teachers and staff.
- Making emotional support available during the day and evening.
- Visiting victims and their families.
- Meeting with the crisis response team to plan the next day.

This list reinforces that while first-responders manage the many incidents highlighted in earlier chapters of this book, mental health responders have their own full plate of issues to consider and response plans to activate to provide the grief and counseling component of school crisis response.

The first-day tasks in responding to mental health aspects of crisis response are the end of the beginning, not the beginning of the end. People grieve in different ways and in different stages. Grieving is a process, not a one-time event, and the mental health support process lead by schools must reflect this process.

Too often, I have observed school boards, superintendents, and principals overlook the fact that grieving is a process while they instead focus on initial mental health activities, and then on trying to quickly move forward to bring the incident to closure (at least from their perspective). From a political and school-community relations perspective, school boards and administrators want to get the incident behind them, out of the media, and out of the minds of parents, students, and staff. Many school leaders, like others in their school community, want to put the incident in their past as they struggle with the idea that such an incident happened at their school and on their watch as leaders of schools.

Having personally talked with teachers, support staff, and administrators who experienced a crisis in their school, however, I have heard far too many human stories of the posttraumatic stress and long-term toll that lingers after a major school violence incident:

- Teachers who had nightmares months after multiple students were slashed and stabbed by an attacker.
- A teacher who jumped every time a book fell on the floor after having heard shots fired from an automatic weapon outside her classroom months earlier.
- A school nurse who triaged multiple victims of a weapons attack still struggling with emotions months later.

Schools that experience major school shootings have massive turnovers of staff in the long term, with some losing 75% to 100% of their staff in the course of 5 to 10 years.

Returning to normalcy is an important part of the mental health recovery for students, staff, and the school-community. Believing as a school leader that you can return to normalcy almost overnight after a major tragic incident, however, fails to respect and acknowledge the longer term mental health aspects of a school crisis.

School leaders, in general, do a good job in preparing for and responding to the mental health needs for students. They tend to do a much less than stellar job in their preparations for planning for providing mental health support to teachers, support staff, administrators, other caregivers, and themselves. The adults are human, and just like the kids will suffer grief, trauma, stress, and mental health concerns deserving of planning and attention should an incident occur.

Poland and McCormick (1999) provide extensive suggestions for parents, the community, and the caregivers that should be addressed before expectations of a return to normalcy can be seriously considered. Educators should receive staff in-service training designed to familiarize them with the management of stress from critical incidents, the grief and healing process, and related mental health issues and resources. It will be difficult enough to manage the mental health stressors after a critical incident, and learning the best practices for navigating that time period must be undertaken far before an actual incident occurs.

School officials should be aware of national and state resources available to help with the mental health component of school crisis recovery. The National Organization for Victim Assistance (NOVA) and the National Association of School Psychologists both have response teams that can provide on-site mental health support in processing school crises and moving forward with school and community recovery efforts. Educators would also be wise to identify all local, regional, and state resources that can be tapped into in the event of a major crisis incident in their district.

The Recommended Readings section of this book points readers to several books addressing school crisis management entirely from the perspectives of psychologists and counselors, which deserve the respect and detailed attention from the mental health grief and healing processes from specialists in that field of study. I especially encourage readers to study the work of Poland and McCormick (1999) titled *Coping With Crisis: Lessons Learned* as it goes much further into the expertise of school psychology and school crisis mental health response than I could, or should, ever attempt. Likewise, the National Association of School Psychologists (NASP) is the premiere national organization for school psychology issues and has extensive, updated resources for educators on topics including death and grief support, crisis response, suicide, and the many other areas of teen and school mental health on its website at www.nasponline.org.

SECURITY AND EMERGENCY PREPAREDNESS POSTCRISIS DEMANDS

The traditional response to a crisis at a school has appropriately been for school administrators to dispatch counselors and psychologists immediately following a high-profile incident. In a post-Columbine and post-9/11 world, parents today have additional expectations: Thorough reviews of security and emergency preparedness plans.

School-community emotions run high after a high-profile school violence incident. School-community politics can also come into play. Media attention is often front-page, top-story, and ongoing day after day. Pressures are on school board members, superintendents, and principals to improve security. Media may question school security and emergency preparedness procedures. Parents want guarantees that such an incident will never happen again.

Parents are concerned about the mental health of their children and the adults that serve them, and they should be. Equally of concern is the immediate safety of their children at the school in the days and months that follow an incident. Parents want to know if school officials have taken all possible steps to prevent the reoccurrence of such incidents and whether they are adequately prepared to effectively respond to incidents that cannot be prevented.

School board members and administrators need to restore calm, focus, and community confidence following high-profile school safety incidents. In working with school leaders on postcrisis consultations, my colleagues and I have had to focus not only on evaluating security and emergency preparedness issues, but also parent and media questions and communications concerns. The perception, communication, and political issues in a school environment postcrisis can adversely impact a school's response to a tragedy or high-profile security incident. This poses a high risk of overreaction by boards and administrators if they are not prepared to make objective, not emotional, knee-jerk, or politically-driven, evaluations of their schools' security and preparedness posture.

Some areas we typically review in providing postcrisis consultation to schools include the following:

- Evaluation of district and building level emergency preparedness plans.
- Examination of district- and building-level school crisis teams
- Assessment of current school security measures and areas for improvements.
- Review of prevention, intervention, and support services, and how they integrate with security and emergency preparedness measures.
- Parent input and community feedback, such as a community meeting and parent interviews, in the assessment process.
- Liaison with community public safety and emergency management agencies
- School safety and crisis communications issues.
- Support with media and school-community communications during and after the process and related assistance to help schools return their focus to education.

One of the most valuable activities we conduct as a part of a postcrisis consultation has been a parent/community meeting as a part of the assessment process. This meeting, which is open to the public, allows parents to voice their questions and concerns and to get a national perspective on school security and emergency preparedness issues. It helps to provide context to postcrisis responses and expectations, to obtain parent and community input into our review of district safety issues, and to serve as a part of the healing process for the community.

School leaders who have engaged this process with us have found it to be a turning point in moving the community forward. Unfortunately, there are still some old-school superintendents and boards who, like one superintendent told me, are "afraid a community meeting could get out of control." Of course, this superintendent also was quoted in the media as saying that schools are safer than movie theaters following the shooting death of one of his school administrators and the shooting injury of a second administrator. Fortunately, more progressive school administrators realize that the old-school mentality of denial and avoiding transparency detract from their credibility as school district leaders.

School administrators cannot afford to fly by the seat of their pants with postcrisis response. In today's world of social media and transparency expectations by parents, progressive school leaders realize they need to have the counselors and psychologists ready to go after a crisis, and their plan for reviewing school security and emergency preparedness set to kick in shortly afterwards.

FINANCIAL AND CONTINUITY OF OPERATIONS PLANS FOR CRISIS RESPONSE AND RECOVERY

Financial Considerations

The costs associated with recovery from a crisis incident can be tremendous. Although costs associated with a horrific incident could range into the millions, even a smaller scale crisis can cost thousands or even hundreds of thousands in overtime, physical plant management, and other operations expenses. Some of the specific cost areas associated with a crisis recovery can include the following:

- Manpower and associated overtime costs for those managing the crisis.
- Physical plant operations for extended hours.
- Repairs and replacement of damaged or stolen property.
- Ongoing and supplemental support services, such as additional mental health and related counseling services, increased security and policing services, additional security equipment and technology, outside expert consultation services, and so on.

School business officials should also explore arrangements with its vendors for providing products and services, and expediting them, following a critical school incident. Procedures and forms for expedited purchase orders, delivery, and payment should be hammered out in advance with critical vendors, school attorneys, and school boards that must authorize such payments. When a crisis strikes, the last thing anyone needs are bureaucratic obstacles holding up critical purchases for products and services needed to restore school operations and quickly recover from a crisis.

Officials responsible for school budget management and business services should develop a disaster recovery plan that includes a mechanism for accounting for crisis-related costs. These plans should include creating separate and distinct financial reporting mechanisms (print and electronic, as appropriate) to document itemized costs in the above and other categories which are directly related to the response and recovery of a critical incident. Having advance purchasing plans for expedited responses after a crisis are essential to the recovery process.

Schools *may* potentially recover some of their financial losses from a school crisis in several ways. The key word here is *may*, as there is no guarantee. Some potential sources for recovery crisis costs include the following:

• Project School Emergency Response to Violence—Administered by the U.S. Department of Education, this program funds short-term and long-term education-related services of local school districts to help them recover from a violent or traumatic event that has disrupted the teaching and learning environment. Immediate applications for short-term relief can be sought for up to $50,000 for a period of 6 months following a relatively short application. Extended service grants are available for up to $250,000 for 18 months to help students, teachers, and staff recover from a traumatic event. Costs for additional mental health, security, and other activity costs may be considered for this grant, for example.

• Disaster Aid Programs—Federal and state government resources work their way down to local communities if a major disaster declaration has been made through established governmental processes. Although there is no guarantee, it seems logical that a school district that has thoroughly documented its losses would stand a better chance of obtaining financial recovery support over a district that has no mechanism for documenting and tracking such losses.

• Restitution from Offenders—Many prosecutors and courts will want an accurate cost of school violence and crisis incidents to use in judicial proceedings to seek restitution from offenders. Having concrete numbers not only demonstrates the extent of impact of the incident itself, but also serves as a tool for seeking reimbursement for the financial losses.

Continuity of Operations Planning

Schools are also increasingly advised to develop formal Continuity of Operations Plans (COOP), particularly in light of potential pandemic health emergencies, terrorism, and other long-term hazards such as weather and natural disasters.

COOP planning for schools could take up a separate and distinct book onto its own. School leaders need to develop plans for continuity of school operations. Areas of consideration may include such considerations as the following:

- Continuity of the delivery of educational services in the event instruction cannot continue in the traditional format or in existing school facilities for an extended period of time.
- School governance and leadership in the event there are severe losses or long-term incapacitation of school board members, the superintendent, the superintendent's executive team, or building principals.
- School staffing in the event of a massive loss of teachers or support staff such as counselors, psychologists, bus drivers, safety personnel, and other support services.
- Physical plant major repairs, demolition and replacement, and so on in the event existing facilities cannot be used for extended times or must be replaced.
- Damage and losses to school buses and transportation facilities, fueling availability, processes, and so on.
- Electricity, gas, and other utilities.
- Telephone, Internet, data, IT facilities and operations, and other communications restoration.
- Temporary and longer term office space, equipment, and so on.
- Payroll services.
- Purchasing processes and vendor payments.
- Banking processes.
- Mail and package delivery.
- Insurance processes.

COOP planning involves many detailed aspects. This is a newer area of consideration for schools and, unfortunately, those tackling it are in their infancy in doing so in far too many school communities.

Financial and Continuity of Operations Plans should be in place before a crisis incident occurs. This is also why school business and finance administrators should be represented on the district's crisis team. Schools need to have a structure in place from which to document, track, and potentially recover the financial costs associated with a school crisis and its recovery. And they need a solid plan on how they will continue to operate if a catastrophic incident occurs that dramatically alters the physical, governance, and operational aspects of their schools.

LITIGATION PREPAREDNESS

Unfortunately, we live in a litigious society. It is not a matter of *if* you will be sued, but rather of *when* you will be sued, especially following a school crisis incident.

Legal counsel should be involved in the complete crisis preparedness process. In the preparation stages, counsel should have input into, and review of, emergency guidelines. In the postcrisis crisis stage, counsel should be involved in the following processes:

- Review of documentation development.
- Review of public information dissemination procedures and content.
- Liaison with prosecutors for criminal charges, as appropriate.

It is likely that, in addition to school attorneys, school leaders will also work hand-in-hand with not only school risk managers, but also insurance representatives, as insurance claims and related issues will likely be raised for an extended period of time following the crisis.

School officials must remember that, as difficult as it is to do, they must make every effort to document details of their response to crisis situations. Ideally, school officials should also have ample evidence of the many steps taken before an incident to reduce the risks and to prepare for managing a crisis. Although litigation concerns are legitimate, those concerns must also be balanced with caring and compassion in responding to the crisis aftermath, including not being overly restrictive in parent and media communications following an incident.

SCHOOL-COMMUNITY POSTCRISIS POLITICS

Schools are political entities. In fact, most parents and many others in school communities do not fully realize just how political schools are on a day-to-day basis. The time following a crisis is no exception to this rule.

In our postcrisis work with schools, and in simply observing the dynamics in the media and talking with those who have experienced a critical school incident, the extent of school-community politics can be intense and long-drawn. We see it rear its ugly head in a number of ways:

- Political posturing by, and divisiveness among, school board members.
- Parents with personal grievances using the climate to advance their own issues and grievances with school staff, administrators, and boards.
- Internal professional and personality disputes surfacing in behind-the-scene attacks to place blame and criticism on how the incident could have been prevented or how it was managed.
- Community members with beliefs and grievances against the school district who use the interest to further their goals (opponents to school funding requests, persons or groups who oppose the current board and/or administration, etc.).
- Posturing and political maneuvering by other local, state, and even national-level elected officials and political appointees who call for new legislation or actions in response to the incident or who are critical of the school district's leadership.
- The exploitation of school incidents by special interest and advocacy groups who use the crisis as an example to further their social or political agendas.
- Exploitation of the media and its coverage of the incident by any or all of the above individuals and interests.

Other potential political dynamics exist, but this list highlights some areas for behind-the-scenes personal and political agendas that could surface in the debates, discussions, and calls for action after a school crisis. Unfortunately, the average parent often never knows these things are going on.

School officials must be prepared to recognize and navigate these incidents. More than once we have seen school building principals dramatically impacted, and in some cases losing control of their ability to be in total control of their school, after a high-profile school safety incident. School boards, superintendents, and principals must have the foresight and political fortitude to avoid making political and knee-jerk decisions while staying focused on the best long-term interests of school safety.

Part IV

Future Directions

Local schools need to strengthen their capacity to prevent, manage, and recover from school crises. Many of the things that need to be done require leadership and cost more time than they do money. But outside entities also can directly and indirectly help provide support to local school districts to accomplish these tasks.

The safety of our schools is directly related to academic achievement, solidifying schools as credible community institutions, and advancing society by promoting environments driven by learning, not climates focused on fear and personal safety. School safety therefore contributes to the operational continuity of our schools, and in turn the continuity of the economic engine the education industry plays in the American economy. State and federal government agencies can, and should, support local school safety planning and programs.

The academic community also needs to step up to better support school safety. Academic research is sorely lacking on school security and emergency preparedness issues, not just prevention and intervention programs. Academia also needs to strengthen its preparedness of teachers and administrators through higher education coursework and certification programs on school safety prevention, security, and emergency preparedness issues. Both the research and education preparation have improved minimally, at best, since the 1999 Columbine High School tragedy.

17

State, Federal, and Academic Support for School Safety

Our state and federal governments have a legitimate interest in supporting school safety. Do we need state and federal education agencies with their hands in the day-to-day management of local school safety issues? No. Elsewhere in this book, I stressed that local school leaders must own much of the day-to-day costs of school safety. But given the vast amount of resources state and federal government agencies put into many other areas of education specifically and societal issues in general, they should also contribute to research and financial support for advancing prevention, security, and preparedness measures in our schools.

State and federal governments can play a supportive role in school safety. Consistency is the key. Unfortunately, we have roller coaster public awareness, public policy, and public funding on school safety. Our legislators legislate by anecdote, rather than with long-term policy and programmatic stability and consistency in mind.

STATE-LEVEL STRATEGIES

State support for school safety should emphasize a focus on direct support to local school districts. More than a decade after the Columbine High School attack in 1999, we do not need states to waste limited dollars on more "centers" or "institutes" to "study" or provide "technical assistance" manuals on school safety. Schools need meaningful resources to directly implement the best practices which have been identified over the past decade-plus, and to provide support services directly to kids.

State governments can do many things to improve school security and emergency preparedness:

- Improve school crime reporting requirements to ensure that crimes are consistently reported both to law enforcement and to a centralized state data collection site. (States should provide training and technical assistance to school officials on crime reporting, proactive audits conducted to assess the accuracy of reporting, and the failure to adhere to crime reporting requirements should be enforced with specific sanctions.)
- Provide a legal foundation for law enforcement officials to notify schools of student crimes in the community.
- Require safe schools plans and emergency preparedness guidelines, and enforce such requirements with specific sanctions for those who fail to adhere.
- Provide resources for enhanced and ongoing security-related staffing, while recognizing that different districts may employ different models, such as school resource officers, in-house school security staff, or school police departments.
- Provide state-certified training for school security and police personnel, and, if possible, for other school safety representatives.
- Obtain ongoing, direct input from school security and school policing officials into legislative and other hearings related to safe schools.
- Provide school security-specific grant funds for security and emergency preparedness training and planning; school security assessments by qualified professionals; limited school security equipment, including such items as communications equipment and cameras; anonymous reporting mechanisms, such as hotlines; visitor management systems; and crime data collection, analysis, and reporting tools.
- Enhance penalties for school crimes, such as assault of school personnel or weapons possession (of all types, not only firearms).
- Improve education requirements for educators in undergraduate and graduate schools by requiring or providing incentives for college education programs to include school safety and emergency preparedness courses, and by supporting school security and emergency preparedness and training for school support staff, such as bus drivers, secretaries, food service staff, and custodians.
- Create education programs for law enforcement officials within police academies and in special programs dealing with school security and emergency preparedness.

- Target education decision makers, such as boards, superintendents, and principals, for educational programs and resources designed to better prepare them for dealing with school security and emergency preparedness.
- Balance security and emergency preparedness policy and funding with prevention and intervention program policies and funding.
- Strengthen prevention and intervention programs, such as alternative schools and programs (even for the elementary level), resources for special education students, mental health and psychological services, conflict management and social skills, school climate, and classroom management and discipline skills.

This list should help guide those who believe that there is nothing that states can do to prevent and manage school crises.

Some states get it, and have been doing a good job depending upon the leadership in the Governor's Office and Office of the State Superintendent at a given point in time. In Indiana, under the leadership of Dr. Tony Bennett, State Superintendent, his Executive Director of Student Services, Gary Green, and David Woodward, Program Coordinator for the Department's School Safety Specialist Academy, school safety certification training is provided to designated school safety specialists from each school district in Indiana. Cathy Danyluk, the Department's Attendance Officer and liaison to criminal justice agencies, has represented the Department for more than a decade in coordinating school and community safety policy and program issues. The Department sends its staff out to local school districts to support their compliance with state education board safety rules and local needs, has provided mini-grants for school security and emergency planning, and has instituted a *focus on the fundamentals* return to practical school safety training in the state. The Indiana School Safety Specialist Academy was formed almost a decade ago, around the time of the Columbine High School attack, and has been a sustained program in the state's annual operating budget for close to a decade.

In South Carolina, the state education department works with the U.S. Attorney's Office and other partner agencies to provide free regional school workshops across the state each year for local educators, school safety, first-responders, and their community partners. The U.S. Attorney's Office and its state partners are approaching their 20th year of providing statewide school safety regional workshops.

Indiana and South Carolina are two examples of sustained leadership on school safety at the state level. Many other states (too many to name) provide practical and useful support for local districts on school safety and emergency preparedness issues. The key is sustained policy and funding support from state education and elected officials, and stability and continuity (not roller coaster responses) in addressing evolving school safety issues and needs.

THE FEDERAL ROLE

Federal government officials improved their efforts to address the security and emergency preparedness components of school safety following the Columbine High School attack in 1999. Although prior efforts focused on the prevention and intervention components, steps were taken toward improving emergency preparedness through the U.S. Department of Education's Readiness and Emergency Management for Schools (REMS) grant program that started under a different name in 2003.

As of publication time with this book, Congress and the Obama Administration eliminated more than $295 million in federal school safety dollars that passed through the state directly to local school districts via a formula grant process and eliminated the REMS grant program. Funds for school-based police officers that increased substantially after the 1999 Columbine attack slowly disappeared in the years following the start of the program. Today, the Obama Administration is proposing what I consider a very skewed policy and funding approach that redefines school safety by minimizing the focus on violence and instead focusing on "school climate surveys" and "bullying" rather than a comprehensive and balanced approach to federal school safety policy and funding.

Federal officials need to stop policy and funding debates over whether to provide more prevention *or* better security, and should instead concentrate their efforts on providing more prevention *and* better security. They also need to recognize that a professional school security program does not automatically equate to simply more manpower and more equipment in our schools. As a four-time Congressional expert witness on school safety, I have recommended a number of things to Congress, including the following:

- Improve federal school safety data by incorporating more incident-based data into federal school safety data collection. Currently no federal mandatory school crime reporting and tracking exist, and federal data are limited to a hodgepodge collection of six or so academic surveys. Improved federal school safety data will lead to improved federal school safety policy and funding.

- Incorporate strong and supportive school safety, security, and emergency preparedness components into the reauthorization of the federal Elementary and Secondary Education Act. Federal education law should include reasonable requirements and resources for comprehensive school safety, security, and emergency preparedness programs. School safety is directly related to academic achievement. Students cannot learn and teachers cannot teach at their maximum capacities if their thoughts and environments are consumed with concerns about safety. A strong school safety component would benefit the whole child and would in turn strengthen opportunities for improved academic achievement.

• Ensure federal school safety policies, programming, and funding reflect a comprehensive and balanced framework designed around a continuum of threats to school safety and a corresponding continuum of comprehensive school safety strategies. Avoid single-cause, single-strategy legislation.

• Create a permanent interagency working group of representatives from the Departments of Education, Health and Human Services, Justice, and Homeland Security to establish a formal structure for communication, planning, policy, and funding decisions combining their respective expertise areas and disciplines related to school safety, security, and emergency preparedness. A periodic conversation or meeting, or a joint publication from these agencies, is not enough. Although each agency may in itself have a number of good school safety initiatives, coordination across agencies can lead to a more coordinated, comprehensive, and balanced federal approach to school safety. A permanent interagency working group, supported by state, local, and frontline experts in K–12 school safety, security, and emergency preparedness, can improve federal policy, program, and funding decisions on school safety and preparedness issues.

• Encourage coordination, collaboration, and cooperation on school safety issues by the Congressional Committee members and staff overseeing Education, Health and Human Services, Homeland Security, and Justice legislation and oversight.

• Acknowledge the threat terrorism poses to our schools. Acknowledge the full range of threats to schools and the limitations of current data on school violence. In particular, be forthcoming with the American public and education and safety officials charged with protecting our children about the potential threat of terrorism to our nation's schools and school buses.

• Restore cut funding for school emergency preparedness planning and expand funding over time to reflect our nation's commitment to school preparedness in the way we are beefing up protection for other national critical infrastructures.

• Require Department of Homeland Security grants and other funding to local law enforcement, emergency management agencies, and other public safety officials to include mandatory requirements that these public safety officials actively engage K–12 public and private schools in local emergency planning.

• Open select Department of Homeland Security grants specifically for K–12 schools for emergency preparedness training, tabletop exercises, school bus security, limited equipment (especially communications equipment), and related needs.

• Require education agency representation on federal, state, and local Homeland Security and emergency management advisory and coordinating committees. Schools and first-responders must plan, prepare, and practice together.

• Increase requirements requiring federal school safety grant recipients to form partnerships, protocols, training, and joint planning among schools, first-responders, mental health, public health, and other community partner agencies.

• Provide improved support for existing federal school safety programs that work, and modify or replace programs deemed ineffective with new programs. When ineffective programs are identified, replace them as soon as possible with programs that do work. Do not throw out the baby with the bath water.

School and public safety officials do *not* need more federal research, studies, and paralysis-by-analysis reports. They do *not* need more conferences, symposiums, and gatherings. They do *not* need more advisory groups, panels, commissions, and hearings. They do *not* need more manuals, guides, templates, and regurgitation of best practices. They definitely do *not* need more earmarked technical assistance centers, institutes, or Beltway contracted technical assistance providers. And they certainly do *not* need more federal websites.

Schools need support and resources in implementing established best practices. Federal policy and funding should be geared toward putting resources directly in the hands of local school districts to put best practices into day-to-day practice. Legislation and funding by anecdote, and roller coaster public policy and funding, often causes more harm than good to long-term school safety.

COLLEGES OF EDUCATION

Colleges providing teacher and administrator programs need to take a leadership role in better preparing school officials on school safety and emergency preparedness issues. The most common response heard when this issue has been raised is that there is not enough time (or money) in the college curriculum for additional required courses. At best, with some rare exceptions, programs on school safety issues are incorporated as a short segment in other courses or as an elective or special topic.

It is logical to believe that at least one reason for the difficulty in recruiting and retaining teachers centers on issues of discipline and workplace safety for both students and staff. To toss new teachers into environments for which they have not been adequately prepared and then to expect them to perform effectively and remain on the job is unrealistic. The first line of defense in reducing school violence is a well-prepared school employee, and colleges must recognize and respond to this need for well-prepared school employees by requiring or providing a unit on school safety in their curricula.

The same concept applies for aspiring principals and superintendents. School safety is a leadership issue. Our colleges of education run many programs on academic leadership, and school safety must be viewed as a leadership issue.

School security and emergency preparedness research is also needed. A number of academicians have been quick to discard school security and emergency preparedness on the basis that, as they say, "There is no research to support that these measures work." Ironically, the reason that there is no research on the effectiveness of security and emergency preparedness strategies is because there have been no researchers interested in or able (i.e., funded) to conduct this type of research. Although communication and coordination has improved over the years between the prevention and intervention communities, typically, academic researchers and the school security and emergency preparedness world rarely interact.

Education, prevention, and intervention programs cannot be delivered with maximum effectiveness in unsafe settings, and a balanced and rational security and emergency preparedness program is necessary for safe educational settings to exist. Yet the absence of research on and evaluation of such programs has lead to us having little to no meaningful data even a decade past the Columbine High School tragedy. The lack of data detracts from the formal research knowledge base, even though there should be some common sense recognition that security and emergency preparedness are necessary in all organizations in today's world, including in the world of education.

Ironically, some academicians use the absence of research as justification for advocating that we not consider implementing school security and emergency preparedness measures. One need only look at the years of research and evaluation conducted on prevention and intervention programs to find countless conclusions that many of these programs were not working successfully, yet the academic world readily encourages the funding and support of more prevention programs, not to mention more new research and evaluation of prevention and intervention programs. To suggest the absence of research on school security and emergency preparedness justifies not having such measures is counterintuitive and disingenuous.

One could therefore easily argue that those academicians quick to shoot down security and emergency preparedness strategies based on a lack of research should then logically also be against prevention and intervention programs, because many of these programs have been found in evaluation and research to be unsuccessful or questionable. It would be ludicrous to suggest that prevention and intervention programs should be eliminated based simply on past research findings, and it is equally ludicrous to suggest that we ignore basic security and crisis strategies simply because there is no research on the subject.

In short, the *absence of research* argument is old, misused, and irrelevant in the big picture—especially in the eyes of victims of school violence and their families, both of whom are looking for answers on how to secure schools right now. Nevertheless, one academician at a national conference on school safety asked me if I was aware of any research that indicated that reducing the number of open doors could prevent someone from getting inside a school. Common sense should tell us that such steps as reducing the number of open doors, greeting visitors, reporting strangers, locking doors to high-value storage areas, preparing for natural and man-made disasters, and other security and crisis measures are all prudent measures to take in today's society and at our schools.

This is not to say that there should never be any research and evaluation on school security and emergency preparedness issues. To the contrary, it would be quite appropriate and past due to research and evaluate the roles and effectiveness of the following:

- School security and school policing staffing models.
- Security equipment and technology in schools.
- Emergency planning and training strategies.
- Security assessments and planning focused on physical security, crime prevention, and other measurers.
- School-police-community partnerships.
- Specific security-related strategies such as many that are highlighted in Chapter 5 of this book.

However, those researchers who have no interest in studying these areas should, at a minimum, stop using the absence of research as justification for not supporting security and emergency programs. Because these individuals have yet to perfect the prevention and intervention fields, they should be less critical (especially with no supporting evidence) of the security and emergency preparedness fields.

WHERE TO NOW?

Looking back at my first two books, published in 1998 and 2000, I realize that although many things in school security and emergency preparedness have changed, many also remain the same.

The specific threats to school safety evolve over time within a school-community. Hot topics, fueled by the media and political agendas, impact public awareness, policy, and funding. Sometimes legislation and funding-by-anecdote changes are good, but in many cases they detract from long-term, sustainable school safety policy and funding.

Although public awareness and funding often change, the fundamentals of good school security and emergency preparedness practices overall remain intact. Many of the best practices in place when I wrote my 1998 and 2000 books are still solid practices today. The body of knowledge and experience we have gained on school emergency planning in over a decade following the Columbine High School attack has grown, and we should likely learn more if we continue to put plans that are written on paper into actual practice through training, drills and exercises, debriefings, and partnerships with others in the school community.

What new threats lie await around the corner? Surely there will be "new times, new crimes" and new challenges. School leaders, and their public safety and other community partners, should focus on solidifying the fundamentals as new teachers, administrators, support staff, and safety officials step into their positions. From there, we can all strengthen those fundamentals with new lessons learned.

In closing, I leave with you a quote shared at the end of most of my workshops:

> *"He is most free from danger, who, even when safe, is on his guard."*
>
> —Publilius Syrus, a Latin writer
> of maxims who flourished in
> the 1st century B.C.

Stay safe!

References

American Association of School Administrators. (1981). *Reporting: Violence, vandalism and other incidents in schools*. Arlington, VA: Author.

American Foundation for Suicide Prevention (AFSP). (2011). *Facts and figures: National statistics.* Retrieved from http://www.afsp.org/index.cfm?fuseaction= home.viewpage&page_id=050FEA9F-B064-4092-B1135C3A70DE1FDA

American Foundation for Suicide Prevention, American Association of Suicidology, & Annenberg Public Policy Center. (n.d.). *Reporting on suicide: Recommendations for the media.* Retrieved from http://www.suicidology.org/c/document_library/ get_file?folderId=231&name=DLFE-71.pdf

Band, S. R., & Harpold, J. A. (1999, September). School violence. *FBI Law Enforcement Bulletin, 68*(9), 9–16.

Centers for Disease Control and Prevention. (n.d.). *Crisis and emergency risk communication.* Retrieved from http://www.bt.cdc.gov/cerc/CERConline/index2.html

Cullen, D. (2009). *Columbine.* New York, NY: Twelve.

Dwyer, K., Osher, D., & Warger, C. (1998). *Early warning, timely response: A guide to safe schools.* Washington, DC: U.S. Department of Education.

Federal Emergency Management Agency. (1995). *Incident command system self-study unit.* Jessup, MD: Author.

Freedom Forum. (1998). *Jonesboro: Were the media fair?* [Online article]. New York, NY: Freedom Forum Media Studies Center. Retrieved from http://www .freedomforum.org/newsstand/reports/jonesboro/printjonesboro.asp

Goldstein, A. P. (1999). *Low level aggression: First steps on the ladder to violence.* Champaign, IL: Research Press.

Hill, M. S., & Hill, F. W. (1994). *Creating safe schools.* Thousand Oaks, CA: Corwin.

Huff, C. R. (1988, May). *Youth gangs and public policy in Ohio: Findings and recommendations.* Paper presented at the meeting of the Ohio Conference on Youth Gangs and the Urban Underclass, Columbus.

Johnson, K. (1993). *School crisis management: A hands-on guide to training crisis response teams.* Alameda, CA: Hunter House.

Johnson, K., Casey, D., Ertl, B., Everly, G. S., Jr., & Mitchell, J. T. (1999). *School crisis response: A CISM perspective.* Ellicott City, MD: The International Critical Incident Stress Foundation.

Kaufman, R., Saltzman, M., Anderson, C., Carr, N., Pfeil, M. P., Armistead, L., & Kleinz, K. (1999, August). Managing the unmanageable: Crisis lessons from the Columbine tragedy. *NSPRA Bonus* [Bulletin]. Rockville, MD: National School Public Relations Association.

Kodluboy, D. W., & Evenrud, L. A. (1993). School-based interventions: Best practices and critical issues. In A. P. Goldstein & C. R. Huff (Eds.), *The gang intervention handbook* (pp. 257–294). Champaign, IL: Research Press.

Lal, S. R., Lal, D., & Achilles, C. M. (1993). *Handbook on gangs in schools: Strategies to reduce gang-related activities* (pp. 7–8) Thousand Oaks, CA: Corwin.

Langman, P. (2009). *Why kids kill.* New York, NY: Palgrave MacMillan.

Martin, J. (2006, September 7). *Schools need to focus on bullying 'hotspots,' not just the bullies.* Washington University in St. Louis [Newsroom]. Retrieved from http://news.wustl.edu/news/Pages/7451.aspx.

National Advisory Committee on Children and Terrorism. (2003). *Schools and terrorism: A supplement to the National Advisory Committee on Children and Terrorism recommendations to the Secretary.* Washington, DC: U.S. Department of Health and Human Services. Retrieved from http://www.bt.cdc.gov/children/pdf/working/school.pdf

National School Boards Association. (2010). *Response letter to U.S. Department of Education's October 26, 2010, "Dear Colleague" letter.* Retrieved from http://www.nsba.org/SecondaryMenu/COSA/Updates/NSBA-letter-to-Ed-12-07-10.aspx?utm_source=Council+of+School+Attorneys&utm_campaign=82252bf4b5-Dear_Colleague_Letter_12_10_2010&utm_medium=email

National Strategy Forum. (2004). *School safety in the 21st century: Adapting to new security challenges post-9/11: Report of the conference "Schools: Prudent Preparation for a Catastrophic Terrorism Incident."* Chicago, IL: National Strategy Forum, Alfred P. Sloan Foundation.

Poland, S., & McCormick, J. (1999). *Coping with crisis: Lessons learned.* Longmont, CO: Sopris West.

Quarles, C. L. (1993). *Staying safe at school.* Thousand Oaks, CA: Corwin.

Reisman, W. (1998, June). *The Memphis conference: Suggestions for preventing and dealing with student initiated violence.* Indianola, IA: Author.

Riley, R. W., & Reno, J. (1998). [Cover letter]. In K. Dwyer, D. Osher, & C. Warger, *Early warning, timely response: A guide to safe schools.* Washington, DC: U.S. Department of Education.

Rubel, R. J., & Ames, N. (1986). *Reducing school crime and student misbehavior: A problem-solving strategy.* Rockville, MD: National Institute of Justice.

Silver, J. M., & Yudofsky, S. (1992). Violence and aggression. In F. I. Kass, J. M. Oldham, H. Pardes, & L. Morris (Eds.), *The Columbia University College of Physicians and Surgeons complete home guide to mental health* (pp. 385–393). New York, NY: Henry Holt.

Spergel, I. A. (1990). Youth gangs: Continuity and change. In M. Tonry & N. Morris (Eds.), *Crime and justice: A review of research* (Vol. 12). Chicago: University of Chicago Press.

Steele, B. (1999, July). *Guidelines for covering hostage-taking crises, prison uprisings, terrorist actions* [Online article]. St. Petersburg, FL: The Poynter Institute for Media Studies. Retrieved from http://www.poynter.org/dj/tips/ethics/guidelines.htm

Steele, W. (1998). *Trauma debriefing for schools and agencies.* Grosse Pointe Wood, MI: The Institute for Trauma and Loss in Children.

Taylor, C. S. (1988, Spring). Youth gangs organize quest for power, money. *School Safety: National School Safety Center News Journal*, 26–27.

Tompkins, A. (1999, April 30). *After Littleton: Covering what comes next* [Online article]. St. Petersburg, FL: The Poynter Institute for Media Studies. Retrieved from http://www.poynter.org/research/lm/lm_afterlittle.htm

Trump, K. S. (1997). Security policy, personnel, and operations. In J. Conoley & A. Goldstein (Eds.), *The school violence intervention handbook* (pp. 265–289). New York, NY: Guilford.

Trump, K. S. (1998). *Practical school security: Basic guidelines for safe and secure schools.* Thousand Oaks, CA: Corwin.

Trump, K. S. (2000). *Classroom killers? Hallway hostages? How schools can prevent and manage school crises.* Thousand Oaks, CA: Corwin.

Trump, K. S. (2007, May 17). *Protecting our schools: Federal efforts to strengthen community preparedness and response* [Hearings before the U.S. House Homeland Security Committee]. Retrieved from http://www.schoolsecurity.org/news/House_Homeland_Security07.html

Trump, K. S. (2010a). *Gangs and school safety.* Retrieved from http://www.schoolsecurity.org/trends/gangs.html

Trump, K. S. (2010b). *Election day security.* Retrieved from http://www.schoolsecurity.org/resources/election_day_security.html

Trump, K. S. (2010c). *Parents and school safety.* Retrieved from http://www.schoolsecurity.org/faq/parents.html

Trump, K. S. (2010d). *School athletic event security.* Retrieved from http://www.schoolsecurity.org/resources/athletic_event_security.html

Trump, K. S. (2010e). *Schools and terrorism: School terrorism preparedness.* Retrieved from http://www.schoolsecurity.org/terrorist_response.html

Trump, K. S. (2010f). *School crime reporting and school crime underreporting.* Retrieved from http://www.schoolsecurity.org/trends/school_crime_reporting.html

Trump, K. S. (2010g). *Steps parents can take to address school safety concerns.* Retrieved from http://www.schoolsecurityblog.com/2010/01/steps-parents-can-take-to-address-school-safety-concerns/

Trump, K. S. (2010h). *Teaching school students to fight gunmen.* Retrieved from http://www.schoolsecurity.org/trends/students_fight_gunmen.html

Trump, K. S. (2010i). *Zero tolerance and school safety.* Retrieved from www.schoolsecurity.org/trends/zero_tolerance.html

U.S. Congress, Office of Technology Assessment. (1995). *Risks to students in school* (OTA Publication No. ENV-633). Washington, DC: Government Printing Office.

U.S. Department of Education. (2004, October). *Letter to schools from Eugene Hickok, Deputy Secretary of Education.* Retrieved from http://www2.ed.gov/policy/elsec/guid/secletter/041006.html

U.S. Department of Education. (2007a). *Balancing student privacy and school safety: A guide to the Family Educational Rights and Privacy Act for elementary and secondary schools.* Retrieved from http://www2.ed.gov/policy/gen/guid/fpco/brochures/elsec.html

U.S. Department of Education. (2007b). *Model notification of rights for elementary and secondary schools.* Retrieved from http://www2.ed.gov/policy/gen/guid/fpco/ferpa/lea-officials.html

U.S. Department of Education. (2010a). *Dear colleague letter: Harassment and bullying.* Retrieved from http://www2.ed.gov/about/offices/list/ocr/letters/colleague-201010.pdf

U.S. Department of Education. (2010b). *The four phases of emergency management.* Readiness and Emergency Management for Schools Technical Assistance Center. Retrieved from http://rems.ed.gov/index.php?page=about_Four_Phases

U.S. Department of Health, Education, and Welfare. (1978). *Violent schools—Safe schools: The safe school study report to Congress* (Vol. 1, p. 75). Washington, DC: Government Printing Office.

RECOMMENDED READINGS

Cullen, D. (2009). *Columbine.* New York, NY: Twelve.

Dwyer, K., Osher, D., & Warger, C. (1998). *Early warning, timely response: A guide to safe schools.* Washington, DC: U.S. Department of Education.

Goldstein, A. P. (1999). *Low level aggression: First steps on the ladder to violence.* Champaign, IL: Research Press.

Goldstein, A.P., & Kodluboy, D.W. (1998) *Gangs in schools: Signs, symbols, and solutions.* Champaign, IL: Research Press.

Johnson, K., Casey, D., Ertl, B., Everly, G. S., Jr., & Mitchell, J. T. (1999). *School crisis response: A CISM perspective.* Ellicott City, MD: The International Critical Incident Stress Foundation.

Langman, P. (2009). *Why kids kill.* New York, NY. Palgrave MacMillan.

Poland, S., & McCormick, J. (1999). *Coping with crisis: Lessons learned.* Longmont, CO: Sopris West.

Index